--WHEN F.D.R. PAID CHURCHILL AN UNEXPECTED VISIT

I opened the door wide, but saw the President look curiously beyond me . . . . Winston Churchill was stark naked, a drink in one hand, a cigar in the other. He beamed cordially, looked down at his dramatic nudity, then grinned impishly and said, "Look, I have nothing to hide . . ."

"As intimate a portrait of Churchill as has ever been committed to print."
—*San Francisco Chronicle*

Originally published at $3.75 by Farrar, Straus and Cudahy, Inc.

About the author . . .

Walter Henry Thompson, one of thirteen children, was born and brought up in London. He went to work when he was only 11 as a clerk, studied for the Civil Service, and joined the Police Force when he was just 21. He was soon transferred to the Special Branch section of Scotland Yard and began his 18 fascinating years as Sir Winston Churchill's bodyguard and "shadow." In this capacity Mr. Thomson has visited, with Churchill, about thirty different countries, and has had a ring-side seat at some of the most important historical events of our times.

ASSIGNMENT: CHURCHILL

Inspector Walter Henry Thompson
of Scotland Yard

POPULAR LIBRARY · NEW YORK

NED L. PINES · President
FRANK P. LUALDI · Publisher

All POPULAR LIBRARY *books are carefully selected by the*
POPULAR LIBRARY *Editorial Board and represent titles by the*
world's greatest authors.
POPULAR LIBRARY EDITION
Published in November, 1961
Copyright 1955 by Walter Henry Thompson
Library of Congress Catalog Card Number: 54-11972
Published by arrangement with Farrar, Straus & Cudahy, Inc.
Farrar, Straus & Cudahy edition published in January, 1955

This book is dedicated to
The Right Honorable Sir Winston Churchill, K.G.; O.M.;
in recognition of his eightieth birthday
and in memory of my many proud years in his service

My grateful thanks to Max Wylie for his constant
and unwearying help and cooperation in the
production of this book

Photo credit: United Press International

ASSIGNMENT:

CHURCHILL

PART ONE

My name is Walter Henry Thompson. For most of my active life I was a member of the Special Branch of Scotland Yard. For nineteen and a half years of this period, my assignment—day and night—was guarding the life of Winston Churchill. For two years before this I was assigned to Lloyd George, Prime Minister of England during and after World War I.

Lloyd George was the first English official to move into Chequers, the country estate given to the Crown in 1920 by Lord Lee of Fareham as a retreat for England's Prime Ministers. Guarding Lloyd George was trying, but guarding Chequers was more so. It is truly ancient, the first structure, still standing, having been built by Rudolphus, clerk to the Exchequer (hence the name) of Henry II. The grounds are enormous, the drive from the main road to the manor being just under a mile. In those days there were no outside lights of any kind, and between the wide stretches of perfect lawn lay thickly wooded areas. Any part of the grounds could easily be penetrated by troublemakers, and the ancient house, which has not been seriously remodeled since 1580, is ideally constructed for assassinations. A police officer, even with his health and a revolver, could feel very alone there. And very unsafe.

In January, 1920, on the night of which I am speaking, this sense of uneasiness was intensified by the midwinter gloom of Chequers. In the rain the building looked preternatural and malign. I lumbered about through the hedges, alert, putting my torchlight briefly into this clump or that corner, but depending more upon my ears and my intuition. The biggest threat to the life of Lloyd George at that time was the Sinn Fein, the Irish terrorist organization. In two years' time, the Sinn Feiners would murder Sir Henry Wilson, chief of the British General Staff, on a busy street in London in the bright of day. Scotland Yard had information on many plots to kill Lloyd George, and the Prime Minister was quite naturally rarely out of our sight and never out of our hearing. Laughter from inside the house came to me through the rain.

I was glad when my relief arrived. Frankly, I always was. I could return to my little room in the village near Chequers, warm up and dry my wet boots. This room was my off-duty retreat. I ate and slept in it whenever the Prime Minister came down from London.

There was a memorandum to call the Yard, which I did immediately. It was a change in my assignment. I was to guard the life of Mr. Winston Churchill, a promising member of Mr. George's Cabinet. This new assignment was to alter my life and change me as a person.

I thought of what a demanding man Mr. Churchill was known to be by all the men in the Special Branch who had ever had this detail. They never had any time off! Mr. Churchill's hours were insane, his demands were reputed to be "casually tyrannical"—if such things can go together. I was tall, thirty years old, married and, as Rudyard Kipling said of some other, "tough as telegraph wire." I was a stout boxer and was being offered money to play football on a professional basis. At these pursuits I spent my leisure. They kept me hard and kept my competitive spirit at a peak, a recommended condition for a policeman. I am sixty-three as I write these words, and regret none of the decisions taken nor the orders given and I'm still tough, but when one has just been through a long bitter war against the Kaiser and is just beginning a new life, it is a most melancholy hour when he hears he must now attach himself to an ambitious politician. It meant, I thought, that I would spend my days listening to speeches and my nights standing outside of doors, in drafty hallways where there is never quite enough light to read the newspapers. This was

Churchill to me then. I did not know, of course, that on top of it all this assignment would one day bring me back to Chequers.

This assignment lasted eight and a half years. Then in 1931 and 1932 another period with him, mostly in the United States, and a third assignment that took us through the whole of World War II. With him I have seen fearsome events, and many that are imperishable.

Members of the Special Branch of Scotland Yard are trained to take in everything at once. Though I had never met Mr. Churchill, I had many preconceptions about him, inevitable because so many of my colleagues had found him "the most difficult man" and because so many had survived the detail "only a matter of days."

When I first met him, he was pacing about his study in his home in Sussex Square in London. I am sure he was already a world-famous man on this spring day in 1921, and he may also have been a great man by that time. Ten years before that he had been First Lord of the Admiralty. And at that moment he had two portfolios. One is enough. But not enough for Churchill. He was Secretary of State for Air, and Secretary of State for the Colonies. It was in this double capacity that we would be departing in a few days for Egypt. Scotland Yard never tells you where you are going, but you always know what you have to do.

As Mr. Churchill moved rapidly about his large study, not looking up nor knowing his privacy was about to be broken, he seemed almost ludicrously preoccupied. His concentration was so frenzied as to approach the burlesque.

"This is Sergeant Thompson," his secretary said quietly. Mr. Churchill stopped walking and looked over.

"You wanted to see me?" he asked.

I did not want to see him at all. I merely recited the orders from Scotland Yard—that I had been sent to guard his life. He asked me how I planned to do that. I told him. Though I of course had no idea of the projected trip to Egypt and Jerusalem, I mentioned the possible security hazards that seemed at that time to be developing for men in public life. Benito Mussolini was soon to march on Rome, and cheap imitations of his bravado, even in England, were springing up in unexpected places and asserting themselves. Sir Oswald Mosley, later to be known as "the Woolworth Duce," was drawing a column of sleek delinquents to follow him to objectives more noisy than clear. There were other dangers and disgraces, communism among them.

Winston Churchill had pulled himself at once from his deep thought. He listened to me as if it were the most important matter then before the Crown. He had the great gift of immediacy. And he had the greater one of dispatch.

"Thank you, Thompson. I've no doubt that we'll get on well together." We did, too, though often through the exercise of restraint.

Mr. Churchill was not much taller than the Prime Minister whom I had just left. Both men were quick of mind and both were always hurrying. Lloyd George seemed to scamper, while Mr. Churchill was more of a lunger and charger. In the months to come, I was able to make comparisons between these two men and come to my own evaluation of what their real strengths were.

Lloyd George's quickness of mind was sometimes his own trap. He would listen to anybody and too often immediately believe him. But Mr. Churchill always, and at once, knew when he was in the presence of an expert. Lloyd George would seek and take suggestions from any man at hand. He was the prettiest talker who ever lived but he also liked pretty talk. To use a common expression, he could be "kidded," for he had the great flaw that is shared by all the great salesmen in the world: they are themselves gullible.

The few times Churchill was taken in, he was caught in errors of his own, never in a misjudgment of the skills of others. He was such an expert at so many different areas of thought that his own belief, gathered through the years, that he was close to infallible seems about justified in the light of what we know today. But his mind was the active and experimenting sort, so Churchill had to find out what he couldn't do by getting smashed up himself.

There is a most literal side to this. He had always been a great lover of flight, for example. To be a pilot himself at an early age was one of his near obsessions, but lacking instinct for the peculiar demands of flying and temperament for the quality of coolness it requires, and most of all lacking the multiple coordinations it demands—he was unfit ever to take off and land. Nothing but severe wreckage ever proved this to him—that and an injury to a close friend.

Winston Churchill's basic thinking was for all time. Even

in those days when I first met him (he was forty-six when I became his bodyguard), there was an enduring and an almost imperial substance to his speech, as if what he said and thought of the wars and struggles that were so much a part of his own life, could have applied with equal sense to many of the prolonged and complicated conflicts that had shaken the Western World in the past.

Churchill always saw the main thing. Lloyd George too often saw only the immediate thing.

Lloyd George would not know for sure today what he had said yesterday. But so extraordinary was his charm and so unbelievable his oratorical nimbleness that no contradiction, no misstatement of known fact, ever seemed to embarrass him. He had all the self-confidence and the engaging recklessness of the true Celt, and was incredibly fast to recoil. But there was no recoil in Churchill. If things didn't give, he took the blow and pushed on in for another. Today he is a very battered old battlewagon, with scars and fractures from Sassoon Dock in India to Omdurman in the Sudan.

Egypt seemed a poor health risk, and I felt little attachment to the journey.

However, and quite contrary to the ponderousness with which the British government arrives at mighty decisions, I soon found myself rocking back and forth in the roughest railroad I know of—the Paris-Lyons-Marseilles—bound for Marseilles, then by liner for Alexandria. On this railroad it is impossible to talk, eat, sleep, shave, stand, sit, or think. One must somehow survive inexplicable discomfort to the journey's end, then forget it all quickly.

On board the train was Mrs. Churchill. Nothing seemed ever to disturb or to dishearten her, but I doubt if she felt any more pleasure at the prospect of the Eastern Mediterranean than I did. Her husband was having a good time. The mission was awkward. The danger was real. The British were at a near peak of unpopularity with the Egyptians at this time.

Chief of this mission was Lord Trenchard. His nickname was "Boom." As a traveling companion he was a column of ice, even less communicative than ice, for literally nothing ever melted from him. I have never known a man less able to reach people nor one so inaccessible. He was a good match for the Sphinx.

I do not know whether we accomplished our mission in Egypt or not (there would be no finding it out from "Boom" Trenchard), but the first objective had to do with aviation. Mr. Churchill, as Secretary for Air, was to determine whether an increase in the scanty air installations of Egypt would relieve some of the pressures of duty and of occupation from the garrisoned Tommies there. They had a dreary life indeed, and if Egypt and the Sudan and the Suez Canal area could all be satisfactorily policed and supervised by an improved air patroling system, it would represent quite a material advance. And save money too.

Mr. Churchill had, as his own parliamentary secretary, Sir Archibald Sinclair. And as his guide, interpreter and general diagnostician for the involved condition of the whole Middle East he had the semi-legendary Lawrence of Arabia.

Lawrence was an untidy little chap, very slight indeed, awkward, aloof, meditative. He weighed but eight stone. He was probably the most important member of our group, for three good reasons: he understood every detail of an unbelievably tangled situation, he spoke Arabic, and he was deeply loved, even actively worshipped, by the Arab world. This "kingship" was not anything that he at any time visibly enjoyed, but it was of much use to our mission many times before our return.

Lawrence had been of great help to the Allied cause during World War I, supported in large part by promises he was empowered to make to assure the continued allegiance of desert groups and in preventing their joining the Kaiser's forces. Lawrence told me that the Germans had so little expected to be defeated that they had built a castle outside Jerusalem to be used by the Kaiser at war's end for his residence when visiting his Eastern Empire. On the Mount of Olives was a stone seat that had been carved for the Kaiser. It was called the "Chair of Imperial Contemplation." I made a point of sitting in this seat by the hour, when we later on got to Jerusalem, and while sitting in it I would wonder how the woodpile was accumulating at Doorn. I was quite conscientious about this and squared some old accounts for outrages beyond measure.

Lawrence told me that Churchill's life would be in danger from the instant we were on African soil. He said we would get excellent help from the Egyptian police but that the Arab masses were dangerous and inflammable. I was instructed never to use my revolver except in greatest emergency but was informed that a show of force by fists was highly respected (if such a display were called for), and that I might make friends for Churchill by beating off such attackers as got near him whereas I would make enemies by firing.

I had not known about this but it worked when needed.

The now-deposed Egyptian King Farouk, whom we have all heard so much about, was a baby of only one year at this time, and his father was Sultan. He did not take the title of king until the year following. His name was Ahmed Fuad, the brother of the previous Sultan Kamil. Fuad served his people until his death in 1936. Contrary to most opinion, Farouk was at first not only competent but popular; but soon destroyed himself in eating and wenching.

The hatred extended toward the British was to some extent perhaps justified in the eyes of those Egyptians who did not entirely understand their own situation or appreciate the protections that limited British influence afforded them. The Egyptians were under the impression that Churchill's visit was to interfere with their internal affairs while our whole purpose (in Egypt at least, though not in Palestine) was to release ground troops. The Egyptians were also disaffected because we had seen fit to deport Zaghlul Pasha to Malta while the Paris Peace Conference had been in progress. The Nationalist Party, called the Wafd, of which Zaghlul Pasha was a headstrong and popular leader, was growing at the time. The necessary methods of British policy, forced labor and requisition of materials, were most bitterly resented. Zahglul Pasha demanded independence. It was too early for that. General Allenby had had to put down several insurrections, most of them bloody.

As the docks of Alexandria and the heat of the mainland began to near us, some of Mr. Churchill's visible excitement about landing was augmented in a healthy way by the true and practical possibilities of airplanes in this region. The age of flight was here, though new. The first flight from Cairo to the Cape had been made only the year before, and Mr. Churchill could trace the route with his finger. Another hazardous over-the-desert flight had been successfully completed from Algiers to Gao (on the Niger), then on to Dakar. A motorized expedition—I believe the Courtot—had just crossed the Sahara to Lake Chad, and the Haardt expedition that was to cross and recross the Sahara with caterpillar motors was then forming. This of course was of great interest to Mr. Churchill (almost anything was, if it looked as if it could be put to work) because it was he who had insisted on the practicality of caterpillar traction years before the war, for safely crossing over an enemy trench or for crushing it in—the instinct that led to the first British tank. Here it was conquering heat and sand and traversing the unmapped horror of the Sahara.

Heat and a swarm of flies hit us as we tied up at the dockside at Alexandria. A large and sullen crowd of Egyptians gathered when we stepped ashore, but there was no demonstration. I stayed directly behind and slightly to one side of Mr. Churchill. Mrs. Churchill and her maid were to my right. Our party stepped into cars chauffeured by British sergeants. Egyptian police, with staves, held the crowd back. There was some shouting and what would amount to boos in our own country. It was not unsettling but these were harsh faces.

"Never let Mr. Churchill out of your sight while in Egypt." I was at this moment seated beside the driver of the car that was to take our party to a hotel. Mr. and Mrs. Churchill sat behind, with Sir Archibald between them. We looked English and uncomfortably hatted, Mrs. Churchill in a gray cloche with black ribbon, very fashionable at the time. The man warning me was standing in the road at my side. He was Russell Pasha, probably the world's most famous detective at that time. Dope smugglers were his most frequent victims. He was as trusted by the Egyptian police and reigning family as Lawrence was trusted in the desert.

We were assigned our proper space in the hotel. I was in charge of the "official papers" which we English, for some reason, prefer to keep in boxes. These I placed in a room adjoining Mr. Churchill's, locked the room, checked the hotel, then talked to the police regarding routes of movement and times for our arrivals and departures.

While her husband ate his dinner, Mrs. Churchill took a brief rest. She heard someone moving about in the locked room where the boxes were and, rushing into the hall, called me. I smashed the door in and drew my gun. The boxes had been disturbed but were unopened and an Arab disappeared through a window at the ceiling level as I came crashing over the threshold. There was not time to shoot him. He was gone.

Mr. Churchill, who had been summoned by the commotion and the odd howling in the corridors, came up unperturbed and I think a bit disappointed that he had missed the show. He hated to miss anything. He asked about the boxes. When I showed him that the seals were unbroken, he ordered extra protection about the place, and asked me if I minded spending the night with the boxes.

I of course agreed and ordered a cot to be put in the place. I shut and bolted the window through which the Arab had flown, drew my revolver, and waited through the suffocating hours for the dawn to break. Except for the temperature it was like many another night.

The day was welcome. We were to take Fuad's train to Cairo. I had had no experience with the Egyptian police, of course, except for the swift impressions I had gathered upon meeting Russell Pasha in the street, and this impression had been a good one. He was English and knew Egypt better than any other man. However, as an Officer of Scotland Yard, I also had some notions of my own and a bit of training behind me as well.

I did not like the temper of the crowd that had been at the docks the day before. But I had noticed, also, a fantastic love of color and an even greater love of what one might call "show of authority."

Sir Archibald Sinclair had told me to cooperate as best I could with the police. I informed the Cairo police who had come over to be with us in Alexandria that our party would leave the hotel promptly at ten o'clock and that the Sultan's train would leave exactly at ten-thirty; that the road from the hotel to the station should be manned by uniformed Egyptian police.

Today I do not know at all who was in the motorcade that went down the main boulevards of Alexandria, but our party went in shabby little cars and dirty back roads, boarding the train from its "off" side.

We got aboard quickly, always wise. The train was well-appointed but a bit garish. All the carriages, as well as the locomotive, were painted pure white. There was bunting around the boiler door and flags spraying out from the cowcatcher steps.

There was a shrill tootling on the whistle and we pulled slowly away, but we were going through neighborhoods so congested that our failure to pick up any speed at all continued to keep me apprehensive. I felt somewhat better when my own party was seated in the commodious compartment (fit for a Sultan indeed, and half a harem). Mr. Churchill busied himself with one of the boxes, the whole bothersome cluster of which I had myself wrestled aboard, and then sat down at a carved secretary and began to read and to perspire. This seemed somehow the proper thing for a cabinet member to be doing in an equatorial country. Mrs. Churchill, always cool and composed and of course one of the best-dressed women of her day, snapped on a fan and commenced reading as if she were home in London. I had the curious feeling in that instant (and a prick of possible disloyalty) that this present picture of Mr. and Mrs. Churchill was not so much an example of their unusual capacity to adapt themselves as an inability ever to realize they were in foreign places. Whatever it was, it seemed very British of them and I liked it. I certainly never felt at home in Egypt.

It was well I didn't. I kept watching T. E. Lawrence out of the tail of my eye and he in turn kept looking out of the corridor windows. We were approaching a grade crossing. I remained standing in the compartment doorway and was not going to move to my own space till the train had picked up enough speed so she could not then be boarded or effectively stoned or fired upon.

There was the sudden sound of splintering glass. Two windows had been smashed, one ahead of the Churchills' compartment and one behind. Fortunately the stoning came from the other side and though my charges might be struck by flying glass, they could not be directly hit. Our speed was an exasperation to me, for we were hardly dog-trotting. Lawrence, with a quiet wave of the hand, cautioned me to hold my position. He went to the end of the car. A huge mass of ugly-looking Egyptians, some fighting for a hold on the outside window ledges, was choking this stretch of the crossing. Stones began to rain up against the sides of all the cars and window after window tumbled inside the corridors and spilt glass over the mulberry carpeting.

Mrs. Churchill had stopped reading. She seemed more annoyed than interested. Churchill laid aside his pencil and turned to Sir Archibald. "Better relieve Thompson of his packages, Archie. He may be more useful to us if he's un-encumbered."

We all exchanged grins. Thinking we might have been boarded by a couple of Arab skulkers, I drew my revolver and kept it just beneath my jacket. My feet were apart to catch the sway of the train. My elbows were in contact with each side of the compartment doorjamb. I would have been very hard to pass. We began to gather a bit of speed. Lawrence came back. He never spoke much to me.

"We'll be all right. There's nothing left to smash." He went in with the others. Porters in red uniforms and gold sashes began to sweep up the mess and toss the debris out the empty frames. Churchill looked up boyishly at me and smiled, then turned back to the austere basilisk who was Trenchard and together they again began to scowl over the Empire's problems.

From my previous night in that lonely flea-ridden "Black Hole" of Alexandria to the dull prospects of the climate we had entered, I began to feel that Egypt could improve herself materially if she could find another location. The British, in all their imperial wisdom, have somehow arranged to place most of their imperial problems in some of our very worst geography. From the moving train the landscape appeared to be cracked open by too much sun. It glistened with vitreous reflections as if this whole sandy waste that is North Africa were trying to cool. The countryside shook and shimmered in the heat. Buildings stood in the air above their foundations. Mirages were soon so common they grew tiresome. Spires and minarets could be seen upside-down twenty degrees off the horizon. Fellahin stood like shrouded scarecrows. The falsetto keening of the train whistle was appropriate to my notion of all these dead stretches of desolation. It all had a scorched lunar look.

I realized I was cross because I was hungry. In order to improve the security of the ride from the hotel to the train, I had been up and at it since sunup and I had missed dinner the night before because of that prowling Egyptian.

Quite suddenly the topography changed, the temperature cooled, and a spicy smell of food ran through the cars. We had left the dead mask of the coast and moved into the delta country. Natives working the fields looked more alive than their brothers a few miles before. And the train could really go.

These satisfactions came and went quickly. We had been clipping along at seventy for but a few minutes, it seemed, when we slowed again. A very correct English colonel with monocle came aboard at a nameless spot in the tracks, showed his pass, and went in to the compartment. The white train panted in the sun. An English-speaking Egyptian conductor passed and told me we were five miles out of Cairo. Apparently Englishmen were no more popular in Cairo than they had been the day before in Alexandria. By prearrangement (not known to us) we were all of us taken off the Sultan's train at this point and driven by cars to the Semiramis Hotel.

There was some sort of demonstration in progress already —there is always some sort of demonstration wherever Churchill goes, I find—but we drove without ceremony to a flowered arch at the side of the hotel and went on in without any more special attention from the "welcoming committee" in front. No stones were thrown but no one rushed forth with a bouquet for Mrs. Churchill either.

Here, while the now familiar annoyance of resettling was taking place, Russell Pasha again cautioned me about the extreme danger that Mr. Churchill would be in for the full duration of his stay. I made an effort to find out what kind of attack it might be and what kind of circumstance or gathering might provoke such attack. Would it be a knife in the dark at night while he slept? Or a shot from the crowd? Poison? Or something ingeniously oriental that Sax Rohmer might invent? Russell Pasha told me I must stay so close to Churchill for the whole of this visit as literally to be right outside his private bath while the Secretary for Air was in the tub, and I realized it was a situation somewhat new to me. And at some shock for what it would call for from my half-filled reservoirs of diplomacy, I realized the situation was a bit new also to Mrs. Churchill.

I am sure the whole nuisance of my being so perpetually about, of being so ubiquitous, was most distressing to her own idea of order and of privacy. My shadow indeed must have been far more trying and importunate than protective, at least to her. Poor woman, she never made any sign or gesture. She did, however, have an icy way she could look at a man when things went to the snapping point of endurance, and on these occasions I always wished I could disappear till she could recover.

I shan't burden the reader with the tired reminder about the policeman's life, beyond saying that there is an indestructible, almost a glacial, truth about it. There is a necessity of being indispensable but not quite welcome; of being forever present and as forever invisible; of being always out of conversations but never out of earshot; of being responsible for new details that no exercise of foresight and no meticulous attention to pre-planning could predict.

The demonstration was continuing outside our windows; there was a rhythm to it now, which I grew to know meant students and anti-British slogans. There was a power failure and the overhead fans stopped. Flies covered me like soot. Hawkers were selling sugarcane in aggravating singsong. Buzzards and vultures stood stationary in the sky three thousand feet above, waiting for animals to die. Donkeys passed, and overloaded carts pulled by huge woeful oxen. Didn't these demonstrators know that His Majesty's ministers were about to be received by their own Sultan? Why didn't they disperse?

An Air Force sergeant poked his head in my door and asked where Mr. Churchill was. I said he was next door. He was waiting for General Allenby, I said, to give us instructions about getting to the palace. The sergeant shook me into a renewed horror of this particular day by saying Mr. Churchill was not even in the hotel.

I sprinted down the marble halls to see a clerk whom I had instructed to tell me of Mr. Churchill's emergence from his own suite. He had forgotten to. I asked Russell Pasha to reprimand the fellow, and rushed into the street looking for Winston.

I quickly deduced that Mr. Churchill had got tired of waiting for the General and that he had gone out to find him. And this was exactly right. He was smoking amiably, enjoying the look of new buildings.

Mr. Churchill and I had a swift conversation about this; about his own responsibilities not so much to me as to any security officer assigned to him. It was not to be the only time that our voices rose, even on public sidewalks, and the best way to leave this unhappy exchange is to say that it was quite brief and thoroughly unacademic.

He promised never to do such a thing again when he appreciated what he had done and the unnecessary peril into which he had so happily hurried. When he saw my alarm and fury, he saw too that there was nothing jaunty about his little walk. Did he keep his promise? If I had known that day that I had to go through the *Blitz* with him, I would have gone back to England.

A few hours later Winston Churchill and Lord Allenby, with a gorgeous satrap whose name and rank I can't now recall, drove to the spacious grounds of Egypt's ruler, with myself and the sergeant in a RAF car right behind. The palace guards, in two huge ribbons of color, stood at attention while the first car came through the gates. There was an immense mob all about, and all shouting. We slowed to show our passes but the gates swung shut just as the mob closed in. I was separated from Churchill.

The palace guards jumped in behind the protection of their own railings and we could not persuade them to let us through. To this day I feel they were afraid of their own people in this aroused condition. All I could think of, and quite disconsolately in that moment, was that while Mr. Churchill was safe inside (I had to presume he was safe), Russell Pasha had warned me not to use firearms except under the severest necessity. But Russell Pasha was not anywhere about to give me the benefit of his views and the mob was now upon us physically, shaking the car's doors, beating on the tonneau with sticks. Our headlights were smashed in. I tried to feel some safety in the presence of this sergeant from the Air Force and indeed could find no fear in his expression. He told me later he had no feeling of fear since the long arm of Scotland Yard had reached clear into Egypt to save *him!* I rose in the seat with my coat deliberately open. At least I would let them *see* I had a revolver. I waved with a show of some urgency to the palace guards. They waved back. It must have been very interesting for them. It must have made the day pleasant.

A rock split our windshield.

"I propose we try to deal with this right now," I shouted.

"I'll do anything you suggest, Thompson," the sergeant said.

I pushed an Egyptian's face away from my own, flung the car door open with force, and flung myself into those directly before me, knocking down two men with two quick blows. The sergeant seemed to feel I could handle this job all by myself. He was most approving of my activity and had even folded his arms.

"Get out on your side!" I shouted. Stones and bricks poured into our car. The sergeant jumped from behind the steering wheel and engaged those on his side as I was flailing and punching on my own. A wooden staff came down on my head. I kept punching at everyone available. Four or five men were lying down beside the car by this time. A huge fellow, rather fat, tugged at my coat with much force, pulling my head over. I drove my fist into his belly and how he howled! As he backed off, I split his nose. The sergeant picked up a wrench and brought it down four or five times. This was a great help. There were cheers and screams.

It was a strange fight. There was laughter and grinning in the fringes but where we were, the whole affair was being attended to with more energy than I had thus far seen in Egypt. I kept hoping to make enough of a clearing to get my coat off and I coveted the sergeant's wrench. We had an unusually busy five or six minutes of this, and though I could see some progress and felt no fatigue as yet, I could not see any end to it. I kept hoping the palace guards would feel some responsibility toward us here at their very gates but they obviously felt it was far too good a show to interrupt.

The sound of police whistles was by this time welcome. A few of the rioters were packed off, but not by the palace guards. It was the Cairo police, a finely trained and versatile organization, as I learned later through Russell Pasha. The palace guards merely watched proceedings.

Churchill came back soon, pink and cheerful.

There were several days of conferences, then a few for sightseeing. One day we went out to the Pyramids. Sir Archibald and I climbed to the top of the largest of these (a most strenuous exercise because of the awkward height of the blocks, about 4½ feet). I refused hot tea, offered by some Arab boys, at the summit but Sir Archibald drank thirstily and next day came down with typhoid fever. This disrupted the schedule a bit and robbed Mr. Churchill of a valuable secretary and a most merry companion.

Lieutenant Colonel Buxton, head of the famous Imperial Camel Corps, was to take us out to the ruins and excavations at Sakkara (Churchill always had to do these things, immediately he heard of them), a two-and-a-half-hour ride directly across the desert as the camel takes you. Buxton was away at this time and Lawrence, a great rider, was anxious to bring off the trip.

I do not at all care for camels. They may be picturesque at a distance but I have never seen them at a distance sufficient to bring out this pleasing characteristic. They smell. They are refractory and disdainful. They are misanthropic, egocentric, and not built for transport. They are built to last a long time by themselves, which is the best I can say for them. Their bite is dangerous as their saliva carries all manner of germs and bacteria, even the spirochete of syphilis. They are in a constant rumble of displeasure, making an oddly oriental gargling sound never heard in the Western world, even in a zoo. They look over you, never at you. They seem patient enough when crouched for loading, but rise by their hind legs first, invariably pitching first-riders over their heads into the sand, a moment always relished by the horse-mounted sheiks in the same way as our recent skirmish with the mob in front of the palace was relished by Fuad's guards.

I knew that I would look altogether ridiculous on a camel and I feel the camel knew this too. But I do not believe I looked any worse than Winston Churchill. No matter where we might be, he could always manage to balloon himself with the most surprising outer garments.

A grisly Arabian Nights sergeant who looked like a retired assassin brought forth two mounts that T. E. Lawrence had picked out. Mine was an immense and bony animal supplied with a purple shawl and a wooden carousel saddle. Mr. Churchill's mount was the same except that his had a few visible muscles and not quite the true pyramid look of antiquity which mine bore.

On a camel there is nothing to grab but the sky. And there is no discernible steering apparatus. You just go whither the other camels go. It is this fraternity feeling alone that delivers new riders to given objectives.

There is a light cord that runs from the saddle to the camel's right nostril but it might as well have been a bell-pull in a dead castle for all the tugging I gave it and the good I got out of it. Once the camel looked back directly at me and looked so meanly I felt for my gun by reflex and stopped tugging. There was nothing to do but suffer through to the end.

I realized suddenly that Churchill, who was on my right

flank at this moment, was precariously close to being on his own right flank in the next stride or two, for he had billowed off to one side of the saddle and was searching miserably about for something to grab hold of. As I already knew from my own circumstance there was not anything a man could do for himself. I watched fascinated. So did a hundred sheiks on horseback. The inevitable moment of separation came, and the Secretary for Air and for Colonies went through the air and landed in the middle of one of his colonies in a fine spray of white sand and wheeling horses. He rolled over and looked around for his hat. Arab sheiks dismounted quickly and offered their steeds, but Winston—who had been fourth in rank among the cavalry candidates at Sandhurst —had come to ride on a camel and he got back on and we somehow got out to Sakkara.

Luncheon was spread out there for us but an hour after dismounting I was still shaking so I could not properly hold a sandwich. Winston wiggled a bit too, as if secretively testing his spine for alignment or his ribs for cracks. The thought of the ride back was depressing.

It was here at Sakkara, with the strange sight and stranger sound of the native diggers chanting in rhythm as they shoveled, that I heard from the junior officers and from some of the English-speaking camel wallahs, of the incredible claims (now the subject of increasing challenge and dispute) of treks that Lawrence "was known to have taken" on camelback. Sir Edward Winterton, a former M.P. who served in Arabia in World War I, has stated: "Churchill told me in the 20's Lawrence would have made a good Secretary of Defense." Churchill was surely fascinated by Lawrence and saw much of him before our return to England, but I doubt if at that moment even Churchill could have summoned enough objectivity to worry about improving the Cabinet.

We got back on the camels somewhat after the lunch period. T. E. Lawrence had introduced Winston to a trick of some sort (maybe he had said something to the camel). In any event, Churchill's seat was improved noticeably. Mine was still what it had been before. Because I truly dreaded our return, I tried to get the secret but when the gaits of our three beasts matched each other enough for me to call to Lawrence, my own animal seemed to realize we were on our way back and decided quite suddenly to gallop all the way home. Lawrence seemed to know what was in the animal's mind for he turned his thumb toward me and said something to Winston just as my long runaway began.

"Go it, Thompson!" shouted Winston Churchill. No urging was necessary. We flew over the sands. I knew, if I could just stay on, I would far outdistance everyone else in the desert. This would at least give me some moments to compose myself before resuming the more formal and sensible duties of guarding Mr. Churchill.

Miraculously both he and Lawrence were already seated in the rear of the car, smoking and chatting, when I arrived. To this day I truly do not know how they beat me. They let me get down without saying anything. I eased myself over to the car. It was like moving a fracture case without benefit of splints, stretcher, or sedation.

It would have been an ideal time for a try on the Secretary's life, for I was nearly blind with sunglare and I felt in every bone as if a stampede had passed over me. Churchill chuckled richly. I didn't want to hear any comment from either him or Lawrence. I felt a tap on my shoulder and Winston's voice at my ear, high and ragging:

"That was a great show of energy, Thompson! I've never known a man to get so much out of a camel. You should enter him in the Grand National!"

My upright position for the ride from the edge of the desert back to the cool of the Semiramis was due to no sense of importance. I merely felt calcified. But Winston had had as rough a time too, and the spirit of fun in the leg-pulling seemed to infect the party—even got through to the Egyptian officials—and was talked about and speculated upon, especially the Air Minister's "flight to earth," for days after.

Early the next morning, and not on schedule, an interesting, and as I soon grew to know, a characteristic, side of Mr. Churchill revealed itself: a strong and controlling power in him.

If dispatch is the central force and secret of this man's success as an administrator as I believe, his compassion is the sign of his main purposes. Churchill is a practicing Christian. It is probably odd to many readers to find the word "Christian" fastened to a man of action and of war. But I noticed this quality again and again. It came from two deeper feelings: a love of simple people and a savage hatred of unfairness of any sort.

It revealed itself one day when we drove with some hurry to the RAF installations outside the city of Cairo. There was something there, or something going on there, that Winston was determined to know about and that, from what I could sense and gather, the RAF was as determined to keep from him. It turned out to be quite a simple thing indeed, but very basic: the unsatisfactory condition of the quarters that were assigned to those NCO's who were married. These quarters were abominable; it is no wonder the commanding officers were anxious to hide this shabby side of an otherwise effective service.

"I'd now like to be driven over to the married quarters," Mr. Churchill would say. And there would be a fussy procrastination, such as another inspection of a hangar the duplicate of which we had just seen, or a diversionary skirmish into the canteen, or into the map room. But they could not shake the Secretary's will to see what he had come for and see it in every detail, creditable and discreditable.

He waved officers away from him, and drew noncoms (and their wives too, standing about in polite and inquiring forlornness, struggling to be cheerful and honorably responsive) about him and into conversation with him, until the whole complaint was in his mind. He went through many of the units himself. His eyes were cameras and the conscience of his mind was their film strip. He saw the full distress of these poor people, recorded it, and before we were ourselves out of the field's area, his urgent memorandum for improvement here was on the cables and tapping out its message to the calm authorities in Whitehall.

The officers who had tried to sidetrack him were dismissed with a monumental disinterest and a handshake almost reflexive in its brevity.

It was in this blunt little exchange in the noonday sun that I realized I would serve this man with all I had, in any danger, and for as many years as his positions might require the protection of the Yard. Was there ever one like him for seeing so much?

Indeed, was there ever one like him?

We drove in silence back to the Semiramis Hotel, Winston now writing in a notebook or glancing into the sky at stunting maneuvers of the RAF. Anything in the air thrilled him.

Arriving in the hotel lobby there was a message from Sir Herbert Samuel, High Commissioner of Palestine. Churchill offered me the afternoon off, then immediately canceled it and decided to take a staff car to the Pyramids again to paint them.

I was most greatly annoyed at the unconscious use to which he could put anyone to do things for him that had not the least suggestion of belonging to his proper office. He would use anyone who would permit it. It is true that I had carried his paintboxes to the dockside while we waited for our ship at Marseilles and stood by holding off inquisitive snoopers at the wharf till the sea-scape was finished. I had at the time thought it to be a capricious enthusiasm that would not repeat itself as it was hard to associate the art of painting with the man's other activities.

I very soon learned that painting was no mere enthusiasm. It was a disease, and before any time at all had passed I had become worn out at the thought of the menial lugging of his damn boxes. It has given me a quite warped notion of this whole side of civilized living to the extent that I would never think of going into a museum no matter what was hanging there.

So he painted and smoked by the hour, while clusters of tourists, dilapidated sheiks and buggy little boys hung about, taking snapshots or giggling.

A group of British Tommies came along, off duty and carefree. With his back turned to them, Churchill could have been nearly anything in the world instead of what he really was. Now, under a green umbrella, he looked like an upholstered toad slowly incinerating itself.

Very loud stage whispers of advice came from the Tommies. They thought the man might be better doing the outside of blimp hangars. They wondered if instead of painting the Pyramids, the man might do better to repair them.

At this sally, Churchill turned and grinned broadly.

"Gawd! It's Winston!" The young soldiers sucked in their breath and wished themselves far away, but he called them over, showed them his effort at close range, criticized what he thought was still missing in the effort, set about trying to put in, and all the time chatted back and forth, getting an amazing amount of spontaneous comment from every one of them. They were being thoroughly "sweated" for impromptu offerings of many sorts, without ever knowing that the magic of the Churchill process of kindly solicitation was also giving the Secretary for Air and for Colonies a true look into the morale of the effectives in the field, and grounds for a guess at their competence. He took many of his best notes from people who never knew they gave them.

"Tiffin" was an agreeable experience. In the Semiramis, I looked forward to these hours, or half-hours, for I could observe my charge under the most ideal conditions, keeping him not only under surveillance but within earshot, and yet keeping out of sight. I could also have my own tea in peace. There were many tubs of palms and flowering plants from the botanical gardens.

I was having my second cup of tea one day when Russell Pasha walked through the lobby, then strode into the enclosed terrace where Mr. Churchill and his party were talking. Lawrence was in full Arab dress. Russell made a sign of some sort to Lawrence who in turn looked over to the semicircle of ferns behind which I was nearly invisible. Pasha nodded a greeting to Boom Trenchard, who looked puzzled as always when people were polite to him, bowed slightly to the rest, and came over to my little table.

Russell Pasha told me that Sir Herbert Samuel had sent special police with him from the Holy Land because of knowledge picked up outside Jerusalem that Churchill's life was going to be attempted sometime during the train trip from Cairo. It was not known whether the attempt would be by bomb or by shooting. My duty would be more than ever strenuous because I was assigned responsibility for the security of the train, not just the official carriage. All the other police that could be made available were detailed to various stations and sensitive spots along the right-of-way. Sensitive spots are locations where trains take water, or coal, where they change engines or crews, or where, due to topography, conditions of the track, or congestion because of junction, trains must be driven at paces slow enough for boarding by unauthorized persons.

A pilot train was to precede our own, a precaution found necessary in this region of expanding railroad services and contracting confidences. Many cow-catchers had been blown off by old-fashioned torpedoes clamped to the rail and detonated by contact.

I asked about the personnel itself, the driving and signal and coupling crews. Russell Pasha said they were all known to the Cairo police. He said, however, that the frictions in

and around Jerusalem were of such explosive heat that there
was nothing a police officer could do but stay fit, stay
awake, and be instantly ready to shoot. He cautioned me to
shoot on even slight suspicion. I asked him to reconcile this
advice with what had seemed almost the reverse of it only a
few days before. He told me we were moving into a climate
of "unclassifiable fanaticism," with much of the feeling
churned up and kept in ferment by the hostile feelings of
the Jews for the Arabs and vice versa.

Not being a politician but a police officer and thus more
accustomed to the essential goodness of man with only occasional, individual deviations into rogue behavior, I had
thought—as indeed the English press had urged us to think
—that the Balfour Declaration had been drafted for the sole
purpose of solving the very problem Russell Pasha was now
telling me was so explosive. The declaration was surely simple enough in outline, and favored the establishment in Palestine of a National Home for the Jewish people. His Majesty's
Government further promised to bring its best endeavor to
bear on the fruition of this hope in a practical sense, so that
nothing would be done to curtail civil rights or to prejudice
civil or religious rights of the existing non-Jewish com-
munities then living in Palestine.

That was the main outline of it and it was put forth only
a few years before Mr. Churchill's visit there. I believe the
date was 1917.

In this very regard, with perhaps too much of the Balfour
remedy coming out (according to the Arabs) to favor the
Jews disproportionately, the Palestine White Paper took
heed a few years later of the plight of landless Arabs, and
suggested curtailment of land to the Jews and the controlling of further Jewish immigration while so many Arabs
were unemployed. And this was a mere dozen years after
the first! And this, of course, because it sought to correct
what was considered an injustice against the Arabs, rekindled
the wrath of the Jews.

It is, however, very hard to know what to do with vexed
populations.

Thinking back over Egypt, we've surely had a rum time
there, too. Even as we were leaving, the Milner Report, that
offered freedom to Egypt with the guarantee of certain
British interests there, seemed to stir up more dark waters
than it settled. When the British released Zaghlul, there were

more anti-British outbreaks than ever before. And the culminating inability of Zaghlul to come to any sort of workable agreement with the then Prime Minister (1924) Ramsay MacDonald led to the British ultimatum of that year. The assassination of Sir Lee Stack, Governor General of the Sudan, was the last straw before the imposing of repressive measures.

People far from these things, and out of the sight and the sound of the collision of them and the import of them, can too quickly dismiss the enduring significance of the phrase, "to maintain the tranquillity of the realm." And I hope no American readers will seek clues in this book to the glib challenge so often put to the English these days (and through the past three centuries as well, I suppose) in such half-mocking phrases as: "What the hell are the British doing there in the first place?" We hear it everywhere.

Let us say that we have made some mistakes but that we deeply believe the good overbalances the evil.

As we packed for our trip to Jerusalem, Mr. Churchill received word from London that an Italian general named Badoglio was preparing a troop movement into Libya. Mussolini's new government represented at this time little more than a successful street parade, headed by a noisy man with patent leather shoes and a bombastic program and backed up with a shouting mob of pomaded and sweaty ruffians. It was, of course, to turn into somewhat more than this.

We were packed and ready for departure to the train that would bear us, without incident, we hoped, to Jerusalem. Lawrence, in the lobby of the Semiramis, asked if our party were on its way down. Winston Churchill was standing on the balcony alone, looking west across the wide wilderness of North Africa.

"If Badoglio is on his way," he said, "we'll have to be coming back here someday." A slight chill went through me. I certainly never expected to hear of Italians in Africa.

This part of the world, with the exception of patches close to the Nile, seems to me to be God's revenge on the impenitence of all the wrongdoing of mankind since Adam. Mr. Churchill had the great detachment of mind to see what he had come to look for, and if he had a few hours to himself and found something either beautiful or striking he would paint it. He was such a traveler and reader of maps, so much a man in motion, that even new places lost their novelty, through advanced study, before they received his personal inspection. I saw him describe, on first visits, the detailed movements of every involved unit in three battles —Balaklava, Waterloo, and Gettysburg—to the astonishment of experts who were with us.

This was true not only of the sections we were departing but the confusions into which we were being sent. At the first great deadlock of forces in the struggle of World War I, just prior to the close of the year 1914, it had been Churchill who strongly urged the idea of the British government that British strength be shifted to the Near East while the armies of France sought to contain the Germans on the Western front. His views were supported not only by Prime Minister Lloyd George, but by the highest military authority that we had—Kitchener himself. With equal force and equally stunning logic, the views were opposed by Joffre among the French generals and most vigorously by our Sir John French.

But Churchill's enthusiasm, his record, his persuasiveness won the government's decision to take this risk. The man was not yet forty.

The assault upon the Dardanelles was beaten off by the Turks from their superior position upon the heights and Winston Churchill's great hopes suddenly collapsed when forces—English, French, and Australian—could no longer hold Gallipoli and had to be evacuated. This was miraculously accomplished without loss but it was a huge failure in an enormous undertaking, and the Straits remained closed to us for the remainder of the war and prevented support from the Allies ever reaching the Russians through these waters. No man entirely knows the inner feelings of Mr. Churchill about this, but I have seen him walk away from conversations when they turned to this sad expedition. We lost everything we tried for here, including three battleships —*Goliath, Triumph* and *Majestic.* The great name to emerge from all this was Mustapha Kemal. For Churchill, it was like losing his own children for he had been First Lord of the Admiralty from 1911 to 1915. I am told by men close to him that nothing ever shook him so hard again until the fall of Singapore and the sinking of the *Prince of Wales* and the *Repulse.*

This is mentioned only to show Churchill's acquaintance with the territories at this end of the Mediterranean Sea.

Archie Sinclair, still suffering from typhoid, was left behind to recover in a nursing home near the Semiramis. Sir Herbert Samuel became most important to our tour, as Palestine's High Commissioner. Because of the warnings we had received through the Cairo police about the planned assassination of Churchill, I went at once on arrival in Jerusalem to Sir Herbert to ask what special precautions he might recommend to us for his own corner of the world.

I met the two special officers of the Palestine police he had sent to accompany us. They did not look like police officers to me. They looked like enthusiastic tourists in uniforms that had been cut to fit other people. Perhaps it is not quite fair to them for I never had reason on this trip to Jerusalem to question their willingness to stand forth in the presence of danger and do their duty. But they surely seemed inexperienced, even naïve. They ate all the time. They whispered a great deal. They had only the most random guesses as to where and how we might expect trouble. Worse, they had no plan at all for how they might meet trouble when it came. They anticipated nothing. They seemed more empty-headed than nonchalant. They were known up and down the train as Mutt and Jeff. The tall one looked like a piece of farm machinery, bent over and abandoned. His arms were surely too long for any kind of physical combat and when he sat down his knuckles dragged on the floor. His companion was pink and full and looked like a heaping barrow of summer vegetables. The two of them fully armed did not seem a good match for an Arabian beggar. And they were English, which made it the more implausible.

We dragged forth from Cairo and headed for the Holy Land. I secured the train as best I could and inspected the travel permits of everyone in the cars coupled to our car. I politely ordered Mr. and Mrs. Churchill to remain in their compartment no matter what kind of outside disturbance they heard and inspected their windows. Mrs. Churchill fanned herself quietly and Lord Trenchard smiled funereally at my concern, the only time I ever saw his expression change. It was not a smile, merely a slight movement in the cheek muscles.

Churchill was all for the new place. Egypt was behind. Sir Herbert had already briefed him on ever new complexities and laid out the inevitable sheaf of plans for dealing with the insoluble. Merely by adjusting his glasses, Mr.

Churchill seemed to adjust himself to the perennial problem of finding a way out when there was none.

Mutt and Jeff walked down the corridor, Mutt chewing a native plantain. Jeff whistled "The Long, Long Trail," then changed to "Baby's Prayer at Twilight," tunes that always made me fidgety even when seriously engaged. He lighted a cigarette (forbidden around Mr. Churchill) and with the smoke curling about his squinty eyes began to finger what looked like a clip of cartridges. Then I saw that it was not cartridges but a new spool of film for a camera. I told him to put up his camera and reminded him that security officers appeared in pictures as little as possible and never took any pictures of their own. He suggested that I cool my views at an open window whereupon I suggested I might reduce him enough to pass him through an open window and took the film forcibly from him.

We came to the Biblical town of Gaza, swollen with beggars and paved with sheep manure. The legendary Samson was indeed fortunate to be "eyeless" here for it is quite the most complete municipal horror I ever saw in the Near East.

There was a large mosque near the station. Our train stopped. Colonel Lawrence appeared at the door of the Churchill compartment. He was robed, burnoosed, sashed, scimitared and slippered. Outside there was a huge mob, howling and squealing. I never could quickly read these mobs. In front of Fuad's Abdin palace, was it all savage ferocity or was there some schoolboy fun in the fight we had, the RAF sergeant and I? When Churchill fell from his camel, I was at first frightened at the sight and movement of the sheiks on horseback. There was something positively minatory in their very solicitude. I feared that they might kill the man if he refused their help.

Here it was again.

"We aren't leaving the train at this spot?" I asked Lawrence.

"Yes," he said. "It's prearranged."

"But it's a true hellhole."

Lawrence peered out the carriage window as if to gauge my estimate against his own. It was a familiar enough city to him, of course, as indeed was every other—from waterhole to domed and pavilioned capitol for half a million square miles. In a strange sense it *was* Lawrence's land, by legacy to him from these Arabs.

Lawrence was not at all disturbed by the appearance of the crowd. He tapped on Churchill's door which at once. Sir Herbert, Boom Trenchard (an almost cosmic incongruity in Gaza), Churchill, Lawrence and myself went to the end of the car.

"What about Mutt and Jeff?" I asked Lawrence.

"They're Sir Herbert's worry, Thompson. Let's just lose them and see if they survive by themselves."

"But don't you feel the need of them? They're a couple of extra guns."

"They're a couple of extra jokers. We're going to the big hall next to the mosque. I'm taking the group inside. These are Arabs. Churchill is going to speak to them briefly. And I'll translate. I think we'll be all right. You come with us to the door. Then stand before it till we come out again. Stand without moving."

I am not going to get into the controversy about T. E. Lawrence. I spent many days and many hundreds of hours with him. I am positive he was a man of unbelievable and inscrutable inner power. I do not know what this was. Tribal leaders, high and low, absolute rulers of unfrequented places as remote, fancied and impenetrable as Hadramaut, as unheard of and unlikely as Khoi and Zakho and Jerziret ibn Omar, would come in splendor or awe and humble themselves before this little Englishman.

Evidence of this magic was present before us even before we stepped down from the carriages. It is doubtful whether the Arabs, with the unclassifiable admixture here in the mob at Gaza of Lebanese, Iraqi, Alaouites, Djebel Druses, Turks, Syrians, Jews, Armenians, Kurds and Persians—whether more than three or four in the crowd knew which was Churchill. Or much cared. We were just a knot of Europeans with hats on. Lawrence was the man.

No Pope of Rome ever had more command before his own worshippers in the Palazzo. And Colonel Lawrence raised his hand slowly, the first and second fingers lifted above the other two for silence and for blessing. He could have owned their earth. He did own it. Every man froze in respect, in a kind of New Testament adoration of shepherds for a master. It was quite weird and very comforting.

We passed through these murderous-looking men and they parted a way for us without struggle. Many touched Lawrence as he moved forward among them. Far off, drums were beating, and a horse neighed. A muezzin's cry fell sadly among us from the single minaret of the mosque.

To me the Middle East—any part of it and at any time of the day—always has the appearance that an insurrection is well started and will momentarily assert itself. It's in the keen-eyed, unwinking look of the bedouin, in the swash-buckling flamboyance of the *keffiyehs*, in the slant of his tarboosh, the flash of his teeth, the glint of his knife. These men moved with the beauty of lizards—hardly at all or too fast for the eye to follow.

The enormous masses of men and materials that had been moved from one place to another because Mr. Churchill thought it a good idea, came to me now in the presence of this exquisitely dilapidated circus, in this hideous Old Testament junkyard of dead economies, black tobacco, and casual slaughter. The places where men must go to fight and die are indeed never picturesque, seem to warn against trespass by forbidding life rather than attracting it; often not even wearing the promise life could be there sustained.

Here where Sir James Murray had failed, and where Colonel Lawrence's undisputed brilliance was to find itself in these deserts that protect the throat of Asia, where the great complex of this phase of World War I was settled—over these stinking alleys and rutted human spillways, was another lighted lamp in this gloomy part of England's reach and her responsibility.

The British had been badly hurt right here; and still smarting, had yet won through somehow when they were about to be engulfed altogether. And this little man Lawrence, here at the touch of a wrist, had done this.

Lawrence was so greatly loved and so fanatically respected that he could have established his own empire from Alexandretta to the Indus. He knew this, too. What his first fealty was can never be known for sure, but his sense that he had been betrayed by his own people or their politicians, or that the Arab world as he knew it had been betrayed, these doubts and despairs were probably a part of his mental and emotional burden to the very day he crashed on his motorbike in Surrey. One merely knew he was special.

On the way to the hall where Churchill was to speak and to receive homages of diverse though obscure substance, I saw him looking about quickly from side to side, not with apprehension (though I was frankly feeling a bit myself), but possibly to locate the "special police" that had been assigned to him. We were hardly fifty feet from the train, the noise of the crowd rising as we advanced. I looked back at our carriages, to place our return journey in my eye, and suddenly saw our two special police—Mutt and Jeff—standing in Mr. Churchill's compartment, taking pictures! I have rarely felt such exasperation or such impotence. What indeed is the responsibility of Scotland Yard in such a situation? Should I inform the High Commissioner of Palestine he had clowns in his party?

I did what I always do. I slogged along saying nothing, independently daring the world to start something. As usual I had to see everything and see it first. This incident always calmed me down and hours or days later managed to amuse me. But there was a bit more security duty than one man should be given and though I had two revolvers (Winston usually handed me his when we were traveling together, but carried it himself when alone—*if* he remembered—and would use it instantly), I also had but two hands.

The red sea of Arabian faces continued to part for us clear to the hall. It was a gathering of tribal chiefs. A great cheer went up, vaguely frightening. Lawrence stood at the battered entrance of this jerrymade architectural anomaly of a public building, deferentially waving Mr. Churchill ahead with a low sweep of his hooded arm. Sir Herbert followed. Lawrence reminded me, with a faint uplift of his forefinger, nothing more, of my duty at the door. Dignitaries of many morals and intentions went inside—sweating, perfumed, transfixed. I stood on the porch, two feet above the remainder of Colonel Lawrence's Arab world.

After two hours of standing, I began to feel certain distresses. Impatience was getting more than noticeable in the crowd before me. Oriental police can become so interested in spectacles of all kinds that they forget their station, and such of them as appeared to be scattered about the "square" —truly an undeveloped rubble—were no longer able to quiet the crowd's shouting and swaying.

Before long, it was apparent that their impatience would break and that they would mob the hall itself, sweeping me in ahead of it—though not before I had emptied my revolvers. Five or six policemen, armed with lead-loaded staves, shouldered and banged through the crowd, sensing the same emergency as I did, and formed a ring between the crowd and the porch. But it was not enough to discourage or retard those in the center. Though they laid about, knocking over some of those who were too eagerly gesticulating in the very front, others merely stepped up and stood above them, maintaining and increasing the clamor. Police on horseback charged in, cruelly insensitive to whom they trampled or the cries that went up. The mounted police drew sabers.

Suddenly I realized what they were crying. It was "Shershil!" "Shershil!" They wanted to see the great man! They wanted to bow to him, to turn on a show of the exaggerated obeisances that were the custom of the land. Again I did not know what to do, and though I could take no alarm as to their intent when their desire was to honor Churchill, I could take no comfort over the way they were setting about doing it. With bitter humor I realized they were going to honor Winston Churchill no matter who might get himself incidentally killed in the ceremony. That he was already being torrentially honored within made no difference, for he was out of sight.

Swords and staves came down on heads and forearms and echoes of screaming that would have demoralized Babel tore the air of modern Gaza. I merely stood still, a gun in my hand, my arms crossed.

The crowd was now being effectively enough coped with to be furious and they began to physically attack the mounted Arabs and Palestinians. One man vaulted the rump of a horse and swept the rider out of his saddle. Bridles were seized with force and the horses' heads pulled down, their riders unseated and beaten. One man reached the porch and I sent him sprawling senseless with an uppercut to the jaw. The noise was now agonized, the faces envenomed, and the guards helpless. Two of them who had lost their mounts jumped to the porch with me and began cutting the air in all directions.

It was at this instant that Lawrence showed himself. He was alone. He held up his hand and invoked the blessings of Allah, smiled easily, even courteously to me and to my two brand new Arabian friends, turned back to the door, opened it, and stood proudly beside it, ushering forth Mr. Churchill.

Churchill just stood there, smiling and nodding like a chubby choirboy with the chores of a long service behind. Riders found their horses and remounted. The crowd cheered and in a joyous rhythm called his name over and over again. They crowded up to him, packing closely upon us. They would not let Churchill move. The cheering and the adulation lasted forever. (The Orient is never hurried.) There was a toot on the train whistle, the enthusiasm having spread that far.

We walked slowly back through Gaza. Thousands followed and pressed about, but the soft words of Lawrence kept the dignity of our little procession unmarred to the official carriages. Churchill stood up at the end of his carriage once more, flanked by me and Lawrence, with the sun and the Mediterranean behind him and the crowd in front. The brightness of the sun seemed to orientalize the spread of color before us and to sharpen the expressions and enrich them. Flashes of teeth, of jewel and dagger, signaled back at the sun. We gently pulled away, the crowd salaaming in tireless exercise, and a stampede of magnificent horses raced the train and stayed beside it for many miles, even until we moved inland toward Hebron.

Eight or nine times we stopped, often because the right-of-way was choked with living bodies wanting to salute the famous man whose name they knew so well but could not ever quite speak. And each time he rose and appeared. Each time too that Lawrence stood by him, the roar of salutation subsided and the mood became quiet and prayerful.

I had finally apprehended that Mutt and Jeff, while authorized for the trip, were not the best of protection even for Sir Herbert, for neither had much of a record at the special kind of security work needed on such journeys, among such volatile peoples. Mutt, the taller, was a mere redcap, the deprecating title assigned to cops in the British military police. The other, Jeff, had won a good record as an officer in the fighting before Allenby's entry into Jerusalem and had stayed on in the country, getting a job with the Palestine gendarmerie. But because both men were now almost useless and perpetually underfoot with their cameras, and because I had had enough of their happy disregard of the job they'd been sent on, I suggested to Mr. Churchill that they be denied the privilege of popping constantly into his own space to take snapshots. He told me to take care of the matter in whatever way I should wish, but to do it quietly so as not to offend Sir Herbert or reflect on administrative judgments back in Government House.

I did not use the American expression that "I would beat their brains out" only because I had not yet heard it, but I did tell them to stay out of the Old Man's compartment or I would scatter them along the right-of-way and take a picture of myself doing so for their families back home, and the honor of their lieutenant back in Jerusalem whoever he might turn out to be. I reminded them they might have been useful in Gaza if they had come to the Holy Land for a purpose other than to fill their damn albums, that we'd had a bit of a "do" there when another gun might have been useful. I told them the car ahead was filled with sabbatical missionaries on a Cook's Tour and they'd better get up in it.

They went away very vexed, and a little snappy with each other. I gave them the baggage detail in the Jerusalem station though I had no such authority, and we saw no more of each other—satisfactory to both sides, I've no doubt.

Our tour of Palestine and of Iraq—the Iraqi question still remains, at least for me, the most confused of any problem to which Mr. Churchill has ever had to attach himself—our travels over these spots of Biblical history were most hurried, often breathless, and crowded with interfering dislocations such as demands for unscheduled speeches (most of which Sir Herbert urged Mr. Churchill to make), laying of wreaths upon monuments in the British Military Cemetery outside Jerusalem, and the double list of places that the Secretary for Colonies had to see and the places he was personally determined to see. '

His first view of the River Jordan brought forth this comment: "Thompson, the energy of that river turned into electricity will indeed make this desert blossom." Indeed, the Jordan was in a fine rage, the mass of its stream being greatly in excess to what I had envisioned from the Bible studies of my pious boyhood. And the swiftness of it was equally impressive.

Most everything in the Holy Land is sad and disappointing, and the landmarks of man are the worst. Mr. Churchill had an appointment with Phineas Rutenberg, a powerful man of the Jewish religion, for the arranging and awarding of an irrigation canal. The desert aspect of the Holy Land is so fearsome as to seem beyond irrigation, and the uses of water and of power were always in the forward part of Churchill's imagination. How to assemble and direct new forces, or how to improve the use of the present ones, was part of the working mechanism of Churchill's mind. World War I, then only recently ended, brought forth the military tank. Without inventing any of its component parts, Winston Churchill and no one else had produced the first tank, and had done so over the most savage criticism of nearly every military expert in England. He saw new power in the river Jordan, as he had seen a new weapon in the tank.

Now he was again to be criticized, this time for impetuous dealing with the controversial Rutenberg. Upon his return from Palestine, and in defense of Rutenberg, Churchill said to the House of Commons: "It is hard enough in all conscience to make a new Zion, but if, over the portals of the New Jerusalem, you are going to inscribe the legend, 'No Israelite need apply,' I hope the House will permit me in the future to confine my attention exclusively to Irish matters."

Hurrying about the Holy Land with Mr. Churchill and with the ever-present Lawrence, I did not of course know that some years hence I would read impressions of these days, and views of the men who guided them, in Lawrence's famous book *The Seven Pillars of Wisdom* and there encounter what I consider the most accurate summary of Mr. Churchill's impact on others. Because it bears reference to these days of hectic experiences, it may interest American readers. "Churchill in a few weeks made straight all the tangle, finding solutions, fulfilling, I think, our promises in letter and spirit, where humanly possible, without sacrificing any interests of our Empire or of the peoples concerned."

To whatever place we might go, this seemed the effect he produced.

The sights were forlorn, a continuation of Gaza. Jericho, for example, is dried mud and not a bit more than that, and a broom could sweep away what could easily be knocked loose with a pick handle. Roads aren't roads, but rather unencumbered stretches in the adjacent desert and usually without markings.

There were two appearances of real beauty: the Dead Sea and the Jewish population. The Jews were a fine and clear-eyed element, strong and free in their movements, the men attentive and quick of mind, their women calm, deep-breasted, of a silent but faintly smiling cast.

Churchill complimented a group of adults who surrounded the beginnings of a new settlement. The work was well started. A throng of children mixed in amongst us, as was common wherever the party stopped. Through Lawrence and another interpreter, Mr. Churchill complimented them all on the great progress being made, then touched a pair of youngsters near him, and added: "You do not seem to have lost much time in other directions, either." Happy laughter rang out as soon as Lawrence had translated the words to their understanding.

At Gethsemane, Mr. Churchill moved away from the party and disappeared. I had to remain close to him but found a clump of flowering thorn-bushes from which I could keep him in view and survey routes of access to him. He remained here for a long time, almost motionless (rare for him) in meditations of his own, and was silent for the ride back from the place. It is enough to remember what occurred here for it to be sorrowful and silence-bearing. The sound of the Crusades is still about one here. So even is the sound of the tamping in of the base of the Cross, the fearful activity of preparing a man for death in this way. Vespasian had been on this very knoll, and Titus too, and the moody, immortal Josephus.

My own mind was melancholy and I welcomed the silence. And more than welcomed tea in Government House. This was in a court open to the sky, but protected by direct sun from the planting of gardens about the roof.

This was the house that the Kaiser had built, mentioned earlier, and his definite expectation that he would soon occupy it was clear to all from many signs that were allowed to stay where they had been first affixed. There was a carved German Eagle over the main gate at the entrance to the grounds. On the door of one vast room was a sign, in German, "The Kaiser's Bedroom," and across from it "The Kaiserin's Bedroom." They were in gold.

Sir Herbert Samuel lived here now! What a world!

I was served tea in a corner of the terrace by myself. I felt tired and sad. In the Orient one does an unbelievable amount of walking, and few people who read their Bible realize that when Mary bathed the feet of Jesus, it was the most refreshing and relaxing ministration she could offer him.

At Mr. Churchill's table there were ten. Mrs. Churchill joined the men presently, looking cool and collected. They rose, and the talk resumed. Soon there was laughter again, and rich talk.

Lawrence had his back to my little table (members of the Special Branch of Scotland Yard do not take offense at these things; they do not take offense at anything but disobedience on the part of their charges—and Churchill had been most tractable of late). They were talking about the Dardanelles again. Soldiers bury their dead but the battles are unconquerable. The names of Asquith, and Balfour, and frequently the name of Lloyd George came up, and because I had served him so recently I was keen to know other appraisals. Alas, these are not for the ears of Scotland Yard, or if they reach the ears, they never get to the typewriters.

In the worst days of World War II, when we had sustained an almost engulfing calamity and had as quickly prescribed its hazardous counterblow, the deadly secret slipped out into my hearing. "I'm sorry I heard that, sir," I said to Winston, who immediately looked at me and smiled: "You are from Scotland Yard, Thompson, and I'm sure you didn't hear it."

The talk ran on down many of the great moments these men had survived—and moments, too, that they'd instigated. They talked of Kitchener's loss in the North Sea, and it was remarked that his nerve had been lost before death caught him; that the debacle of the Dardanelles broke his spirit.

Churchill wanted Lawrence to accompany the party back to England. We were to leave in a very short time from Aleppo, then go to Malta and Naples. But Lawrence was engaged, so he said, for a meeting in the heart of Iraq.

Lawrence by this time had taken possession of my own imagination, after the astonishing displays of his power. These displays were particularly astonishing by reason of being so simple in a land so riotous; astonishing to find a man so meek and unostentatious in a land where custom and show-of-power are so altogether the reverse of this.

I had heard Lloyd George talk of the Dardanelles and Gallipoli. He had powerfully supported Churchill's advocacy of this amazing undertaking. And it had, like most great gambles, *almost* come off. At a time when Sir Douglas Haig's campaign, in the battle of the Somme alone, had cost Britain six hundred thousand casualties, a plan that would stop the Turks and divert the Germans to the Russians in the East made hard sense to many minds. And it was then that Churchill had set Lawrence to work. Who could there be, today, who could say that without these two men here twenty feet from me, the Kaiser might indeed be upstairs in this very palace at this very hour, looking forth upon domains that were his—here from the Mount of Olives clear on to the caravan paths in Baluchistan? How *barely* missed it was!

In guarding the life of Lloyd George, how many times I heard the same said of that wonderful mind and energy. And indeed with equal plausibility. For it had been Lloyd George and no other who, in April, 1917, when the Admiralty was in despair and when in a single month the Germans had sunk eight hundred seventy-five thousand tons of shipping, had insisted on the convoy. That was not the end but from there it was measurable, and it was the bouncy little cobbler's son who did it. Ten months after he forced the idea upon the Admiralty, it was an unqualified success and from that day to the Armistice, the Allies built ships faster than the Germans could sink them.

What carnage! What cosmic stupidity! What last-minute rescue! We seemed to have won everything as narrowly as the Germans missed it.

It was part of my duty to study Churchill. He had made some perfectly awful mistakes, and would make others, some of which I would myself witness while in process of their construction. Antwerp still hung over his head and would still, even by 1921, get parenthetical mentions in editorials. For Churchill was never stingy in giving his enemies an abundance and variety of copy. Everything he said was either quotable or misquotable. I knew there would be plenty of rows. Yet always he had come forth to face his accusers, had taken his whippings, had been in every instance overwhelmingly and disarmingly candid. No man could ever doubt his sincerity or his courage. In the very circumstances upon which they reminisced, the sad, regrettable, avertible disaster that the Dardanelles and Gallipoli were, the Committee of Inquiry had exonerated Churchill. Of all those put under interrogation he had come off best. His basic strategy had been upheld and is today. It was Kitchener (who had been too late on occasions) and De Robeck (who had too soon broken off the action, not knowing the Turks and the Germans were out of ammunition) and Asquith himself (for not driving Kitchener harder, even though he was a field marshal)—it was these men who came out badly, not as villains of course but as policy makers and military leaders guilty of errors of grievous misjudgment.

Lawrence reminded Churchill and Sir Herbert that he (Lawrence) did not seem to know any longer how to get on with the English and it was as well he had made a "previous engagement" in the desert of Trans-Jordan. Lawrence had disgruntled and upset a number of people, first by refusing, and none too civilly, any decorations for his great victory in Arabia. He'd spurned the Commander of the Bath and, I believe, also the D.S.O. And there were some—Churchill himself among them, for he'd rebuked Lawrence for it—who felt he had been discourteous to His Majesty George V. At the Paris Peace Conference, Lawrence had been a bit more colorful than matters required, attending sessions in Arab dress, even to red sash and dagger. His personal behavior was at times close to scandalous, which is difficult in Paris. Winston Churchill, who so much admired this strangely inscrutable and marvelously gifted tactician and wished great honors for him in the government, was more than once appalled in Paris in his sincere effort to get the desert out of the man Lawrence—now that the desert war was won; and to Anglicize Lawrence enough for him to accept a few medals. But Churchill could not urbanize Lawrence. At the same time he would never allow any man in his presence to subtract a tuppence from the true values that Lawrence had brought to Britain's causes. And as recently as 1954, in March, he permitted the reissue of the same flattering estimate of Lawrence which he had made in 1936, the year after Lawrence was killed. Churchill's loyalty to causes and to people was unshakable and was becoming apparent to me that far back and on such little contact as I have described.

There was to be a large dinner that night (I grew to dread these unending bores, but the worst were in the Kremlin!) and it was suggested that, because there would be a number of important Middle East leaders present, a show of medals and decorations would be in order.

That night, as I stood guard and was mistaken variously for a butler or guest (never for a eunuch, I trust, though there had been many about), I noticed that Mr. Churchill was wearing a medal which I had never before seen. And no wonder, for he is the only Englishman to have been given it. General Pershing pinned it on him. It is the American

Distinguished Service Medal. As Minister of Munitions during the war, it had been one of his duties to equip the U.S. troops, to see that they were prepared for combat. He had done this so well that Pershing himself had bestowed the decoration. Bernard Baruch had attended this ceremony and from the day that Baruch and Churchill met, they became and remained friends. Baruch had come back and forth all during the war, as head of the War Industries Board. Churchill always looks him up in America and greatly admires him; but I do not think he felt much more for Pershing than he did for de Gaulle. They had a kindred coldness.

Our stay was suddenly over. Churchill of course went right to work, even before the last of the well-wishers had stopped waving, and we began cutting through the waters of the Levant, heading westward. He was this time a true model of deportment and I enjoyed this short voyage more than any other with him except possibly the trip for the signing of the Atlantic Pact. As usual I had to wait until the official reports were in and explanatory excerpts of them were appearing in London newspapers, not so much to find out where I'd just been as to see how successful the work of Mr. Churchill had been—and to see also what the work was.

I mentioned that one of the objectives as Secretary for Colonies and Secretary for Air had been to survey Egypt, portions of the Sudan, Palestine, and most particularly Iraq, to see if the inauguration of an air patrol could not be an effective replacement for ground troops now garrisoned in great numbers in these remote places.

Some days after our return I was pleased to read in the *Times* (Mr. Churchill is a voracious newspaper reader, and while he is reading his papers, usually in bed and between the hours of seven-thirty and nine or nine-thirty, I am just outside his room, wherever it may be, reading my own) that a full account of the mission was published, together with some figures—as they were submitted to the House of Commons—that represented substantial saving to the Crown.

Our troops in Iraq cost the government about $200,000,-000 a year. Churchill urged the government to hand over the assignment to his air patrol and to return to their homeland the armies of occupation. You will remember how miserably housed he found them to be. This struck a welcome note from a sentimental view of things, but from the fiscal it was even more convincing. The air patrol could do the work faster, oftener, with a show of much greater striking power. And it could save the government $165,000,000 a year! It was passed at once.

This was the happy time of return to his homeland. There were of course numerous problems, some ugly, that were on his desk each morning and in his mind each night. And as Secretary of Colonies, the Irish question was very much a problem. But it was the return to his family that brought deep and moving gratifications to him. World War I was over and England, if not intact, at least was not breached; at least was still free and unshamed.

He and Mrs. Churchill had been through the agony of the loss of a little child—Marigold Frances, who was born in 1918 and died in her third year—but the solidity of the family was real and happy, and assured as well, for there were two daughters surviving, Sarah and Diana, a son Randolph, and a third daughter Mary, not yet born but due.

About this time I saw at close range the strength of his stoicism. It came about as a result of the pain of disappointment. Winston Churchill was so obviously the logical appointment for the Chancellorship of the Exchequer that no man thought Lloyd George could withhold it from him, or that he would conceivably want to do so.

It was in late 1921. Lloyd George's Cabinet was not too sturdy, and Tory opposition was building to challenge the Coalition. Leadership of the House goes with the Exchequer office (usually, too, succession to the premiership). Churchill was already considered, not only by the press but by most of those in the House itself, as Parilament's *de facto* leader anyhow. He was a Liberal.

Lloyd George feared that the Conservative machine would and could end his painfully assembled Coalition. And he did not give Churchill the post of Chancellor of the Exchequer. I am sure it crushed Winston. It astounded the British Isles and was the subject of editorials in American newspapers.

By this time I had become very attached to this man and had looked forward each new morning to his cheerful: "Good morning, Thompson, got your gun?"

That morning the office workers about him, the secretarial staff and clerks, all shared the desolation they knew he suffered. I dreaded seeing him. I could not arrange a proper sentence in my mind, yet I could not let such a momentous hurt happen to him even though it was none of my duty to remark on it.

He must have seen the distress in my face and wished to spare me the embarrassment of speaking of it, for he brightened roguishly, peered up at me by peering over his glasses (I always felt a foot above him for he crouched so) and said with a twinkle: "It is obvious, Thompson, you have little influence with the man you last protected. See that you improve this."

I must say I went away with a lump in my throat that he could be this gay when the circumstance was so bitter. But it was characteristic of his aptitude and inventiveness for making up a phrase on the spur of the moment.

Character summaries, and reviews of his personality and accomplishments, began to appear in quantity about this time. All of them spoke with affection, admiration or gratitude but some of them, because of the imputation of motive (personal ambition was common among these), hurt him deeply.

Of these latter, Harold Begbie's, in his book *The Mirrors of Downing Street*, was typical:

With the exception of Lloyd George, Mr. Churchill is the most interesting figure in the House. From the start of his career he was an element of great promise. Sometimes he disappointed his admirers but he never destroyed their hopes. No man is more difficult to shout down. From his youth he fiercely loved England, war and politics. Politics, to him, are almost as exciting as war and quite as dangerous. In war you can only be killed once, but in politics many times.

He has many qualities of real greatness—but has he the unifying spirit of character? He has truly brilliant gifts, but you cannot quite depend on them. His love for danger runs away with his discretion. His passion for adventure makes him forget the importance of the goal. Mr. Churchill carries great guns, but his navigation is uncertain. His effect on men is one of interest and curiosity, not of admiration and loyalty. His power is the power of gifts, not character. Men watch him but do not follow him. He beguiles their reason but never warms their emotions.

It was expected, and I think today by Mr. Churchill himself, upon recalling conversations held among his party on the trip back through the Mediterranean, that Lloyd George would surely give the Chancellorship to Winston. It was agreed everywhere, not only casually among passersby, if one chanced to catch their talk, but informally by those in the know, those at policy and influence-bearing levels, in the press, and about government buildings.

In point of experience he seemed to know more (for his age, forty-seven) than nearly any man in English history. Surely he carried most every secret there was, could find intelligent flaws in the plans of others, and was welcome among men of every degree for one most engaging attribute: he would give sober reply to any question put him, which gave the interrogator the impression, always true, that Churchill had himself long considered that same question and could bring the approach of answer to it, if not the answer entire. He always knew where the road was, if, as some will insist to the end, he did not always know where he, or England, was *on* that road.

What man in British history—and I am sure if Mr. David Lloyd George were himself alive today to read these thoughts he would not feel I was slighting him by the comparison—had ever been trusted with the responsibility of so many offices, requiring such diverse abilities and contrasting qualities of decision? And at so early an age? He had been in one ministerial capacity or another for nearly the full length of his political life since he set about having one at all. It began with the Undersecretaryship for the Colonies. Then he was made President of the Board of Trade, later Home Secretary, and after that—and in succession—First Lord of the Admiralty, Chancellor of the Duchy of Lancaster, Minister of Munitions, Secretary of State for War and for Air, and Secretary for Colonies.

Yet the next step in this proper progression, the step that now seemed most inevitable, was not offered him.

He took this, as the Americans say, "on the chin." He took more too before long and if there is a man who is more noble in defeat than Churchill, I am unable to name him.

Though Winston Churchill in defeat is noble, with nothing to do he is a kicker of wastepaper baskets, with an unbelievably ungoverned bundle of bad temper. It is better to stay away from him at such times and this his family seeks to do. And such of his retainers as can take the day off, or find an emergency miles or counties away.

I did not so far forsake my own responsibility at this time

as to wonder if it might serve to subdue him a bit if he were reminded he was still in danger, but it was apparent to all that if something active and preferably difficult were not supplied him soon, many would ask to be relieved from his employ.

Then in the course of a few months, the quixotic course of events took many turns, some of them doubling clear back on themselves. Lloyd George's Coalition fell. Bonar Law's Conservatives moved into power.

Churchill was neither a Cabinet minister nor a member. He was plain Winston Spencer Churchill.

On his way to Buckingham Palace, where it is the custom of retiring ministers to kiss His Majesty's hands upon returning the seals of office, there were some moments when we were together and some manner of resignation to his fate had taken place in him. His humor was back, and his urge to fight. I reminded him that he was, because of membership in the Privy Council, "Right Honorable," and some of the glint of the man came back at once.

"They don't want me here! We'll see about that! I'll have to try somewhere else. But I know where I'm going. I'm just not clear about the date. Pack a bag, Thompson. I'm going to fight for my old seat at Dundee."

In England a candidate does not have to "run" in the same district in which he lives. He may "stand" for Parliament from whatever district is to his liking; any district where his chances seem favorable. Winston had stood for Dundee before.

That night he had an acute attack of appendicitis. The General Election had already started. I sat outside his room in the nursing home and was not able to believe my ears when I heard him shouting my name as if he might be at his own desk.

He wanted my newspaper!

Then he wanted his secretary. He wanted several, not just one. He kept sending all manner of people to telephones, insisting they answer little questions written to them on slips of paper; insisting that they come to the nursing home right away. He kept a schedule and expected others to. When his doctors told him he was sick, he told them he knew it and that was why they had been called in. Presently his visitors began to arrive—one after another, all day, all evening. It was one of the most complete demoralizations of the floor and the most awful rout of any theories of proper visiting hours that had been seen there.

The more his doctors insisted he was too ill to do so much, the more they were reminded it was now their doing and none of his. When the chief nurse complained, he told her he would have Parliament look into the matter and she could expedite her own cause along with his, if she'd leave the distraction of rules for people who had time for them.

He was vastly good-natured again and in a few days was vastly noisy. All of the wheelchair cases made detours to take in this interesting room, and there was always a heterogeneous half-circle right outside his door—most difficult to classify since numbers of them, and both sexes, were in anything from surgical gowns to bowlers.

Running against him in Dundee was a nondrinking Scot named Scrymgeour. I had heard of him and presently saw much of him. Too much. Dundee was his own home. He was a fanatical teetotaler. I believe he was the only teetotaler ever known to have been raised there. Winston, though far behind in the campaign, must have felt he had a chance, even with such a late start. And there would no doubt be a good many things said about liquor.

Churchill announced to his doctors that he had ordered a special coach to be attached to the regular Scottish express and that he was going aboard the train that evening. They were most deeply concerned, more than the ordinary solicitude that doctors might be expected to expend on a man of his importance. They were concerned because they knew how weak he was, how much he'd tax himself the instant he left, and how quickly collapse might follow if he did this.

He was reminded that his stitches had not yet been removed. "Then I shall wear them in remembrance of you," he most dreadfully warned them. (And of course he would have.)

In those days I had great strength (much of which is fortunately still with me) and I was grateful for this because it was called to use before we ever got much rest again. We carried him aboard his train on a stretcher.

There were but six days left in the General Election. Winston Churchill did not feel he was likely to win from Dundee so much as he felt that no Prohibitionist could think to be seated in the Mother of Parliaments from this particular constituency. I must say—and I have nothing against a man having a drink and take one a day myself—that Dundee is the most drunken of cities, at least for its size, that I have ever seen in the British Isles.

In Scotland I did not suspect the security risk with Mr. Churchill—especially since he had resigned his two Secretaryships—would be a severe one. And this was true. But there was a noticeable antagonism, even though there was a nice crowd to welcome the man at the station when we got there.

His corps of electioneering aides came to him to discuss the strategy of what was left of the campaign period, and the routes and locations of halls, meeting rooms, churches, and school buildings at which he was to speak. He had had some forewarning about these matters while still confined in London, and it was then—with the steady stream of people coming and going—that he had been readying, if not speeches, at least full notes to discuss with the audiences he would find in Dundee; notes that would show his familiarity with the nature of their desires and grievances and show them, if he could, his capacity to represent them.

My strength came to his service when I had to carry him, or nearly so, from street levels to his hotel room; up platforms at the sites of public meetings; up stairs in halls of assembly. My arms, sometimes, were his legs. The struggle was in his face at all times, and signs of pain were there often enough. But what always burned through was the dominance of the man, the "carry" and the "send" of his personality.

He would simply not allow appendicitis to interfere with an election.

There is a time when things go against a man and there is no explaining it, either then or years after. I cannot offer any reason for the coldness that Mr. Churchill there experienced. It mystified his aides. Members from the Liberal party were dejected.

Had he been too popular too long? Was there an unaccountable surfeit of him, in the headlines, on people's lips? Or was there an equally unaccountable reversal of reason and tradition (and an upending of economic sense, Dundee being a Scotch whisky city) in sending Scrymgeour to London to persuade Englishmen everywhere to stop using spirits? It is possible that he was too often, perforce, carried to stages in chairs. A few times even weeks after the surgery, he had to be transported by stretcher. He looked very bad, and though he spoke well, it was plain to all that he could only endure a few moments at a time. And hecklers this time were too much for him. He just wasn't up to them. Or to the fun of it.

Those who have had appendicitis may know the exact degree of discomfort he had to carry. I never had this but it seemed that, though there were no signs his pain was unbearable, it was nearly continuous and fatigue and sudden movement made it worse.

People shouted from the back of halls: "Stand up, Winston!" He would try to rise, and half do so, then slump down again, and half smile. It was not a show. It was not a tragedy. It was bleakly brave. Nothing ever comes right in this way.

I do in retrospect believe he might have defeated a far more substantial opponent, if brain had engaged brain, but a platform of Prohibition was so appalling to think of that no one could sort out the real from the illusory.

The people themselves didn't seem to know what kind of campaign was going on. An ill man was struggling with an empty one. That might sum it up.

Aides and tellers who stood outside the various voting stations scattered about the city and its environs tried to hide from him their fear that he would be turned out when the record of the count came in. It was awful weather. There was no rain but the days were dark and polar and Dundee is hardly cheerful even when it would insist so itself.

The pessimistic predictions were all realized. Scrymgeour had displaced my charge. I also felt the discouragement. It all seemed too much and too packed together.

He served some champagne, not to devil the victor, but to thank and cheer those who had helped him and who had quietly taken care of the sad paperwork and endless grinding errands that go into this phase of public life. He went into a stony sleep of a few hours, then it was time to lug him to the train again. This time we did not need a stretcher. It was a good fast ride. I was glad of the confinement and the enforced immobilization. Later I looked forward to ships and planes for the same reason.

By this time I was becoming used to the schedule with Mr. Churchill. I had wisely adopted a plan never to think too far ahead. With Churchill, his driving purposes, his swollen agenda, it was the only way to do. Even members of the Special Branch of Scotland Yard have a private life, at least the rules in the Branch recognize time off and the wives of members expect to see their husbands from time to time.

But with Churchill all this was different. In a practical sense there was no time off (not in a literal sense), and this seeming paradox can be cleared up when I say that "no practical time off" merely meant that there was never any time to myself that I could count on.

I had always loved football, for example, and had myself played quite a bit of the game, even for a professional club when I thought I might make a young man's career of it, but it was hard for me to get to a game with any belief that I'd see it through to the end. I was too often called away by Mr. Churchill's office. Mr. Churchill had "not had opportunity to notify you of this plan." Plan? It might be Cairo, or Dundee. Or a quick speaking trip, or an accepted invitation to an unguarded country place where my services would be needed for the period of his stay.

So it was that although I did have time off, I could never be sure of it. I might get into some work clothes to dig in my garden, get part way to the toolshed and be called by the Yard to be at a certain place without quite enough time to get there, even though I knew how to get to it. Often they were places new to me, and places new to a Scotland Yard man are few indeed.

There were times when I felt that the impetuosities of Mr. Churchill hurt his own career, but I grew to know that when tempted with such judgments it was because I was myself short of sleep or that I ached somewhere from doing too much. At this time my arms ached from carrying a heavy man about Scotland where he'd no right to have sent himelf in the first place. I never had to do this again, though he was dangerously ill more than once and nearly died in Tunis during World War II. In such times, after Dundee, he kept sensibly inactive until his normal strength returned.

I was in no way surprised therefore, when upon beginning to unwind a bit myself and with two days off in prospect in which he promised me he would not leave his rooms (with the Yard to supply me relief), his secretary telephoned that he was leaving at once for the Mediterranean and I should be ready in a few hours.

It seemed we had just taken care of the Mediterranean! But I then discovered he was taking his family, that he was going to the côte d'Azur, that he had taken a villa there, and the journey had nothing to do with the Mediterranean's problems.

There followed a five months' holiday in Cannes.

Rest? Yes, somewhat. For me. But for him? I do not believe great men ever rest—I do not believe that they can. His family had a wonderful time. I felt very close to them all during this period, for the pressures of government and daily answerability were not upon him nor upon those around him (government pressures can be felt in the Churchill kitchen soon after they reach Churchill's desk!). The family's grief over their loss of little Marigold Frances had been somewhat assuaged by time, and the empty place in their family unit was taken by the arrival of little Mary, a truly enchanting baby. She was as fully alive and instantly responsive as her father, and guarding her was an additional duty I often found necessary and to which I assigned myself for a time each day.

Many people, when they discover I was bodyguard for so long to a man of such energy and color, have asked me about this period in Cannes. Did Mr. Churchill gamble? Did he gamble heavily? Did he have unlimited funds for it? Did he budget himself and stay within a stated sum or risk money? Did he win or lose? If he won, what did he do with the money? Was he an habitué or a "psychic" gambler? What were his games? What did Mrs. Churchill think?

Mr. Churchill most enthusiastically enjoyed gambling while at Cannes and went to the Casino innumerable times, always playing one or another of the tables, and preferring chemin-de-fers over roulette. It has been freely reported that he "lost heavily" and inasmuch as I was physically very close to him at every one of his visits to the Monte Carlo gambling tables, I always saw what he won and what he lost. He lost very often. Everyone who gambles can count on this much at least. And he lost oftener than he won—a not uncommon ratio either. But he lost heavily very seldom, played his stretches of luck while they were full, and knew when to leave the games.

He knew this so well that his winnings, while not immense, were more than enough to pay for the rental of his handsome villa for the full period of his family's stay in it—just over five months.

He loved the color and noise of gambling, the drama of

it, and the challenge of instinct against a blind adversary. The rooms of Monte Carlo disturbed and unsettled me. There was a depravity in the atmosphere, and though wealth and breeding were from time to time apparent (European and Oriental royalty too), most of the gamblers were poor and frightened, and pursued their pleasures as if in great pain. There was excitement but little fun, Churchill being one of the notable exceptions to this. He was by no means a "born" gambler in the sense of being unable to leave a game alone; nor in the sense of inveterate. For after Monte Carlo, I never saw him gamble again. I saw him make and take bets, but never again formally address himself to a table in the presence of a croupier. He loved to bet, and did so on any issue, with any man, all during World War II, on such current excitements as number of German planes shot down in a raid, or number of Germans taken in a battle, or a date on which a disputed objective would fall to us. He often loved to bet on the content of the speech by the next speaker and would jot down his guess. One time, when he was exchanging his predictions, he wrote, "The next speech will be innocent of content" and it was agreed with much laughter that he had won.

Churchill's days were spent in writing, painting, and bathing (he loved swimming, especially salt-water swimming, beyond all other delights I am sure), and in visiting people nearby. There weren't many guests, and this always made my own job lighter: less strain, less to watch, fewer "targets."

Everywhere one looks along the Côte d'Azur it is peacefully or excitingly scenic. There is almost a bit too much of its special kind of beauty to be continuously beautiful. One's eyes sought interruptions in it or neutral reliefs from it. Mr. Churchill would ask for his painting gear—a kit that grew more and more burdensome and seemed to me to grow heavier perhaps faster than his skill improved—and off he would go to a rock or promontory that commanded a fine curve of the littoral. There was always the unbelievable contrast of white sand, metallic sky, purple water, red rocks, and the ever-swaying green of subtropical foliage that lined the shore. The glare and glitter that came from reflected sun against the white of the villas and the innumerable shiny toadstools that were the massed and massive beach umbrellas were too strong to be directly looked upon. Here he would paint, many hours at a time, never a word coming out of him, but sometimes great grunts and wheezes and long sighs, like a locomotive finally giving up in a roundhouse.

I am a contemplative man, and these hours never bored me. And on one occasion, I innocently became drunk on the job, though to this day I do not believe the Old Man quite knew it. Perhaps he thought it was sunstroke.

It was near a place called Beaulieu. The Duke of Connaught's villa was located here. The Duchess of Marlborough, Winston Churchill's cousin, had a new house going up (she had recently married the millionaire Balsan) and she wished Winston's opinion of the work in progress and the site. He had a good opinion of both and had brought along his painting box in the car.

He asked me to take the stuff to a shoulder of the slope that runs down to the sea at this place. It was hot and we had received an excellent lunch, an elaborate, outdoor, soporific meal. Mr. Churchill set up his easel, got out his brushes, arranged the subject matter of his next picture in his mind, and began to paint and to hum. I felt an immense sensation of peace, always the most dangerous of symptoms for men in my work. This was in no way improved when Mr. Churchill's host, having seen me very much alone from the porches and terraces of the villa, came to my spot on a boulder and set down something that I did not at once notice.

He had left me a large bottle of white wine in an ice bucket, had said in French it was for my own use while Churchill painted, and had gone back to the cool of the shade. I, being almost wholly unacquainted with wine either as to flavor or efficacy, took an experimental sip to find it uncommonly delicious.

I drowsed and sipped for more than two hours, in fact until I realized Mr. Churchill was finishing up another "go" with the Mediterranean. I tried to get up. The sun seemed in the wrong part of the sky, and the whole stretch of water was aslant. Loose stones that I couldn't see kept jumping against my feet, and stationary objects moved away from my grasp as I reached for them. I had an embarrassing time trying to fold the easel and get everything back into its proper slot and square. I got a great deal of paint on myself, though I had not done so before. I slid on some moss and fell and bruised myself. Odd noises, including some muffled chuggings not heard before, came from Churchill. I believe he was looking at me sharply, but when I tried to look sharply back I could not focus. He left me then and the sound of a summer swarm went along with him.

He never mentioned it, and I never had white wine again, nor did I ever again feel the sensation of having the earth rock and lift. I, of course, had to rock and lift along with it, and trudging back to the garage with the paintbox, checking my weight against the sudden shifts of the ground beneath, I made an impression on the Duchess' servants they can probably still recall.

These days passed happily and uneventfully for me. It is not so easy to tell how they passed, though, with Mr. Churchill. I am convinced that his mind is never still; that what will seem some placid contemplation in some other man is, in him, the most active and advancing sort of forward meditation. He is always thinking about something in the round, but also about some specific aspect of it, and always toward a solution or a crisis. I am certain all his reflections are dramatic, for all living to him is such. He was in these quiet days, for example, making a great deal of money. Everything he wrote he sold. And he began to discover that he need not be at the mercy of a mere editor or a mere magazine, for his own writings improved circulation when his name was featured. He found that you could also get paid *for amount*. In his magazine work, where his output through the years has been enormous and will continue to the very month of his death, he began insisting upon more money for longer pieces. He began to suit the amount of what he was going to write for a given editor to the amount the editor was going to give him. He became one of the highest paid article writers in the world.

Along with this instinct, he also had several financial windfalls. His mother, Lady Randolph, had died and had left him a small fortune. Another fair sum, with annuity, plus an Irish castle and innumerable cottages in Ireland, fell to him about this time, an inheritance from his cousin Lord Vane-Tempest. Before he ever had a chance to occupy his Irish castle, or even make a show of taking possession, the Irish got to it and thoroughly despoiled it, burning part of it, smashing its fittings, pulling the rest down altogether. Churchill, hearing of this, said nothing and it was later discovered that he gave the rest of this inheritance away to people who had been living nearby or upon the estate, though he did not know them.

He also, during this period, began writing *The World Crisis*, though I did not at that time know the magnitude, or even the nature, of what he had undertaken.

It was upon my own discovery, months later, that he was well into this vast history of World War I, that I conceived my own notion of the fertility of his preoccupations. With me, as with the average man, such would be simple daydreams. But it is apparent now that while he would be standing upon the shores of the Mediterranean, making all manner of guttural sounds and scowling, his *painting* was, in an odd way, an organizing and constraining focus for the thinking that was going on at the same time and that bore no relation to the activities of his hand and eye. Neither suffered, for his paintings are uniformly good, and while there is more than one opinion of his thinking, there is no disputing that it was and is earth-moving, spectacular, and very often prophetic. It has the classic line that contains the massiveness of continuous and informed thought.

So it was that while much appeared to have been done fast, almost nothing was. Certainly never a picture. Nor a book. Why his books seemed to surprise his immense readership, when they did appear, is no secret at all to those who were close to him during their composition. We merely knew that Mr. Churchill was working. And he was working all the time.

Meals seemed little different, and while there was rich laughter in the man and all those who were to be entertained at his table looked forward to it with pleasure as all those who had just had the pleasure looked back on it the rest of their lives in agitated and delighted remembrance, there was a bit of a scheme to this too. He liked provocative people around him. He liked to be buttressed with opinion. He loved argument in the logical style but he loved it too, in the ready invention of conversation that needed to be maintained on multiphasic levels. He loved the presence and the company of men who also enjoyed the mental endurance race this kind of talking exacted from one's inventiveness. So luncheons in their way were hours of greater significance than the passing to and fro of compliments, anecdotes, and gaieties given and exchanged. They also fed his mind and taught him not only the tricks and skills of his adversaries but the weaknesses and foibles of his friends as well. Men never felt they were being studied by Winston Churchill, yet he never ceased studying them and he had enough personality to steamroller those he could not outguess or outthink.

In the last of the happy days we had near Monte Carlo, the jaw began to set once more, the forehead to pinch and contract, the periods of dictation to lengthen, and his secretaries to begin looking more and more weary earlier in the day. He was getting ready to re-enter the lists. He was a man out of a job. And this he could never stand.

We were suddenly back in England and, before I could get used to the familiar weather, we were again barnstorming in some of the roughest elections any Englishman has ever gone through.

I hate election campaigns more than any other single thing in my work. I always have. Mobs are never predictable, and of course they are never manageable. And you cannot arrest a mob. Nor knock it down. Great damage can be inflicted on both candidates and innocent bystanders and there is little chance to catch those doing the harm because it is difficult to see it coming. It is not, for example, like setting up the security to cover the routes of the King's processional, for in such cases the advance planning is months in the making and there is protection on every square and corner, every embrasure, every roof. All traffic stops.

But elections are helter-skelter. You jump from a horrid street in Soho to a more horrid street right behind the Houses of Parliament, and *you alone* with your gun and your very good health are the law, and such guarantee against missiles or murderers as there is. I did not mind the danger of these campaigns (Mr. Churchill always looked forward to it and kept hoping exciting things would explode about him without warning), but what I did mind was the possibility of my impotence in its sudden presence; by the press of people, for example, or by my being thirty feet from a center of hostility instead of three.

People ask me if Mr. Churchill, in times of danger, was not usually armed, and this is my answer. He was when he remembered to carry his weapon. He was an unusually fine shot, with either rifle or revolver, and later became deadly with some of the most lethal of the automatic weapons that we were to develop, including the Sten. He loved firearms, and I believe loved the sound of them. He practiced target shooting in the basements of his various residences, and never refused to "have a shoot" with me when I felt it was time to check his handling of arms. Being a good shot is like being a good pianist: one cannot grow rusty and return suddenly to dependable controls. One can leave his guns alone for weeks and, by practicing a few hours each day for several days, recover all his skills, but he cannot recover them immediately. So while it was all right for Mr. Churchill, in periods when he was not a protected public servant in high office, to ignore this somewhat realistic side of survival, I never recommended it, knowing these periods would be brief.

Acquaintances of mine in the military, some of the great marksmen of England, often go to the shooting butts without so much as a target-load, and merely sight the targets, from all the shooting positions, for hours at a time, for the more perfect command of muscular composure and the Spartan demands upon the eye. Violinists learn lightness of bow by bowing for hours without the bow quite coming into contact with the strings. I have seen my son do this many times. So it goes with the control of our bodies whether we are pianists, acrobats, or professionals with the bow and arrow. We must first of all become animals again. It was very natural for Mr. Churchill, at least in the realm of contest with his fellows, whether a "friendly" election that landed scores in hospitals or a global war.

Stanley Baldwin had succeeded to the Prime Ministership of Great Britain upon the illness and death of Bonar Law. Mr. Churchill put up his name for candidacy at West Leicester, and in a bruising and confused campaign, he was defeated by Pethick-Lawrence, a Labor man, in a drab industrial town. But the fighting look stayed with him and I knew he would run again as soon as something resembling a fair gamble presented itself. Churchill all this time, except when actively campaigning, was writing at a prodigious rate—six or seven hours a day—and he completed what later appeared as the second volume of his four-volume study of World War I during the ebbtide between his defeat at West Leicester and his next sortie.

I shan't soon forget those days and nights. The political temperatures and the immediate situation confronting him at that time would be of little interest to recall in any detail, even for English readership. But to make it clear to readers overseas, it will be enough to say that Mr. Churchill, who was always much easier to offend than to rout, had been so offended and so little routed by his defeat at the hands of Labor, in the person of Pethick-Lawrence, that he turned around, renouncing Liberalism as he did so, and proclaimed himself the leader of a new party to be called the "Constitutionalists." Here he had no intraparty distractions for he was the only member the party had!

Friends pointed this out and suggested he needed a constituency from which to make his new bid for Parliament. They suggested Westminster, not at all what Americans envision when they hear this word, and in some ways the most contradictory nest of contrasted purlieus that London holds. It is in the center of London, of course, and contains the Abbey and the Houses of Parliament. But it also contains some of the city's vilest slums. A clash between sidewalk disorderliness and civic and architectural pomposity.

Mr. Churchill had several opponents. One was a Captain Otho Nicholson. Another was Fenner Brockway, a Socialist of little consequence; and there was Scott Duckers, a Radical of no more.

His headquarters, a terrible assignment to me, was the London residence of one of England's richest men, James Rankin. Society stamped all over the premises, each running Mr. Churchill's campaign in his (and as it developed, more and more, in her) way, for titled ladies, women of great wealth, and aimless and retired but self-styled zealots flocked to this pile of inefficiency. I remember Lady Wodehouse, and Lady Blandford, and Lady Bessborough, and Lady Harmsworth. But the nearness of the slums and the dedication of party workers seemed to bring an infusion of ape blood to this particular set-to, and I lost over twenty pounds before it was over.

One of Churchill's political meetings was mobbed and then routed. Knaves from Soho battered down platforms, brass knuckles appeared, and clubs and staves and modern improvisations of Little John's single stick. And thugs! I even saw many I knew by sight, from previous overflows of ill feeling for one cause or another, or for money they wanted but didn't own. And secured anyhow. Crooks.

Churchill's political platform was more durable than those

from which he spoke, but here again he attracted support that sometimes won him more trouble than votes. Because he was out to liquidate socialism, fascism and communism, he immediately attracted attacks from the strong-armed mobsters from those very elements. For the most part, they were followers of Commander Oliver Locker-Lampson, England's most colorful hater of communism in all its forms. Prizefighters, hearing that the big rich house on Victoria Street was owned by quite a sport, attended Churchill meetings and roughed up anybody that raised a voice against him. Locker-Lampson had recruited them, seeing they would be needed. Lord Darling, the more or less famous croquet expert, formed a group of protectors to supplement Locker-Lampson. They brought their mallets. They stood guard for Winston ready to whack anyone trying to rush the stages or the stands. But many times mobs of Communist hooligans just went right over the lines and broke up meetings.

Lord Balfour supported Churchill. So did Leopold S. Amery, his Harrow schoolmate. This helped. So did the Countess of Bottsley, who rushed about the slums with pails of signboard mucilage and a brush on a stick, pasting up life-sized pictures of the Churchill children, gathered at mother's knee—and over their smiling innocence VOTE FOR DADDY. Lord Darling became more involved, put aside his mallet and spoke. Even the Duke of Marlborough went about, tapping on sagging doors with a gold-headed stick.

Hecklers would appear in halls, and other hecklers would rise and begin clubbing them. Locker-Lampson was of the greatest physical comfort to us all. Churchill hated to have heckling interfered with because he was so good at giving it back. On one occasion he got a big laugh when a heckler became so entangled in his attempted abuse that he could only splutter and before the expletives could be arranged for delivery, Churchill had flung at him: "My friend should not develop more indignation than he can contain!" And the same evening (Mr. Churchill was cultivating a not very successful mustache at this time and quickly abandoned it), a shrill and striking woman rose and shouted, "I don't like your ideas or your mustache!" To which Winston had this to send back: "Madame, pray do not distress yourself. You are unlikely to come into contact with either one."

In such times, I always managed to find a small box, or plank, or stone which would give me another few inches of height advantage. Being over six feet already gave me some in most groups, but this added amount provided the sweep of the crowd to my eye at every turn of the head, and I am sure this small advantage was of great protection that very night. Sir Philip Sassoon, grandson of the more famous Sassoon against whose dock in Bombay Churchill had torn his shoulder so painfully many years before, received severe cuts about the face, and Locker-Lampson, whose militant disregard for party manners of any kind was a continuous embarrassment and a continuous protection to Churchill many nights in a row, was painfully beaten after having been knocked down. But he was his own charge and he had his own mob to protect him. He was the most seasoned warrior of them all, whose combat record even then included battlefields as far apart as Lapland and Persia. And like Churchill he was of American extraction on his mother's side.

Churchill had just silenced the woman and the crowd was momentarily slaked when a wedge of true ruffians two of whom were anarchists known to me from my earliest days at the Yard, began banging people right and left on their way to the platform. We were outdoors, just finishing the meeting near Long Acre. I could see our campaign car and its driver. I shouted to Winston to leave the platform and follow me to the car. I pulled out a truncheon and labored a way through for us—Churchill right behind, then his brother Major John Churchill, his gay redheaded friend from North Paddington, Brendan Bracken, and another Special Branch man convoying at the side and rear. We bowled over people all the way, piled into the car, and drove away. Our destination was King Street, Covent Garden, for another meeting. The mob swarmed about, chasing us as we drove off.

Of a sudden I shouted at the driver, as we made a sharp turn, and grabbed the wheel trying to correct the route, but I was too late. And he cursed my interference, for he felt the tension equally as we did. But I knew this section like my own room, and he was driving us right into a dead end!

The mob swarmed in upon us and engulfed us there. I sprang to the runningboard, and knocked down so many who tried to manhandle the occupants of the car that I grew tired. Working away at the fringes of the crowd were hundreds of young Churchill supporters. Their sallies and line penetrations finally began to help us and the two Churchills and Bracken, who were at the forefront of the melee, helped to hold off the crowd till the driver could find room to turn and maneuver the car. There was a final spurt of action against the huge Brendan Bracken; his arms went up and down, striking. Then he fell, stabbed to the bone in hip and thigh.

Ambulances were sent for to pick up the injured. And of course to take Bracken.

We never caught Brendan Bracken's assailant. Street brawls are in some ways the most vicious and the most dangerous sorts of attack that public figures can encounter, for there is no isolating the assailant as such. Spur of the moment ferocity can be generated right there, even boiling up in a man who had no such intent half a minute before. I much prefer the armed man, lurking. Him I can take. We have a number of methods. In fact, all the men in Scotland Yard's Special Branch must know how to disarm two armed men, the police officer himself being quite weaponless.

Some of the younger men who were supporting Mr. Churchill's party now began to outnumber those who had struck physical blows and who, having done so, had retreated. And the younger men were beating open a path of retreat for our automobile. There was still much screaming in the air, and a few missiles, and the inevitable happy squealing of some crone leaning out from the safety of her lodgings, enjoying the excitement without knowing its cause.

I was shortly to receive a most blinding blow in the jaw myself. After getting Bracken away, the Churchill brothers, another Special Branch man, myself and the wayward driver headed for a small hall near the Berwick Street Market. This is a very unrefined section, no better than the one we'd left, and Winston went straight to the platform and right to work on the gathering that was already waiting there.

He was of course most solicitous about his friend who'd taken such deep wounds in the leg, but as for himself there was no hint of distress. The incident had not been enough to ruffle his composure. He made a fine speech.

A young man of about my height and build attempted to brush right by me, with a quick and half-whispered sentence about a message for Churchill. I merely put my arm out so he could not pass me. "Sorry. You mayn't pass here."

He smiled and seemed to retreat. In fact he did draw back three or four feet. My eyes were sweeping the crowd again and in a second or two returned to those in my immediate presence. Here once more was my friend.

His fist hit me a jarring blow right on the jawbone, rocking me back. I did not go down, nor lose sensibility, but I staggered under the blow, for the man was strong, and his full shoulder and torso came on through with the punch. It was almost classically delivered, I must say in fairness to him, whoever he was.

Perhaps because of some of the excessive enthusiasm my charges had already been exposed to, I put a few more pounds behind the counterpunch than were needed. Before the young man went down, he went up about two feet and a fine "We-e-e-e-e-a-a-a-aw!" came out of him. He crashed back into a lamppost, and a uniformed constable who knew me rushed to the scene, bent over this semiconscious zealot, and then took him off to interrogation. He stumbled wearily down this dingy street, holding both hands to his face. I had a bit of a swelling myself, and a pair of green-yellow eyes for some days, where the inflammation seemed to take root.

There was an all-night torch and klaxon procession, quite hideous in its din and, it seemed to me, quite uncivilized in its purpose. Certainly in its method, for we were trying to protect the life of a man who was seeking a perfectly legitimate seat in the Mother of Parliaments in the oldest democracy in the Western world. Therefore the sound of whistles, of blasphemy, the smell of powder and of sweat, the roaring, and the flashes of maroon in the night sky all merged into a satanic incongruity that belongs to other people—certainly not to mine.

Our dedicated driver, his hat gone forever and his goggles too and his windshield smashed to powder, somehow managed to get us to the front part of Caxton Hall. Electioneering was all over. This is where the count comes in. There were rumors that it was the tightest race ever to occur in Westminster. I could believe it. I had the feeling, even at the start, that though Nicholson was entrenched here the enthusiasm was for Winston. I had the feeling that in a mad melee like the one we had been in (days of it!), my charge would win and obliterate the real agony he had sustained in

Dundee not so long before. That campaign, with the physical pain that was such a part of it, had been such a heedless thing! No place to set controls.

And somewhat the same sort of thing here too, except that Churchill the fighter was in this one, not Churchill the casualty. And he'd rocked the audiences with fast sallies many a time—and for many days running—loving the comeback and the insult, and giving one vulgarity for another, his own just a bit richer—a bit more proconsular, as it were. They'd liked it. So I felt.

Waiting in Caxton was quite as much agony for me in its hours of suspense as the longer ordeal of Dundee. Somehow Churchill didn't mind losing at West Leicester and treated it about as he might if he dropped a sandwich at an outdoor tea party.

Waiting upon destiny at Caxton, Churchill won my inner sympathies all over again. The man was still tired out and in general appearance far more prepossessing, for he had been rolled about by the mob a good bit and the King Street scars and the small knobs and bruises of this dirty fighting had marked him a bit.

I was close to him constantly, though he kept bobbing about like a cricket before a scythe. And I was most pleased when two men rushed to him and began pounding his back, pumping his arm up and down, and shaking him by both shoulders in a most disorderly and un-English fashion, but of course with the unmistakable meaning that Churchill was again in Parliament.

Nicholson's officials rushed about with a distracted and abused look, as if their pensions had been annulled. They demanded recounts. They got them at once. These recounts, in constituencies like Westminster, do not take long even though the counting is hand counting. But it seems long. And though I was desperately anxious that this time it come out right for Winston, I was close to physical collapse myself, and wished only for rest, the luxury of one undisturbed supper, and ten hours of sleeping that nothing would interrupt.

Unbelievably the recount handed the victory back to Otho Nicholson. And this meant some more, and possibly premature, celebrating all over again. I now had to remain standing to stay awake, though Caxton Hall was so boiling with excitement a wild bull in its midst would have been unnoticed.

Unbearably, Winston Churchill lost his third election in a row. He lost by forty-three ballots! Nearly seventeen thousand were cast!

I have taken American readers to these unfamiliar election campaigns in England primarily to show the *quality* of Mr. Churchill's stoicism. When it was my duty to pick him up and take him along home (he was nearly dead of fatigue), I felt far more paternal than custodial and I did not trust the level of my own voice to say a simple "I'm sorry, sir," for my sorrow was very deep. Seeing him refuse even a show of disappointment on the outcome of it all merely made it worse. Dundee was indeed bitter, but it was endurable because it was inexplicable. And it was also a first reversal. Westminster was different. Westminster had been riotous, with the clash and clangor of steel and mace, the clamor of churning millions. Westminster had been a thrill, enriched with billingsgate, dramatic surprise, and the foreseeable thrills of a planned and lively escapade. It *should* have come out right. And it just missed.

Could you tell by looking at the man? I believe Mrs. Churchill could tell; I could not.

At his door, after a silent ride home late at night and with a light rain coming down, I stood quietly. I suppose there was some sort of sickening smile, rather mummified by now, on my face. His own face was serene. Some thought of his was trying to mutter itself into articulation—but it was still well inside him. We were both bruised, myself rather comically so. I told him I was sorry. I said it quickly without thought, so there'd be no inflection to it. He thanked me in the same way, looking right into me. Then he looked beyond, in the direction of the Parliament buildings, and he saluted them with a long wave.

"You know, Thompson, they really can't run that thing without me. I've lost again, so nobody will be thinking to shoot me tonight. We'll rest tonight. I may try Epping."

I drove away. I did not even *think* of what he meant. I had been punched in the jaw but he had been struck in the heart, so it seemed. He had lost three times. Most men would seek other work!

The Yard did not order me back until late the following afternoon. There was a little identifying to do of some of those held over for the electioneering fracas, but after this was disposed of, I had a chance to read the newspapers without fear of sudden bells, or the interruptions that the very opening of a door usually mean. Yes, it was of course true that Winston had lost a race that was historically close but everywhere one looked—irrespective of what party a newspaper correspondent belonged to—the man Churchill was more popular than ever. "Giddy moral victory," one wrote. Well, he'd take his breakfast with less than the usual glower, and that would please Mrs. Churchill as well as the domestic staff.

I thought of another thing: What had Winston Churchill accomplished in the course of these mortifying raids into back districts? What had he gained in public stature? He had gained something in these two years that was to make the man unbreakable. That was one thing. And he had been quietly and diligently laboring on *The World Crisis*, the four-volume history of World War I.

In the course of a very few weeks things happened almost too swiftly to be properly digested, to be sufficiently savored. There was a rash of victories. First off, Epping did return Churchill in a walkaway victory, his Constitutional Party philosophies having acted as a stimulant to the Conservatives. If Churchill wasn't pro-Conservative, he was surely anti-Socialist. And Ramsay MacDonald ("The Boneless Wonder"—what a cruel appellation!) evaporated.

Before Churchill had quite got used to his own seat, Stanley Baldwin was back in the big job again. The first thing he did, certainly the best thing he *ever* did, was to name Winston Churchill Chancellor of the Exchequer.

A moment before, all those who were close to him and working hard in their various ways for him and for his beliefs were trying to swallow the lump in their throats for the sequence of political deprivations he'd been through; for the pain he'd had; the courage shown; the losses taken without a grimace. Now there was no time to celebrate his easy victory at Epping till a greater celebration was called for when he was granted the seals of office of the second most responsible job in the British Empire. The Chancellorship of the Exchequer is the traditional step next behind the Prime Ministership.

I was well caught up on sleep before these larger responsibilities fell upon Mr. Churchill and so the acclimatization of myself was a most pleasant experience to go through.

There is a great deal of pomp and even much more traditional ritual that is observed in the changing of governments and I shall not detail it for American readers. The accession of a Prime Minister is an occasion for a good deal of dignified and slow-moving ceremonial, not of course in any way comparable to the elaborate and almost oriental pageantry and heraldic observance of a coronation (familiar now to Americans through motion pictures and television), but it does, as many English customs, take quite a long time. I did not mind the gradualness of the process by which Winston Churchill became the Prime Minister's right bower.

What set things in motion was a telephone call to Mr. Churchill in his home in Westerham. King George V had asked Stanley Baldwin to form a new government, for the second time.

The motor ride to Conservative Central Office headquarters was a happy and expectant one, Mr. Churchill of course knowing that one of the important Cabinet posts was to be offered him. Palace Chambers, the place was called. Mr. Churchill hummed all the way. He sounded like a mass of insects. His humming was the most astonishing thing for it was impossible to tell what was intended, as to the nature of the noise itself or what the tune was, if he really meant to be humming a tune at all. It seemed to force itself from the closed lips and set jaw we know so well, and also to be coming out of the nostrils. Churchill's humming is a bleak, unsettling thing.

We pulled up before Palace Chambers and Mr. Churchill went inside. It was a little before eleven in the morning. He was gone for more than two hours.

I began to speculate a bit on my own life, how it would vary—not so much in hours as in geography—if he were to get this job or that one, and the closeness with which he had skirted the Chancellorship of the Exchequer under David Lloyd George kept this one office suspended before my own mind.

There would be an interesting familiarity about being Chancellor of the Exchequer, for Churchill's own father, Lord Randolph, had had that very post when he was only thirty-six. He'd resigned the office three times, Lord Salisbury, the Prime Minister at that time (1886), finally accepting the third resignation. Churchill's father Randolph is one of England's most complex and wistful characters and badly neglected by today's commentators.

In any case, if Winston *were* to succeed to the post, he was already outfitted for it from a wardrobe point of view, for Randolph, upon his resignation in the previous century, had refused to surrender his robes of office when he quit. He somehow just wanted the robes, and he took them and kept them. This had never happened in England's history.

Another father-and-son connection concerned India. Randolph had been Secretary of State for India (under Gladstone—how the Churchills all hated Gladstone!) after having been an M.P. under Disraeli (whom they all loved) for four or five years, serving from Woodstock, the sweet village that is close by the family estate of Blenheim. All the King's ministers, great and forgotten, drifted through Winston's life during his boyhood and early manhood, for they were part of his own father's life and circle: John Morley, Balfour, Chamberlain, Mr. Edward Carson, Asquith, Lord Rosebery. And Lord Randolph, of amazing appearance (he was spare and exophthalmic and he wore handlebar mustaches that came out well past his bloodless cheeks, then dropped down nearly to the collarbone) was one of the very few in England who would stand up in the House and sass Gladstone to his face. And loved doing so. Much of his reputation, in fact, was derived from the sense of Parliamentary eagerness that stood in the atmosphere whenever the Prime Minister was about to be engaged by the sickly though sulphurous member from Woodstock. For Winston Churchill's father was one of the readiest and most eloquent of living men. He nearly drove Gladstone crazy, and did drive him out of the Prime Ministership.

Jennie Jerome, Randolph's wife, the fabulous and still discussed American girl, had no more fear of the breed of English she met, lived with and immeasurably grew to love than did her baldheaded and cyclonic husband have for Gladstone.

Randolph's own father, the Duke, found his son impossible, unpredictable, and far from promising, and one day when he found Randolph taking off in the most unconventional get-up ever seen in the county (it included a cooking skillet that was suspended by cord around Randolph's waist), he asked him where he was going. The Duke was immediately told. Randolph was "off for South Africa to dig for gold." That is where he went. Did he actually dig? Yes, indeed. Churchills always bring a discouraging plausibility to their pronounced insanities by returning with proof of results. Randolph Churchill, to be sure, did not very much enjoy digging for gold and complained of the arduousness of it many times in later years, but he dug up $35,000 worth of it. He used the money to go to Japan and, with the remainder, upon his return to Blenheim, he bought a string of horses, began breeding them, racing them, and winning race after race. But he rarely saw his own animals go, and once, after a big win when his friends sought him, they were to find he was not even in England. He was in Norway, alone, going through fjords in a canoe.

He died at forty-six, his work pitiably unfinished. Guedalla called him the "Peter Pan of British politics."

The shove and pressure of memories of this man and his family, their surpassing energy, and their determination to see, and do, and be everything all at once and to die burned out or run through, occupied me for the two hours and better that Winston was inside Palace Chambers talking with Stanley Baldwin.

When he came out he was bent and beaming. He said one thing: "We'll have to move from Westerham, Thompson." It didn't matter to me, of course, desert nomads having far more peace than I did. But if he had told me where the Churchills were next to settle, I'd have known the post. Specific addresses go with many of the Cabinet posts, Ten Downing of course being the best known British address there is, and Eleven Downing the best known next to it.

I discovered that I was now working for England's new Chancellor of the Exchequer only by reading it in the newspapers the next day.

The Churchill household was of course overjoyed, and past disappointments died out like the din of King Street and the roaring of klaxons in Soho. No one thought of what had passed—only of now and tomorrow.

"Now" included his investiture, and the ancient ceremony of the "Pricking of the Sheriffs," during which the new Chancellor wore the robes of his father Lord Randolph. Soon after he "kissed hands," his family moved into the huge place at Eleven Downing Street. It is, to be sure, old-fashioned but it is friendly, tastefully decorated, and commodious enough to absorb huge parties without strain and with minimum distress to guests. However, it is not easy to assume the security responsibility for such a busy man, especially in a house so large a newcomer needs floor plans to find his way.

Agleam under a new top hat in an incredible day of sunshine (April, 1925), I walked with the Churchills—the new Chancellor, Mrs. Churchill, Randolph, and Miss Diana—from their home to the House of Commons. It was Winston's first Budget Day, an event of special significance in England.

Everybody shouts things at Winston Churchill. Bus drivers stop, lean from their cabs, and give him advice. Children pluck his sleeve. There is a happy flutter of solicitude on all sides. I walked slightly behind, and to his right, armed of course and quite proud to be among this little company that carried so much meaning. Winston carried the Budget itself in a dispatch box, somewhat too much of a size to be handled easily in one arm. And he was under the necessity, often, to raise his topper and acknowledge the enthusiastic hand-clapping that his passing down the street had started.

"Let me take the box, sir," I suggested. He pulled back in some horror, hugging the cumbersome thing the closer, as if I were suddenly proposing to grab the godfather's baby at the moment of christening.

"No, no! There's but one person to guard this box and it's me!"

What he had was very much and utterly his own. Once, ten years or more later, when he was heavily engaged with his hands full of paper details of many kinds, I opened his dispatch box, which I'd brought from security, and offered it to him open and he bawled me out roundly in the presence of a multitude of people, including military bigwigs. "*I* open this! I alone. No one else! Ever!"

He was nervous in his maiden speech. But he looked up into the gallery, to his beautiful wife and to his children and smiled lovingly. Their presence seemed to soothe him, or to return him to the moment, and steer him through it.

And since it was Winston Churchill, there was the inevitable ingredient of the dramatic. Only the Prime Minister and the Cabinet knew what Churchill was going to say. And this was to be the day when England would be told that His

Majesty's Government was to return to the Gold Standard.

The immediate reaction to this (which I took to be the one that would continue) was tumultuous in its approval. It was a great day all around for the Churchills.

Alas, great men's great days are hard won and short-lasting. Right after declaring the return to the Gold Standard all manner of heckling began, some of it with serious force of argument behind it. The preceding Chancellor of the Exchequer, Sir Philip Snowden, a man whose brilliance Winston privately admired to the fullest degree, was important in all opposition arguments, in challenges to the Churchill forces as to where new money would come from and in assembling furious objection to the uses of some of those sources. One of these sources was to be liquor. Mr. Scrymgeour, the unlikely Scotch Prohibitionist who had defeated Mr. Churchill in Dundee, was of course sitting in the House. The American-born Lady Astor went after Churchill on the liquor problem (Scrymgeour did it daily) and on one occasion, when acknowledging that more money in His Majesty's coffers was his first concern, Churchill said calmly enough: "It is imperative that I should refresh the revenue." And, perhaps enjoying the discomfort of Lady Astor, whose tongue is not only versatile but sharp, he produced from the Speaker's stand a bottle of Scotch whisky and added to his previous sentence: "I do so now," taking a fine pull before replacing the bottle.

He stopped his speech in midstream, looked right down at Lady Astor and told her that she was "noble" but that "I do not think we are likely to learn much from the liquor legislation of the United States." The House roared on both sides.

Another time, sitting in the gallery, I was immensely impressed with a speech by Winston that had come off at his top-level best. And I was enjoying the comfort of realizing that he had won the argument. He was sitting below, enjoying the same thing, listening to a harangue from some now-forgotten member of the Opposition who was taking Winston's logic and his character apart, one bone at a time. It began to bother Churchill who, while the greatest talker in the world, is also its worst listener, and he began to indicate his disagreement with what he was listening to by the most violent and continuous shakings of his large head. Everybody in the House of Commons saw what Churchill was doing. The speaker too saw how seriously the House's attention was being pulled away from himself and disastrously dissipating his argument. He came to the edge of the platform and looked right down at Churchill who continued shaking his head. The speaker aimed his forefinger at Winston and remarked to him, in a sort of squealing outrage: "I wish to remind Right Honorable friend that I am only expressing my own opinion!" And Churchill, looking up impishly and half-rising, said: "And I wish to remind the speaker that I am only shaking my own head!"

There could be no more serious business that day.

Philip Snowden has several mentions in the story of his own life, which came out many years after these tests, of the excitements that went into them. But I never saw Snowden top Mr. Churchill. Mr. Snowden, in the mellowness of his later years, saw himself as a more substantial adversary than I saw him to be with Churchill in front of him. Snowden was heartbreakingly crippled toward the end, and even in the days of his greatest mental and fiscal robustness (it was conceded everywhere that he was a far better "money man" than Churchill) he walked painfully with two canes. It was hard not to allow one's response to the Snowden argument to be influenced by the Snowden appearance. And Churchill was far more merciful in his response to the Snowden heckling than he was to the others. He let the others have it right on the nose time and time again. He held back on Snowden.

Old men like to think they were exciting when they were younger and some of them were, but I do not now remember Snowden as bringing to the battles of the House of Commons very much of the sense of impending suspense of it. He brought sense and facts, but it was Churchill who came in with the show.

Churchill put a tax on horse bets and instantly provoked the wrath of half of England's women! Many women threatened to quit betting (this was, of course, before Churchill himself owned a racehorse) and he picked them right up on this and reminded them that the Crown would not object to their "increased usefulness in their own homes."

However, things were serious in the economic life of England. In foreign exchange the English pound was worth only eighteen shillings, and England's most famous economist, never in agreement with Churchill about what money was, where to get it, what to do with it, published *The Economic Consequences of Mr. Churchill*, in which he balefully predicted a great depression (which England very soon had) in the export industries. In bitter sarcasm, John Maynard Keynes logically saw disasters almost everywhere, and after charging Churchill with having sold out England to the bankers, ran through a list of melancholy prophecies that read in part: "To begin with, there will be a great depression. This in itself will be helpful since it will produce an atmosphere favorable to the reduction of wages. The cost of living will fall somewhat. This will be helpful too because it will give you (Churchill) a good argument in favor of reducing wages."

And in the coal industry, this very thing happened. Churchill countered that the government's return to the Gold Standard had no more to do with conditions in England's mines than "the Gulf Stream."

It was just as hard for a practical scholar like Keynes to argue with Churchill as it was for Snowden. Snowden once went after Churchill for a recommended abandonment of Free Trade principles and challenged him for this change in view and position. "There is nothing wrong in change," the incumbent Chancellor told the ex-Chancellor, "if it is in the right direction." In his improvisation of saving diversionary tactics, Churchill was as resourceful as Lloyd George, but with Winston, though it was never so acrobatic, it was even more impressive somehow because it *sounded* so dynastic, so imperial. There was a squirrel quality about Lloyd George but about Churchill there was something Ciceronian, something Roman.

One night after Churchill and his family were all locked up and I had checked all the fifty-six security points in their enormous house, Scotland Yard notified me that some extra men were to be assigned to the Churchill family and to all of Mr. Churchill's movements, public and private. Only specified visitors to Eleven Downing Street would be allowed inside, and they only with the proper passes. I asked what accounted for this sudden tightening of protection and was immediately told that the miners' walkout was taking place, during the night shift, that very night, and that this action would be followed at once by the General Strike.

In England there has never been a time like this was, before or since.

It created an overwhelming depression of spirit. One could see it in people's faces. However, Englishmen seem to go right on being Englishmen, and if they have one virtue that is ascendant over others, it is their ability to endure.

I lived in Sydenham. I did all my commuting on a motorcycle, frequently picking up other members of the Scotland Yard force who were going my way. I had a very clear idea about what the General Strike would do to the city of London. There were no trams, busses, trains, or undergrounds. Miles away from the city, suburban streets and village lanes were choked with people trying to get to work, waiting on the mercy of anyone who had a conveyance, no matter what.

In a matter of seconds I had three young men in my sidecar and later picked up a fourth who sat behind me as a pillion rider. They tried to pay me. I refused. Later when I cleaned the sidecar I found a quantity of silver coins that had been surreptitiously dropped en route; hundreds of them for the hundreds of lifts I'd given during the Strike. Englishmen hate to owe anything.

I am not up to describing the confusion the General Strike brought to the Treasury. But since Winston loves confusion if he can take charge of it and since he missed his morning newspapers more than he missed his food, he added the problem of getting news to England to a list already too long. He became an editor. That he had never run a newspaper before made no difference to him.

All during the General Strike, because of Mr. Churchill's determination to run everything, I got to bed at four o'clock in the morning. Never once would he leave his newspaper before 2:30 A.M. and he rose before seven. Once I went sound asleep while standing up, leaning against a doorjamb, just listening to the sound of those damn presses, and toppled over with great embarrassment into a pile of paperboxes.

The General Strike was the most awful upheaval of her own doing to scourge England since her own Civil War and I do honestly believe Winston Churchill enjoyed every single minute of it!

What brought Churchill's *British Gazette* into being was simple enough. None of the newspaper workers wanted to strike but did because they were afraid to disobey their unions. Although all of the newspaper owners and editors very much wanted to send out the day's news to England and repeatedly met for the purpose of coming to a working agreement that would pool their manpower and bring to one paper some sort of consolidated British view on things in general, the union leaders prevailed as to the workers. And they struck. The newspaper owners and editors could not agree to disregard, even for a time, their political leanings.

It was the militantly independent editor of the *Morning Post*, Gwynne, who wrote the Prime Minister and, strike or no strike, offered the full physical facilities of the *Post* if the government wanted to make use of them.

That was the actual moment when Stanley Baldwin sent for Churchill and they discussed how to use what they had been offered.

Mr. Churchill didn't want to hear about the problems. He just wanted to run the newspaper. In no time we were off to the building of the *Morning Post*. On my very first sight of the structure, it was apparent it was a worse security risk than a county bazaar. One could enter anywhere without a pass, without challenge, and carry anything whatever into the numerous dark floors. I cautioned Mr. Churchill about this. I cautioned him four times. He merely thought I was cross and sleepy, which was true, and went ahead singing abominable melodies through his nose.

Churchill first visited the presses, then met the staff, then went to the editor's office. The full staff of the *Post* was on hand, very proud to be working for such a man under such conditions. He went through the place very much as he went through His Majesty's battleships.

Everyone began excitedly to do his job; to do more than his job. They planned to run record editions from the start. Deliveries? Already Mr. Churchill was organizing an emergency fleet of automobiles. They were instructed to pick up their bundles and dump them at the doors of dealers—individual subscribers and buyers being obliged to come to these shops to get their own copy. Local distributions would have to take care of themselves.

But England herself was cross and dangerous, not ready for a long siege, not wanting one, and the unions far from equal to supporting their own membership with anything but the briefest tussle with the government. I knew there would be acts of violence.

Churchill's first frustration came a few minutes after he had taken over. The telephone rang. I stood guard in the doorway (we had immediately instituted a system of passes); all the other telephones were busy. I picked up the one that was unattended. It was the union informing the office that the union would not allow the *Post* personnel to work for the government.

I told Churchill. He whirled around, getting his arms up and his chin down and called Beaverbrook. Presently Beaverbrook's night superintendent from the *Daily Express* appeared (I believe his name was Sydney Long). This man could not be touched by union control and sat down by himself and all alone played the linotype machine like an organ while Churchill stood at his shoulder. It was only two pages but it was a start and Churchill grabbed the first one out of the maw of the machine and ran hawking it through the house. He was hard to keep up with. He enjoyed these moments. I did not.

People say Churchill was and is a master of detail. This is not true. He is impatient and even contemptuous of it. But he never misses an element in the *continuity of function*. Here were fine examples—days crammed with them—of this unique skill at work on a hard and practical matter. What did he do? He had called the Automobile Association to lug the papers to their consumers. He finally agreed that we might expect sudden flashes of sabotage and though he seemed to care very little who might get hit on the head, he surely wanted nothing to happen to the machinery in the plant. For standby crews of expert machinists, he did what few other men would think to do: he called a submarine base and asked for their best mechanics and in a few hours we had an interesting, interested group of experts from Davenport, ready to tackle a job new to them. The few workers who had defied the unions were so overworked they were wearing out. Churchill called trade schools, even universities (where he thought students might be studying the printing arts in various practical ways) and he was quite right about this. We had a lot of very well-educated men running all manner of toys all over the building.

He would work all day in the Treasury (thirty or more phone calls to the *Gazette* being average), then jump into the Treasury car and we'd whirl over to take the day's pulse.

And it was indeed going up. This was not before the days of the wireless, to be sure (1926), but it was before England as a nation was sitting at home each night listening at six o'clock. So they *devoured* Churchill's paper. He could have printed anything.

I called the Yard and said we were insufficiently secure. While I was on the telephone, I could hear windows being smashed. Employees, plus many luckless passersby, were getting hit on the head and beaten about the body. And there was a good deal of stone-hurling.

Police reinforcements began appearing in comforting numbers and occupying strategic spots. Knowing Churchill, I thought it would not be long before elements of the Irish guard appeared and they presently and accommodatingly came over. The Irish might have hated Churchill in their own way, but they could not hate him here where they could see him and hear him.

Churchill was always unceremonious about his departures. He would just be gone. Now he was gone. I chased down the dirty floors and hallways, overtaking him on his way to the machine room. There were a lot of beer mugs on the floor. Winston peered into them. They were all empty. He inquired what this meant and found that beer drinking, typesetting, and press-running were occupations that went together. He was told the men had enough beer. He didn't believe it. One of his long-remembered sentences rolled out of him then as he stood in the middle of a cluster of sweating workers in dungarees.

"Nonsense! There *is* no such thing as enough beer!" How they cheered! He quietly saw to it that there was an unending supply during the remainder of the Strike.

In a few days his newspaper had become world-famous. And in a few days it grew from two sheets (our first edition was a "folio" and by now almost as rare as Shakespeare's) to eight. In circulation the rise was meteoric. We grew from roughly a few thousand to a record runoff of 2,209,000. Beric Holt, an official of the *Post*'s permanent staff, was a steadying influence on Churchill's exhilaration all during this newspaper crisis. Holt was enthusiastic but he also knew how to do everything, so the actual chores of assembly and distribution (of a newspaper with nothing but pro-government editorials that the public had to take, no matter what it thought of the government) were part of his daily exercise. Churchill energized. Holt steered.

One morning Churchill called up the British Navy. He always enjoyed an excuse for doing this. We had such an involved security situation by this time that Churchill felt nothing less than a fleet admiral should supervise it. So he appointed Admiral Hall to this strange assignment and in no time he was on the job, joining the rest of us and finding some sort of excitement in this landlocked adventure.

Though none of the other London newspaper offices were running, they were all open and staffed. It occurred to Churchill that they could reprint or photostat what he was creating from his own corner of Fleet Street. In this way, three other famous dailies—the *Daily Mirror*, *Daily Mail*, and *Daily Express*—appeared. They were single-sheet editions, to be sure, but their banners were on the newsstands and in the agents' windows and counters again.

Socialists in the House of Commons (and Churchill of course went each day to the House, for at least an hour, often three or four) went after him repeatedly, not being able to sit still while the government was enjoying such an unprecedented editorial monopoly with unwarranted immunity for it. It was just too much luck, they felt. Churchill made the most of it.

When the Socialists rose in fury against him in the House of Commons (and wasn't it odd that the Chancellor of the Exchequer should be publicly scolded by Socialists for running a newspaper?) for being so biased in so many of the expressed views of this organ, he shot right back at them:

"The State cannot be impartial as between itself and that section of its subjects with whom it is contending."

This sentence seemed somehow very much like the sentence with which he so effectively silenced Philip Snowden, "There is nothing the matter with change, if it is in the right direction." Boiled down, what he'd said to Snowden was question-begging of the worst sort. And here, to the Socialists whom he loved to rag and lacerate, he'd done it again for does it not mean, "How can you expect us to be impartial when our office necessitates our bias?" Or close to it? This threw a confusion into them.

In retaliation the pro-strike agitators threw something more substantial than confusion in the presses one morning. Mr. Churchill and members of his staff were touring the machinery room. Suddenly there was an unearthly metallic screaming and a great rhythmic thumping. The floor shook up and down. Great whines and whinnies came out of the presses and their supporting frames shook in agony.

Into the most sensitive part of the mechanism a knowing person had thrown a small steel bar. The results were ruinous.

Winston lighted a cigar and regarded the dying giant. He realized that only the machine's designers and builders (it was a Hoe press) who knew every rod and connection in her could repair the damage in time to meet the next edition. He realized, also, that these men were on strike, as was the whole nation.

What should he do? When England is in doubt, it calls for Churchill. When Churchill is in doubt, he calls the Navy. He asked his admiral to come down.

"Can this be fixed at once by the Royal Navy?" he asked Admiral Hall, daring him to say no.

The Admiral of course said yes, it could, and called for a land convoy. Then he phoned the Chatham Dockyard, describing what was on its way to their machine shops. We stood by while the mangled unit of the machinery was isolated from the body of the main assembly, hoisted by block-and-tackle, and set in a truck.

A whole fleet of cars carried this to the seaside at the Chatham yards, with cars loaded with police officers riding before and behind the critical cargo itself. The "convoy" was under civilian command of Beric Holt who told me later he was glad not only for the time off but for the protection of the extra police. The poor fellow had been cruelly knocked about the day before by the mob in front of the *Morning Post* building when he had rushed to the rescue of his colleague Robert Gray, at that moment being manhandled by eight or nine men. Holt had laid about with an iron stick until he went down, and the police had finally pulled these two from the melee.

The same afternoon the machinery came back from the Royal Navy all shined up, wrapped in bunting and with a Union Jack sticking out of her top! And the edition appeared as if nothing had happened!

Churchill was criticized again in the House over the continued attitude of the *Gazette*'s editorials. One could see his answer readying itself even though one was too far away to hear the premonitory growling. The Opposition had not cared for Mr. Churchill's assumption that the State and the Baldwin government were the same thing, or even remotely so. The Opposition of course insisted that the striking workers represented the true nature, and the majority makeup, of the State. When the petti-fogging got to the breaking point, Churchill rose and lashed out with a stinging statement—one of his briefest—that was copied at once everywhere. It was not answered by the Opposition, and I felt it was the psychological instant at which the General Strike was broken. He said: "I decline utterly to be impartial as between the fire brigade and the fire!"

Sensing his advantage here, Churchill made a hurried call on Stanley Baldwin, sat up late that night writing in the editor's office, and the next morning—over the signature of the Prime Minister—the following appeared on the front page of the *Gazette*—in the largest type the paper had: "*Every man who does his duty by the country and returns to work will be protected by the State from loss of trade union benefits or pension. His Majesty's Government will take whatever steps are necessary in Parliament or otherwise for this purpose.*"

The General Strike ended soon after this edition. There was a good deal of quiet celebrating in the offices of the *Morning Post*, whose plant and whose proprietors had made possible the physical assembly of the *British Gazette*.

Winston said goodbye to all, raised a toast, and informed me hurriedly that I would have to stay on a few more hours. He was taking a large party to the theatre.

I hate these assignments more than almost any other because of the tempting distraction of the show itself and because of the deceptiveness of theatre crowds. This is very different from cinema shows where anonymity is more likely not to be penetrated, and our training in Scotland Yard, later picked up by air forces all over the world, had long ago sent us ahead of our charges so we would be perfectly accustomed to the dark and thereby better able to protect the man or woman we were paid to keep in sight.

When, however, you are bodyguard to an important man, who is making a spectacular and well-advertised appearance in a famous theatre at a show that is a smash, bodyguards have a poor time. The target is lighted up.

The show was *Lady Be Good*. It was at the old Empire

Theatre on Leicester Square. And its stars were Fred and Adele Astaire. No pair of performers from America's shores has ever so captivated a British audience as these two did. (This was when Lord Cavendish, who later married Miss Astaire, first met her.) As to Adele Astaire herself, I do not think that even the happy excitement over Mary Martin, many years later and in a quite different show, was any stronger or more spontaneous. In any case, both these American girls were taken to the hearts of Londoners, still are and will always be talked about lovingly by theatre-goers.

In such times, I never have a seat and I move about as invisibly as possible, probably considered an un-uniformed fireman or a back-office flunky of some sort.

Churchill's party arrived late and was seated after the show was well started. I remained unobtrusively in the side aisle and conned the house, having already checked the theatre's management. I was pleased, upon looking through each row and spotting various of my colleagues, when Adele Astaire recognized our "public hero," stopped the show, and came to the apron of the stage.

"THERE HE IS," she cried happily and Winston rose in that rumpled slump of his, bowed and was most thrillingly cheered. Adele Astaire called for three cheers for Winston and what a mighty sound it was! What a thrill! What a man!

Then the pit orchestra struck up the opening bars of "God Save the King." There was an exhausting relief about the evening and many happy tears and Churchill of course received hundreds of congratulations as he sat in the stalls with his party. The *Morning Post*, now appearing under its own name again, wrote of this hour: "It was an eloquent testimony to the delight of the London public at the unconditional withdrawal of the General Strike."

One of the old Empire's managers tapped me on the shoulder to say that there were some "unpleasant" characters in the lobby. I went out with him. Here, with eight or nine others, hands in pockets, was my old friend who had struck me in the jaw that night on Berwick Street when Churchill was trying to get a seat from Westminister.

A fine cold fury suffused me. I could have taken on the whole packet of them. I had no thought in my mind at that instant but to break as many heads as I could hit. I kept walking across the lobby of the theatre, a cheerful background of music behind. I walked right toward the man and ignored the others, though they watched my approach with some curiosity. I drew back my right arm with no other purpose than to drive my fist right through this unfortunate man's skull if he should remain still for me. Then he recognized my purpose.

"Look out! It's *him!*" he shrieked and he bolted into the street. The others, in wild conjecture believing me to be the devil at least, hared after him. I am sure he became a model citizen and grateful voter. Among the thousands of miscreants I viewed in later years—big and little—he was absent.

There was something about the termination of the General Strike that had a poor ring to it. Winston never takes anything that isn't his. But he hates to have anything taken from him that *is* his. Winston Churchill had been in one nerve-wracking conference after another all during the Strike. Many of these were with some of the toughest talking and toughest looking men on this planet. I remember, for example, secret meetings in such London houses as Sir Abe Bailey's (the salty South African millionaire) when I first met "Jimmy" Thomas, the Colonial Secretary, and A. J. Cook, the miners' leader, who said he'd settle for anything Churchill himself thought was fair and sensible.

Where had the Prime Minister been during the General Strike? He had been for the "cure" to Aix-les-Bains on a holiday.

Winston Churchill broke the Strike and made the settlement but Stanley Baldwin took the credit for it. Winston resented this very bitterly. Any man would. His resentment was never publicly stated because Winston continued to serve Baldwin. But some of the shock of ingratitude and pomposity swept up to me in my eyrie in the House when Baldwin as Prime Minister announced the end of the Strike to the House. And he was only a few hours back from the baths! He did so in such a way as to exclude any suggestion of the mighty contribution that Churchill, his Chancellor, had made to the government. He seemed to imply that since this settlement had been arranged during the Baldwin incumbency, it was a Baldwin doing. And it was no such thing.

With the evidence of many days of the sunshine of southern France on his face, while Churchill looked dead and ashen and almost useless, I realized I could never care too much about Baldwin and that if I was later assigned by Scotland Yard to the protection of Stanley Baldwin, I would apply for other assignment.

The Duke of Westminster, who had a residence near Dieppe, invited Mr. Churchill to his place for a weekend. A great fatigue had settled on the Chancellor of the Exchequer —a reaction to his drive to settle the Strike, and he happily accepted the Duke's invitation to escape telephones, meetings, people, and papers to sign. He also liked the Duke very much.

He decided to drive the car himself to Dover to catch the boat for the Channel crossing. This is always a bad sign. It either means that he is cross and subconsciously wants to smash up something, or that he is dangerously elated and things will get smashed up anyhow through careless exuberance. Mr. Churchill has an immense grasp of the advantages and uses of the machine age; a real genius for putting whole mechanized organizations to work, whether it be a navy, an air force, or a fleet of emergency automobiles to distribute his *British Gazette*. But he has no personal sensitivity about the machines themselves. He strips gears and rams head-on toward anything. He could never learn, for example, to fly an airplane though flight has been one of his greatest enthusiasms. He is a great shot but a poor dancer. He is a strong swimmer but he sounds and looks like a North Sea flotilla maneuver. He has the most beautifully kept hands I ever saw on a man and they have great strength, but the very few times he tried to play golf he cursed the turf till it sizzled, never once hit the ball a clean whack, and sent gouts of grass into the air.

Did he ever, in fact, solo when he was first getting the feel of flying? No, he never did, though flying officers have told me they are sure he was thinking of it. He would have cracked up. If things had not gone the way he felt they should, his temper would have blown up in midair and the retaliatory forces of gravity would have been waiting for him when it was time for the two to meet—Winston and the earth, that is. He was a bit less than fair when he took over the controls in the early days, but was useless in the problem of landing or taking off. There was no sense of "glide" in his makeup; no lightness of touch; no kinship with the invisibility of this fluid element.

His driving was no better, and when he drove (I always

endeavored, usually successfully, to persuade him against it)
he was forever just missing things, or not quite missing them
and denting cars—his own and others. People shouldn't be
in his way, was his theory. "Here I come—look out!" might
have been painted on his windshield. In actual collisions, he
does not to this day believe any of the damage could have
been any of his doing. He does not take blame very well.
But then, why should he?

So we drove, myself in some misery, hurrying for Dover.
Churchill was driving as if all he hated was Stanley Baldwin
and all he wanted was to find Baldwin suddenly in the right
of way so he could ram a "thank you" out of him. There
was a lot of road repair. We were near Croydon. Winston
went through ruts just as if they weren't there. The road
narrowed. Construction lamps were burning. Cars were in
single file. There were mounds of shoveled earth about.
Winston did not care for the delay the situation indicated.
He saw an opening between the line of cars and I suddenly
realized we had jumped out of the road and were progressing right down the sidewalks of Croydon. It was apparently
the plan of the Chancellor of the Exchequer to bypass the
single file of almost stationary cars and merely rejoin the
procession when he could conveniently be head of it!

It was indeed most foolish of him. He had forgotten that
pedestrians have privileges on their own sidewalks and are
not accustomed to seeing motorists, even Chancellors, drive
right down them. We got into a nice mess in no time and had
to make an abrupt stop (Churchill was unusually good in the
technique of the abrupt stop) and of course looked up into
the face of an outraged local constable.

"You fool!" the constable shouted. Then he swore most
richly for some seconds.

Churchill's head hung down in deep discouragement. He
did have the civic sense to say he was sorry (though I'm sure
he was not at all sorry—just nettled at the delay) and the
matchless voice of the man identified him at once to the
constable.

"Sorry, Mr. Churchill." Then the majesty of the constable's office and the disgusting guilt of the violator
brought forth, in gentle sarcasm, a caution that withered
Churchill and kept him silent clear to the Channel. The constable looked into the car in the most falsely paternal way
imaginable and said softly: "*Do* try to stay in the road, sir."

At the dockside at Dover, there was a group of Irish extremists waiting for Winston. I knew one of them by sight and three by photographs. Half a dozen others, to reduce suspicion of those who had come to attack Churchill, were wearing Sinn Fein badges on their coats, being ostentatious in their anti-British calumniations. They were drinking, swearing, and spitting into the ocean. When they saw Churchill and me, they went aboard and into the ship's saloon. I stepped back ashore and called the Yard. Scotland Yard cleared a sergeant who was on customs duty at the port and I held up our departure a few moments while my colleague (we of course never "know" each other) could get into a disguise.

We communicated with each other by methods familiar to us, my purpose being to see to it that the men who had come to harm Churchill were informed that I was his bodyguard. I passed through the saloon a few moments later, looking like Scotland Yard in every dart of the eye and action of the hand. Some of the ship's officers came with me to embellish the appearance of our "security tour." I opened a valise or two, asked one of the officers to show his weapons, which he did (though I had to loan him a Webley), had the proper number of whispered conversations, the formal sweeping of the saloon with the hard eye, the inspection of passports and pocketbooks that had no meaning.

In less than a full minute the Irish knew I was the man to follow, for where I would be there would be Churchill also. This was the purpose of the excursion through the saloon, the first leg of the small journey to nowhere.

Churchill likes to know when he's in danger. It exhilarates him. He gets extra lively and almost boyishly concerned. The danger simply delights him. So we never tell him.

He ate breakfast in a restaurant in Calais after the crossing, quite by the station where the Dieppe train was standing. Between the Dieppe train and the main right-of-way for the Paris train stood a goods train. It was detaching a car from a string. At the proper moment and by prearrangement with the stationmaster at Calais, when the Paris train came through, I hurriedly boarded it with a large supply of hand luggage. Winston Churchill was in the gentlemen's retiring rooms on my orders while the Paris train stood in the Calais station.

Though the Irish for those few moments had lost physical sight of their quarry, they had never lost sight of me. And two of the bags I had with me as I climbed into the Paris train bore the name of Winston Churchill. The Paris train started. I was aboard. So were the Irish. But not Winston. I walked through it on a security tour. Fearless Fosdick. All the Irish were riding with me. I examined tickets, peered into bags that were none of my business, followed conductors, turned pieces of paper this way and that, and once again was very much in charge of the life of a man who at that moment was not even in motion. I am particularly impressive in dining cars.

In the Gare St. Lazare, I was greeted by other members of Scotland Yard who appeared as French baggage clerks and station manager's personnel. They took me and Winston's baggage directly into the manager's office where I was momentarily invisible. I went quickly through a side-door and directly into the cargo space of a goods van, sat down in the dark after dropping a tarpaulin flap, and was driven to the Gare du Nord where I boarded a train for Dieppe. At Dieppe I stepped into a taxicab and was driven out to the estate of the Duke of Westminster.

Winston had been there for a few hours by then, having been driven there by one of the Duke's chauffeurs and guarded in my absence by my colleague who had come aboard in Dover in disguise. I relieved him. Mr. Churchill, upon seeing me back with him, grinned happily. He was dressed in hunting pink and velvet cap and immediately charged away, with the weekend party and a whole sounder of hounds, on a boar hunt. I followed in a car. I also am always properly dressed for everything, considering my work, and own nothing but a suit.

But that is a good example of a Scotland Yard inspector's journey to nowhere. It had accomplished its purpose: it had kept danger away from the Old Man.

Winston Churchill's popularity could of course not stay at a high pitch for an indefinite time in a nation like England where every man is absolutely positive he is right and says so continuously. One of the newspapers had called him a "genius without judgment." Stanley Baldwin called him a "hundred horsepower brain," more perhaps in the spirit of a man who can't harness all the power he's been given. He was called an opportunist, and it was said he was "jaywalking through life." Winston didn't seem to care too much what people said of him so long as they went on using him.

The final volume of *The World Crisis* had now appeared, a great success financially and critically too. His magazine work was commanding ever larger figures, and the legacy from Vane-Tempest, his Irish cousin, made possible his purchase of Chartwell Manor.

When Churchill purchased this great house and the huge stretch of ground which surrounded it, his life seemed to open out in a new way. A new dignity entered him. I think he had longed for years to have some place of his own to go for holidays and weekends; a place where he could really work the earth with his own hands and tools; where he could relax. At Chartwell he did just that.

I was with him on the long and excited walks that preceded his buying of the land itself (there were many parcels not attached to the original grounds which Mr. Churchill wanted to have). One could see that much work—all of which he anticipated with huge excitement—was going to be needed. He read lists of projects out loud to me.

"We'll have to mow that." "We'll have to plant that." "That ought to be leveled and scraped." "New hedges in here." "We can divert this runnel and dig out this little bog and put in a pool, Thompson." "The house of course will have to be extensively altered." "I want several acres of perfect lawn, Thompson. Please get up early and see to it."

After the purchase of the estate, he did not move his family in for some months. The alterations were about as comprehensive and expensive as he had said they'd be. Winston loves to get into workclothes and he is a horse for day labor. So he and I, with a whole army of gardeners, stonemasons, diggers, planters, and bricklayers, spent hundreds of hours turning this fine place into a perfect English country home.

Here was peace, beauty, and architectural dignity. There was none of the dead and rusty grandeur of Blenheim, nor any of the impassive though impressive gloominess of Chequers.

Being able to help gave me a proper kind of exercise I had been missing while jumping about the Houses of Parliament, and rushing through the Mediterranean, election meetings and to the innumerable colleges and universities that were forever offering him a new degree or a graduation speech invitation.

It was good for Winston Churchill too, to get close to the ground and the fine smell of it, and to work it and plant it and make it bloom and yield. His great natural strength because of his hard training at Harrow and Sandhurst had not at all begun to abate, but he had the stoop of government and he had areas of fat that could not be worn with comfort. As his lawns improved, his fat melted away and the gratifying hardness came back to him.

He loved to stand on his porches and shout at us, giving wild and encouraging instructions. I was head lawnmower (I have tremendous arm power) and it was fun to use my arms again. As our labors went forward and the lawns came into being, Winston's expression of pride of possession was a pleasure to look at. It was not at all his office or Exchequer face. I suppose it was more the face that his "Clemmie" had married.

The house is built on a level with the roadway, with a bank of trees and flowering shrubs going high up from the front. At the rear the ground goes right down in a V-shape, to rise up again on the other side of the property into a handsome cluster of great old trees. At the time Winston took possession there was one large lake running along the bottom part of the grounds, and a smaller one at the side of the house which was fed by a number of springs which had been directed into it.

After we got the lawns all finished, Winston ordered a concrete dam to be put at the end of the big lake—the inlet end of it. This of course formed another lake and in a most surprisingly short time. It delighted him. Once he began changing the surface geography of things, he couldn't stop. The mixing of cement fascinated him. With a hoe and a sandpile this man was altogether tireless. The humming through the nostrils began all over again, frightening off the birds.

"Over with it!" he'd shout, with a great barrow of sand, cement, rock, brick, stone, or lumber, and he'd spill the burden with a caveman's joy into an unsightly but purposeful pile. He was a great exhorter of his own crews, often showing them how to lay brick when he did not yet know how to hold a trowel.

When he wanted a swimming pool, he at once set about to

dig it, then line it, then run the water in. When it was too cold to swim in, he at once devised a complicated but sensible system of conduits to carry warming water directly into the new pool. This had the same dependability that North Americans assign to the rest of our plumbing. Few swam there, though Churchill very often did so in the years following, and put up a diving board from which he would launch his happy hulk first into the air, then into the complaining waters, where he overwhelmed them in a flailing trudgeon that showered onlookers twenty feet away.

It was in this period of primitive rediscovery of England's earth that the legend of Churchill the Bricklayer began. It was like so many other things. He just loved the visual gratification that bricklaying brought him. You could see more progress every few minutes. Winston could lay over two thousand bricks in a single day. British unions don't permit more than eight hundred.

In any case, his first "wall," which he finished in four hours before lunch one morning and which he proudly fashioned without guiding strings, level or foundation, looked less like a wall—to the amazed but silent bricklayers who were too paralyzed to say anything—than it did like a funnel of mine tailings after a disaster. It was a thoroughly awful wall that would fall down with the very first rain. Winston, of course, because he'd built the thing, went off to his luncheon quite sure it was the best thing since the Romans.

We gave up our own lunchtime to pull down his work and put it all back together again, working with the regular beat of output that pronounces the professional. A little before twilight, Mr. Churchill came out again, bringing with him a Cabinet member whose identity I don't now recall, and pointed out his great skill and speed and sureness of eye and steadiness of hand and delicacy of trowel work. "One morning's work, and behold: a classic entity!"

Churchill's manual skill did somewhat improve, to be sure. He had a way of watching other people doing their job and of imitating without revealing ignorance by asking. The newspapers were picking up running stories about Chartwell—the pool, the water heating, the dams, the lawn —but no one had the courage to tell him what we thought of his bricklaying and what we had done about it. Actually I never did summon the moral courage to look Mr. Churchill in the face and tell him we'd torn down his poor wall and built a proper one.

It is even possible he would not have at that time believed it anyhow. Pictures of him in all manner of workclothes were proof that the man had taken charge of nature single-handed and, because he was famous and was of course in the forefront of all the press pictures, the imposing proof of accomplishment that made up all these backgrounds was ascribed to Churchill's own enterprise and personal zeal. The bricklayers, carpenters, and gardeners might have been so many Gilbert and Sullivan decorations waiting to sing.

To me, there was some delicious recompense in that it made up somewhat for his getting no praise from Stanley Baldwin for breaking the General Strike when he had done most of it all by himself.

Not for ten years did Winston know the real truth about his wall, when he read of it in a book I wrote. He was a fine sport about it, after the first stab of pain, for he had the satisfaction to have been a member during all that decade of the Bricklayers' Union. They had been so impressed with the photographs of "his" labors that they were proud to include anyone so distinguished as a Chancellor of the Exchequer in their membership. There was a brief challenge about it from the union's council, querying the right of an amateur to enjoy professional standing and the union's protection that went with it. This turned into an amusing row. The union itself seemed to want the "bricklayer-statesman" in their company, the council not to, and the Socialist element in the membership was strong enough to force the president to ask Churchill, who by then had paid dues, to resign.

Churchill was hurt at first, then majestically furious. He reminded the whole union that they had sought his membership and he'd lay bricks with the best of them in a public exhibit to prove his competence. He said he was to be considered in this matter for exactly what he was and that he was a bricklayer and nothing more and those who were dragging in his "incidental duties" as King's Minister were laying down a smokescreen over the dignity of organized, skilled labor.

He never did resign. He still pays dues. And he has thoroughly learned to lay a straight course of bricks, the use of plumbline, the level, and guiding string being part of his own equipment now. But at first it had been like his driving, or his flying, or his golf: massive energy but no touch. He's basically a rammer and a pounder.

How about his painting then? I'd say it's like his desk-work, or his rifle marksmanship, total concentration on one small area with one fixed purpose, no machinery, nor involvement with people. Here is Churchill, the contained man, at his best. But give him a swimming pool or a war and look out.

His family began to materialize. They had motored out on many afternoons to inspect the progress of their new home. Mrs. Churchill, whose expression seldom changed from its beautiful and almost severe serenity even when we were fearful we would have to set civilians to shooting invading Germans, was thoroughly taken with her new place in the country. The children of course devoured it all and tried the lakes one after another, Randolph sampling every stream to see what fishing the property had.

Winston's great love of water, salt water for swimming when he can get it, but moving water at any time, seemed an almost primitive thing in the man. I had noticed his instant response to the roar of the Jordan on our first long trip together when he could only hear the power of it without yet seeing it. The same expression was duplicated when he first beheld Niagara in North America. Here at Chartwell the natural water system, and the filled basins that gravity had deposited about so generously and that spilled from one to another, was as much a continuous occupation to his mind and fancy as an elaborate system of toy trains is to an inventive boy. When he found such a quantity of water escaping his own swimming pool and losing itself to no observable advantage in the lower ground beyond, he built another pool there to catch it and hold it. He put goldfish into them. Some of them became very large and they became so familiar with the appearance of Churchill that they would swim to the side of the bank and take food from his hands. He has painted this. There was enough steepness of ground so that the interconnections of these ponds, lakes and pools—six altogether by now—made happy waterfalls everywhere.

A short distance from the main house are a number of cottages and outhouses. One of these latter he turned into a studio. It is fourteen feet square but very lofty. He put slats of wood about the interior walls and many of his paintings from the time he commenced are now fixed to these walls, another of the activities of this busy and happy man during this interval. His paintings reveal his itineraries, and often when my own duties were done and I was either awaiting my relief or departure with him for London, Paris, Washington or Toronto, I would go into this simple but lively place and sit. I liked to see where I'd been! And what a gallery! Pompeii, Waterloo, Stromboli, the fjords, Dutch canals, Ulster, Balmoral, Devonshire, Kent, Passchendaele, Festubert, Ypres, Vimy Ridge, Mons, Messines, Menin, Scapa Flow, the Minches, Rotterdam, Rome, the Acropolis, the Theseum, the Caryatides, the Tomb of Cheops, and the Assuan Dam.

Over the years he has gotten over the difficulty of having to finish at one sitting. He has developed a system whereby he does not have to return to the scene itself, as he had to, for example, in the Holy Land, or at the Pyramids the first time. From about the time of the late 1920's he evolved a scheme of outlining the picture. If he feared interruption, or knew he could not soon come back, he would dab in the various colors (their exact shade and quality) from which he could pick up the scene from memory and reconstruct the whole. Many times, when I've had the opportunity to appraise his technique, having been myself to the site of the original and seeing what was done and what was left undone, I have been surprised at the marvelous results he has obtained from this method.

The case in point was demonstrated to its best advantage at Marrakesh, during World War II. Marrakesh is slightly inland from Casablanca and Mr. Churchill had gone there to recuperate following his extreme illness at Tunis when we all thought we'd lost him. At first his recovery was exceedingly slow. He was too weak to think of painting, so, perverse man that he is and thoroughly un-Christian patient, painting was the first thing he thought of. Marrakesh is a savage city, full of wonder, hideous in its histories and ugly to the eye at close range, but most romantic when softened by half-distances or the gathering pity of twilight. Winston very much wanted to paint a picture of Marrakesh, showing as much of the city as possible. As there was a tower attached to the house where we were staying, he requested my colleague and me to carry him in a special chair to the tower's top. We did this. A marvelous view was obtainable from this height. Lugging him up the several hundred steps was not easy but when you work for Churchill, nothing is easy and everything is worth what it costs. Suddenly, as he painted, his strength gave out and he asked to be carried down again. This of course we immediately did.

He did not return to this canvas for three years; not till after the war. But his method, with the optical reminders he had sketched for himself in the tower, was good enough so that Marrakesh is the most admired of all his paintings by professionals who have studied his whole output. It's dazzling, Moorish, and sad. He recalled the sight of it and his emotional impressions of it—all in only a few moments after he pulled it out and looked at it again.

Winston paints almost anything except people or violence. He loves water and is one of the few who can get the *sound* of water onto canvas. Yet he has never painted a storm, or wild water, that I know of. Shore margins and mirages are his favorites here. The signs and symbols of man's life and presence are usually in his pictures somewhere: houses, buildings, cathedrals, a suggestion of population. He loves ruins and could not be pulled away from Pompeii. He studies his subject only briefly, then works with great speed. He never fights his work. The paint goes on and stays on with the blunt and self-assured enthusiasm that his trowel brings to his bricklaying. He slaps it into place and there it stays. As to content, his pictures are always a spontaneous reaction to a single theme: pool, temple, ship, harbor. Though he works at high speed, there is no sign of carelessness. Winston Churchill's own life has been dramatic—often melodramatic—yet his paintings are peaceful. There is not a riot of any sort in a single one of them, in color, activity, or suggestiveness. So I would think that the man's inner spirit is superbly calm and that he paints from it—never from the mind or the intellect, never certainly from the surface excitements that propel most men in the uses of their leisure. While his results always produce a contemplative quality, there is no religious overtone there, no subjectivity, nor hidden hints that greater meanings will emerge from longer study.

I do not know when his painting started. He was a good painter when I first met him, but I am told that even as a very young man, his dispatches to the London papers from the scenes he witnessed as a war correspondent in the Boer

War were often decorated with sketches that were filled in and used as illustrations in his newspaper articles. I have heard his friends say that Winston is a good portraitist and this may be true, though I could not say. I have looked for many hours, with nobody at all about, at nearly all of his paintings (the majority of them are in his studio in Chartwell) and the only portrait that comes to mind is that of Sir John Lavery.

Churchill's attitude toward his own work is an interesting and not uncommon paradox in all men of abundant talent: the shield of modesty and the mirror of pride. He won't part with his own work. Few own a thing he has painted, though I would estimate his output now to run over four hundred and fifty canvases. So, while being miserly in the possession of his own work, he rarely signs it, even by initials. He won't sell what he paints. His wife Clementine once urged him to put up one of his works for auction for a benefit of some kind and his painting "The Blue Sitting Room" drew a bid of twelve hundred and fifty guineas.

Churchill has only rarely lent his work to exhibits. And then only when he has the protection of anonymity. Here, I think, he liked to stand up under the pressure of competitive skills and see how good he was considered to be by those who did not realize they were examining the labors of a Prime Minister. The vanity-modesty dilemma again, an odd but constant ambivalence in him. Possibly too Professor Thomas Bodkin, the art critic, director of the Barber Institute of the University of Birmingham, may be close to a great truth about Churchill, one which I missed in my twenty years of daily contact and conversation with him. I have come upon the thought only recently and the more I consider the paragraph, the more sense it makes to me: "He may think, for all I know, that his reputation as a statesman might suffer from his activities as an artist. In this country a love of music or the visual arts is still too often considered to be evidence of mental instability. Had Mr. Gladstone composed symphonies or Mr. Disraeli carved statues it is unlikely that either would ever have found himself at the head of one of Queen Victoria's governments."

None of his work is catalogued and it would be my guess that upon the passing of this man, his work as an artist will tumble into the most terrible confusion. It is the most unprotected part of his total output and his vulnerability here (in lack of safeguards) is both fascinatingly and tragically un-characteristic of him. After his death, it will not be possible for any living person positively to say just when this or that picture was executed. There will be disputes as to where they were painted. Yet they have great value in associations of contemporary history, as I think you may agree from the incident I have recorded of Marrakesh. Front or back, though, most of his canvases contain neither date, title, clue, name, or initial. This seems very wrong to me and I hope, if he again finds any period of relaxation, that he can go through his Chartwell studio, Chequers and Number Ten Downing Street, where there are about fourteen of his pic-tures, and label every single one of them as to date, circum-stance, location. I suppose they will acquire their own titles, which is not important. But surely time and place are of par-amount concern.

I never did get over my annoyance at having to carry all the stuff he used. I suppose it's a foolish resentment but I never could get over it. It seemed coolie work, especially in Africa where millions of available coolies obviously thought so too. They just couldn't understand it. Neither could I. And Winston—since I never complained—didn't need to understand.

The Commander-in-Chief of the Mediterranean Fleet, in the late 1920's, was Admiral Sir Roger Keyes. We were to visit him at the British Island base of Malta, preparatory to joining the fleet for extensive exercises and maneuvers. I was enjoying the ride on board a handsome Italian liner named the *Esperia*. I was thinking that my lot was perhaps just a bit better than was that of my other colleagues in the Special Branch. It was a fine morning. Then a British destroyer was sighted ripping a white streak through the surface. She pulled up alongside. In no time at all, Churchill and I were aboard the destroyer. A few moments later we were at breakfast on the heights of Valetta, and it seemed to me that every day I was lugging Winston Churchill's damn paint-boxes about. Actually, it was for only two days.

I suppose, as I get older, I am getting the feeling that I did all the work while he got all the fun and glory. So be it.

The fleet coasted back after maneuvers, rounding the Ital-ian boot. Mr. Churchill was to be a guest of King Victor Emmanuel and to meet Il Duce too later on. The King did not know how much longer he was to be allowed around his own palace and country.

I was not given any particular instructions about the protection of Mr. Churchill during this stay in Italy. So many special detectives (Italians) followed *us* around that it gave us all a sense of comic-opera security. Mobs went alongside us, laughing, taking pictures, waving signs. On one occasion Winston accepted an invitation of some English friends to spend a few days and nights in their villa near Florence. Just to be sure, I checked Scotland Yard and was informed to insist that Winston not leave the villa after sundown. He was having a good time there and so did not resist the order.

This liberated me evenings, an unusual and welcome change. I poked about all over Florence one night. Returning home late that evening, I heard a burst of gunfire, and a lot of screaming and running. Knowing it could have nothing to do with my own charge, my interest in the matter was more boyishly investigative than professional.

A mob of Blackshirts were quite obviously killing a group of their enemies in a large house right beside the main thoroughfare. It was not at all my fight but I could not resist wanting to see who was killing whom and how it was progressing. It was all in perfect accordance with my own views of the way Italians were supposed to behave, and with Mussolini at the threshold of power it seemed altogether correct. Presently flames began shooting from many windows of the house. I could smell petrol. People ran in and out, then only out. Several men who had been stabbed but not quite killed struggled screaming into the garden before me, clutching themselves, looking blindly about. Three of them toppled over dead.

I had many impressive passes, instantly recognizable by European police anywhere and upon showing them to the Carabinieri who came up upon the retreat of the Blackshirts, I was left alone and unnoticed. An English-speaking Italian detective, who recognized me as of the Churchill party, told me without concern or interest that it was a "private affair" between the Fascisti and a nest of their enemies. They had killed a whole family, including all the girls and the children too.

Even with such an ugly exposure to what later on became my favorite abomination of all time (Mussolini was far more loathsome, even though far less dangerous, than Hitler), I must say in all truth that when I was close to and in the physical presence of Benito Mussolini, he impressed me as no other human I had up to then ever met.

I am past sixty now and it is indeed hard to countenance what I have here written. Yet then it was not only not hard to be impressed with the man; it was the universal reaction. I know Churchill was not in the least impressed with the so-called "long-walk-to-the-Presence." Churchill likes to take the military clank out of heavily decorated aides and flunkeys, when he thinks they need it, by jabbing them in the belly or blowing smoke into their faces, so instead of clanking fearsomely they merely tinkle sweetly like toys. He then goes past, never looking back to enjoy the apoplexy of surprise and outrage he's left there whenever he decides to ignore self-importance.

So, when challenged by the advance brass of Mussolini's outer chamber for daring to be smoking at all and especially for thinking he could walk in on Il Duce that way, he simply passed his smoldering cigar to the astounded sergeant who had challenged him, pushed his gun up, and walked in by himself, lighting a fresh cigar while he closed the door with his foot.

I was not in the Presence for the interview but I was on hand that same night. The occasion was a grand reception for Winston Churchill at the British Embassy. Our Embassy in Rome is a pretty good one. Most are dreadful but this one, in beauty and stateliness, is suitable to house the representative of an English King. Somewhat to give me a rest from my chores, the Ambassador had declared me his official champagne taster. I tasted all the champagne the corps of butlers opened, using the Russian technique of engulfing an hors d'œuvres between swigs. I had a pretty good time that night.

About ten-thirty, with all the guests assembled, there was a great bleat of sirens, and a sudden bold show of police. As Americans would say, they "cased the joint." It was unbelievably rude and fantastically unnecessary. I suddenly realized what was known to many others: it was the "dramatic preamble" to the entrance of the Big Man.

And at the psychologically right instant, just after his special police had swept in and swept out and before the host of the evening could intercede, Mussolini strode in alone. It was of course almost comical. But he got away with it. He dominated that whole embassy floor. He was swaggering and he was pompous but the fanaticism of the man, and the flame of some passionate purpose, the look of strength and boldness, were altogether real and compelling. It affected every man and woman in that gathering. I suppose that he was thoroughly rotten right then and there, but it did not show; not anywhere. He was a Roman. He had a sheen and an exterior appearance Napoleon would have envied. And he knew how to wear it. Perhaps that was the main thing.

He nodded to me as he passed. It was one of my duties to collect the invitations from arriving guests, though why I should want to know who was genuine and who was not was never made clear to me. I suppose it was thought—since there has always been an almost comic-opera enthusiasm for gate-crashing at Italian embassy parties of all kinds—that Scotland Yard could tell the difference between a guest and an impostor at a glance. I don't know whether Mussolini had a card or not; I never thought to challenge him. He was the one who did all the challenging.

Il Duce was one of the few uniformed men in the place and this helped him. He was passed quickly to all the guests of primary importance. He was a conscientious lingerer over women, a swaggerer and a heel-clicker by instinct, and he jingled about in the bright lights, his medals, some of them known to be self-complimentary, gleaming and ringing like a county fair jewelry stall in a wind. Winston, who had been reading something handed him by his companion of that moment, now removed his glasses the better to see the Conqueror. There was no other way to explain the look that came to Churchill's eye than the phrase: Who's kidding?

But I was impressed. At least until I happened to be near the King and Mussolini. They were walking in the Palace grounds. I was waiting for Winston. The King accidentally dropped his handkerchief on the grass. Mussolini immediately stooped to pick it up, whereupon His Majesty said, "No, no, do not pick it up."

"But your Majesty," cried Mussolini. "You know I would do anything for you."

"I prefer," said His Majesty, "to pick up my handkerchief myself. It is the only thing belonging to me that you have not put your nose into."

An attendant whispered a translation of this amusing exchange to Mr. Churchill who in turn relayed it to me, with great amusement, as soon as we were away from the palace.

Well, things very often went very quickly with Winston Churchill. We got back to England but it was no time at all before he was very much out of a job. This time he was out for good.

So it seemed, too, for though he was still an M.P., he did not exercise power of any memorable influence at all for more than tén years.

The circumstances of his leaving public life in 1929 and remaining out of it till the beginning of World War II are better known to contemporary historians than they are to me. I saw him often and served him, on his lecture trip through America, but I don't know what went on in his mind during the long interval.

It is hard to see a busy man assigned to idleness. But Winston was suddenly no longer Chancellor of the Exchequer. He was suddenly nothing. The economic decline had subtly changed the public's attitude toward him. He did not know much about money or economics—not very much more than how to make a good living for himself and his family somewhat as the Roosevelts have always been able to do. Because depressions and Chancellors of the Exchequer are supposed to be able to explain each other to their public and because Winston could not do so, he began to lose favor. His fear of the rise of socialism and communism was increasing and his hatred of it was increasingly outspoken. His genuine affection for the workers was thereby doubted by them; even the Tories felt he was becoming too Tory. And Churchill's colorful impetuousness, so deadly right so many times throughout his whole life, seemed to make him everywhere more vulnerable. It was claimed all about that his methods were like a weathervane.

"They don't want me around, Thompson," he said mournfully one morning. "They need someone to take the blame. They need someone big to take the blame. There is going to be a great deal of blaming and they seem determined that I shall receive it." And that is how it went.

Ramsay MacDonald's socialism moved into the Houses of Parliament. Winston Churchill, though still an M.P., stepped down from government office.

He called me into his study early one morning at Chartwell Manor and told me lugubriously that the "authorities" would like his reaction to their suggestion that perhaps the time to withdraw special protection from him had now come. He did not tell me that the authorities had suggested he dismiss me, as the public and its new Prime Minister had dismissed Winston, but that was it.

We both, of course, understood this right away. Englishmen don't take on in such circumstances. And it may be, too, that our feelings are more restrained than those of men of other nations or races.

In any case, so long as there was no one around any longer who wanted to assassinate Winston Churchill, I could not be regarded as other than an unnecessary public expense.

We shook hands and I left.

Reporting to Scotland Yard, I was immediately reassigned. I chased Communists for two years, a bore if ever there was one. We call this "following the activities of political bodies of extreme opinion." The only interesting man I tailed was Sir Oswald Mosley. He was a Fascist, not a Communist, but he looked to the rest of England as if he might disturb the peace if he could. He was a great speaker, a well-disciplined thinker, and a quick-minded theatrical man with a lot of education, far more than Mussolini had or any of the Russians for that matter, except Lenin. He aped, without knowing it, the hand gestures and the very gait of Il Duce and separated himself from comparison to the Italian by a studied simplicity—and almost funereal simplicity of dress. Mosley had the reserve of the professional executioner about him. Mussolini always looked like a rooster and could strut anywhere, even in his own bathroom. You knew Mussolini regretted he had not invented the goose-step. Mosley, though, moved to the rhythm of the saraband.

There was a solemnity to Oswald. He somehow had the look of the church—or perhaps the cemetery. He was pale and sad and his force seemed truly an inner one—not as easy to diagnose as false as Il Duce's. He could hold audiences, but he seldom shouted. When he did shout, the effect was stunning in the extreme.

Like Mussolini, he waited for the right moment to enter. And he always managed to have a main aisle down which he progressed always alone. No hangers-on at close range, ever.

It has been the great mystery in my whole life why any-one should *want* to be a Communist, a Fascist, or a totali-tarian of any kind, nameable or unnameable, when Com-munists themselves are the walking proof that there is no comfort in it, no money, no sense, and no future; that there is nothing but insult; the merciless tedium of intellectual depravity; the merciless twist of physical depravity; and not a single dish upon which the human mind or belly can feed in peace either by himself or with his fellows. I have never met a Communist who was not a bully, a coward, or a fool, or, most common, a secret failure to himself.

My meditations on Communists and Fascists were broken in on by a most happy contrast of ideas. Scotland Yard had received an inquiry from Winston Churchill as to my pos-sible interest in accompanying him on a lecture tour to the United States and Canada.

I at once said I would be delighted to do so but how could such a pleasant prospect be legitimized? What had Scotland Yard to do with a man who was no longer a King's Minister?

There was a partial answer to this question. There were several secret societies in India who had for sometime wanted to kill Winston. These societies had cells in America and Canada. Churchill had been opposed to the India Con-stitution Bill, feeling at that time the Indians were not fit— no matter how willing to try—to embark on the expensive business of running themselves. Then too, he didn't want to lose India anyhow. It was not unlike his feeling about Egypt.

The Indian Terrorist Society—quite courageous and for-midable, even if uncertain of aim—was a well-organized group with several hundred members, many of them men of fine character and education. It was believed, however, that they would have nothing on their conscience if they could bring down Winston Churchill by whatever means.

Even though at this time he was an ordinary M.P., he was considered by the Indians to be their greatest living enemy. It was Scotland Yard's information that attempts on Churchill's life would be made in America, if he actually arrived there for a long tour, and that these attempts would most likely be made in one of four cities, New York, De-troit, Chicago, or San Francisco. The terrorists' headquar-ters were located in this latter city. Detroit and Chicago had substantial numbers of Indians living within their limits, many of them students in the large universities, and there were many other Indians who were in North America with legitimate travel and study permits absorbing American industrial techniques.

I was most pleased that, when informed by the Indian Office of His Majesty's Government that attempts to assassinate him might be expected and some of the plans were already known, Churchill at once asked for my return to him.

Very soon I saw him again. We were both delighted.

"So you're coming with me, Thompson? I'm more than glad!" He looked it, too.

This was fine. But the first difficulty was the money. Winston had no official position and in no way represented the Crown. The situation grew increasingly confused. Then it cleared up. Winston was to pay all my personal expenses, while the police authorities paid my salary. It was somewhat as if I were still chasing about after the blackguard Mosley, only with two pleasing differences: I liked the speeches better and I had an expense account.

Something happened about reservations. Winston won't ride on anything but a British vessel if he can avoid it. But he couldn't get berths for all of us (he was taking members of his family, too) in time to meet his first early speaking dates, in and around New York. There was a certain amount of interest by the American radio, too, as early as that was —1931. Churchill wanted the money and so had to make the unpleasant compromise of getting on any ship that would deliver him in time to meet his contract.

He cursed and swore and banged his cane about when he discovered to his great disgust that of all ships afloat, the only one that would fit the situation was a German liner, the *Europa*.

My own hatred of Germans, which has now become pathological, was never up to his. Many have heard Winston in the midst of his fulminating improvisations, assigning their true villainies to Germany's generals, but no editor has ever been able to print any of it.

In all truth, we had gorgeous accommodations, superb food, fine companions, and service of a kind I'd never seen before, afloat or ashore. I shall not pay the Germans another compliment and am relieved here to report that I do not need to. But they can run a ship and I'll never say they can't. It is hard for a Britisher to admit this, but it's true.

We were due to arrive in New York harbor about eleven o'clock one morning. I got up before four o'clock, cleaned my revolvers, reloaded them, and made a slight repair in my holster, a special one that I made myself. With a gun in one hand and another one on the dresser before me, I turned my attention to Churchill's private arsenal. There was a great pounding on my stateroom door. Outside it was pitch-dark of course, and a good sea lifting and sinking beneath us. From such noise I thought we were at least sinking. I ripped the door open and stood there half-dressed, amazed, and loaded down with guns. Forty people stood right in front of me, about ten of them women.

Who do you think they were? The American press!

"Where's Winnie?" "Get the Old Boy up for us, copper!" "We want to see Churchill!"

All this without warning of any sort at all. Not a single request had ever come to us that my charge was to be seen before we arrived.

And I could not figure how they had got on board! I still had a "mid-ocean" feeling. I hated the American press right then and there and for a considerable time after, though we've made our peace. But we didn't make our peace on this trip. They were in all ways indecently adhesive, unbearably rude and thoughtless, even cruel. I could not get used to it at all, and if they had realized that we were just a couple of decent people, one of whom had come to lecture and would be around for months, they would have had much more material from us than they got.

It was my first experience with American newspapermen and their manners. I suffered. But I think it was they, perhaps more than Winston, who lost out. They wanted copy and Winston, if he never was anything else, is copy all the time. But the importunings, lies and dodgings and the calculated insensitivity made him ill. And it set my guard up and I never let it down once.

They couldn't understand that I refused to wake Mr. Churchill. Nor would they understand I would say nothing about his trip or its itinerary. Or what he planned to talk about. They knew where he was to stay in New York and told me reporters and photographers were already waiting there, but that they themselves had come aboard the ship many miles at sea with the pilot and quarantine officers and that they did this every time anyone important was on his way in to visit the States. I thought it was a terrible way to live and said so. I promised they would have a chance to chat with Mr. Churchill but warned them it would be brief and that I would under no circumstances think of knocking on his door, hurrying his bath or breakfast, or disturbing his peace in any way. He's cross as a bear when his rising routine is interfered with.

I went back into my own stateroom. There was a steward there, making up the place with suspicious enthusiasm—a steward new to me. Suddenly I realized it was one of these clever American tricks, and for a few seconds it worked, too. One of the reporters had somehow found a steward's jacket and cap, and had slipped into my quarters to look about or pick up information in whatever way he might. He was no more German than I was. I just picked him up under the arms, planted him hard outside my door and slammed the door.

Later, after normal risings and a somewhat normal breakfast (I warned the Churchills to stay inside their suite), Winston met the press in the lounge. Here there was a noisy but useful interview, and a rapid exchange of questions and answers. They liked their subject. The group went out on deck, where newsreel photograpers ground away and held microphones close to his mouth to catch what he said.

Churchill had a certain sympathy with it all that I didn't feel. And even I calmed down a bit when I learned that this group had been up all night (it was a horrible November day) and had come out past Ellis Island to meet the ship far out, traveling in a small and far from seaworthy launch.

We docked, were counted off and packed off in five different cars. A half dozen celebrities and city officials were on hand to welcome the great man. There was something too military about it all. There was no warmth of welcome, and there was far too much glint to the cordiality of it all. And several hundred police! It seemed absurd.

Suddenly we were all in motion, all at the same time, and in a whirling parade that rocked up Broadway with enough sirens to waken the dead. It seemed a most awful way to get to a hotel. I learned since that private individuals, if properly connected, can receive this much attention and that the motorcycle escort is a very common sight.

In the Waldorf-Astoria hotel we had a few hours of peace. I was overwhelmed by New York the first time I could peer out a window, and when off duty spent many hours looking at the immensity of it—immense in the vertical sense.

I had certain matters to go over with the police and with the detectives who were on the hotel staff. Mr. Churchill seemed glad to be rid of me for a time and said so. Mrs. Churchill was going to take a short rest while her husband planned to run up Fifth Avenue and call on his best American friend, Mr. Bernard Baruch. I reminded Mr. Churchill that he was not allowed to do this alone, irrespective of the time of day. He became very agitated with me and in his determination to make this one call all alone, he was supported by his wife. I looked out the window. The night had come. America was friendly by habit. I gave Winston into the hands of the local police, which I should not have done.

There is always a good deal of confusion about baggage. Churchill's valet and I took care of most of this. I took care of some more of the reporters who were living in the lobby. After forty-eight hours without rest, I went to bed.

My telephone rang. It was Mrs. Churchill with the distressing news that Winston had met with an accident and was in the hospital. "The Lenox Hill Hospital," Mrs. Churchill said. Naturally I had never heard of such a place. I rushed to her suite and we immediately went to the address.

This is what happens when police officers permit themselves to do things contrary to their own best judgment. Never once in my entire life had I allowed one of my charges to tell me what I was to do or not to do. But this time, because of their insistence, and perhaps influenced psychologically by my own newness to America, I had allowed the Churchills to set their wish and judgment over mine. And Winston immediately got himself into a bad accident.

I do think, because he was a private citizen and not an official of the British government, that I had subconsciously permitted certain leniencies and that I planned, though still subconsciously, to give him more leeway than he'd received on any other trip or tour with me. But no matter how it is looked at, there is no excuse for this, and I have never given myself one.

Fifth Avenue was, and I believe still is, the street in New York on which his friend Baruch lived—at 1055. Fifth Avenue is a delight to walk upon, especially upon the park side. It goes for better than two miles and a half and except for a few transverse roadways for passenger cars, a pedestrian never has to look for traffic. He may walk in peace.

Churchill apparently rode most of the way, then started to cross over. He isn't too much of a walker, as you have no doubt gathered. But the night was so fine, and the invitation of the park's unexpected size (Winston had not been in New York since his strangely successful and most lucrative lecture tour at the conclusion of the Boer War when he barnstormed as a bit of a youthful hero)—these late autumn glimpses caught him and held his attention. Being English, he forgot about the direction of American traffic. It nearly cost him his life.

He stepped off the walk into the roadway, looking the wrong way for traffic. He looked south. There was a screaming of brakes. Then a shock of collision. Churchill was flung up and forward. Then he crashed down heavily upon the asphalt pavement of Fifth Avenue. He tried to rise, then fell back. He was unconscious, and later semiconscious. Fortunately for him, and for us all, it was not a hit-and-run driver who had knocked him down. It was a poor but honest Italian American by the name of Mario Contasino, a taxicab driver, who at the time was out of work. He helped Winston. He was waiting still, and most nervously, when Churchill recovered consciousness and there were many pleasant exchanges of courtesy and appreciation.

At the desk, bleeding and covered with dirt, seeking admission to the emergency section of the hospital, an exasperating thing happened. Churchill was challenged, before he was given assistance, as to his ability to pay the doctors. I suppose this is understandable, since Lenox Hill is a private institution, but the man was bleeding all over the floor, he was in terrible pain, and the extent of his injuries was unknown. Yet he had somehow to prove his financial competence to meet bills not yet rendered in order to get onto an operating table.

"I am a British stateman and a friend of the King," he said faintly. This got him some attention.

His accident was not publicly known until the next day. This was a good thing. King George V, immediately on being informed that Winston Churchill had had a bad accident in America, called the hospital. Somehow this information went through the hospital like the news of a new warden's appointment gets to inmates of an old jail. I was on hand during these days, of course, and it was lucky I was in the corridors at these particular hours.

An enterprising newspaperwoman had done what her colleague had done two days before on the *Europa*—only this girl, instead of dressing like a stewardess, put on a nursing cap and came right in. The ruse was too clumsy, but it was only one of a number. After I threw her out of Winston's room, he took the call from His Majesty, reporting that while he had been knocked about very soundly, with a painful shoulder sprain and deep lacerations of the face, chest, and nose, nothing appeared to be broken. He limped for many days after his several days' confinement there.

Newspaper reporters hid in the laundry bins, in the wardrooms, and came in wheeling loads of tea things, unordered. Some would come in white jackets. All the chambermaids were suspect. And outside Winston's door I had twice to propel people away, just because their clamor of questioning was making it impossible for the poor man to rest.

Once a load of fresh linen, unusually heavy and seeming to move strangely when its attendant left it standing in the corridor, revealed a reporter crouched inside, hoping to be wheeled right into the sick room and there either to overhear something worth sending his editor or to manage to chat with Churchill long enough to say he'd seen the man first.

It would have been a good scoop. Winston got the scoop himself, this time, for while hoping for a good press in the United States and Canada, he felt he would surely get it anyhow. The accident had helped already. And he scooped the others by writing the story of his accident. Floral tributes supplied nearly every patient in that whole nursing home, and while these were being acknowledged by a clerical staff which was thrown together partly by the hospital and partly by the hotel, Winston himself dictated the story of what had befallen him on his first day in America.

He sold it to *Collier's* for about three thousand American dollars, enough for him to take a rest trip to the Bahamas. Here he painted and swam. One day, in Nassau, when nearly run down by a young Negro driving too fast, he leaped out of the way and grabbed the top posts of a board fence.

This was the only time in my life that I have seen Churchill in the clutch of old-fashioned fear. He shivered and shook. Sweat poured down his face and darkened his cream colored shirt. It was shock. It left him weak and shaking. It seemed almost malarial in its symptoms. He was thinking, of course, of the accident he had just sustained and survived. He looked rather piteously at me and said: "They almost got me that time, Thompson."

Churchill could not start his tour without more rest. He was advised to remain in the Bahamas for three weeks. It was a good feeling (it always is for an Englishman) to see British soil again; to be on it. It cheered him. And me too. In Nassau I was most lucky to get into a game of soccer, the first I'd played since giving up the game to spend my life with Scotland Yard.

Churchill and I saw our first rum runner, the fleet that was enriching and at the same time contaminating American life. We later met the man to whom all of these particular cargoes of fine whiskies were delivered. He seemed very civilized. He told me that if either myself or Mr. Churchill wanted a drink at any time in New York, to just ask any policeman where the nearest speakeasy could be found. He gave me a card, not one of those that suggested you ask for the ever-present and indestructible "Joe." It had a phone number that we were to call for our order to be delivered. (Later, back at the Waldorf in New York I used this number to restock Mr. Churchill's modest supply and in less than ten minutes, the man had come with "the goods." Very excellent whiskies, too, and uncut. It would not be possible to fool Mr. Churchill about fine whisky, or champagne.)

We came back to New York to start the lecture trip. I shall say little about it. It is a poor way for a new man to become acquainted with a new country. Too much travel, too much hurry and not anything which the resident population would in any sense call typical. My first duty was to check all my firearms with such authorities as could permit me to carry and use weapons in a state-to-state tour of some length.

I took two or three guns to the New York Police Headquarters. I told them who I was, and which guns were mine and which Winston's. I thought I would procure licenses of some sort, to cover us officially under any conditions.

"But nobody is permitted to carry firearms in the United States," said this twinkling Irish captain.

"What about the five persons who were shot down by sawed-off shotguns in Chicago only yesterday?" I asked. This charmed them.

"Oh, them." Then, "Chicago."

"But right here," I protested. There had indeed been a daylight killing of remarkable enthusiasm right in the middle of 49th Street the day before.

The group of New York police officers thought I was an unusual man and said so. They told me I could not have a permit but that I should just go ahead and use the weapons I had brought with me and do so on as economical and infrequent a basis as possible. They said if there was shooting, to let them know and they would do all that was needed in order to "square it."

I asked them how in the world all these shootings could be going on all round without the police knowing just which citizen had a gun and which did not. It would seem to make their own selection of suspects a far more difficult job than it is for Scotland Yard. How would anyone, I asked, carry a gun without the police having cognizance of it?

These police officers seemed to disbelieve that our methods in Scotland Yard could possibly be as effective as I had stated but they nonetheless seemed to take to me and offered to show me something I had heard of only in the cinema—the famous big-city morning lineup.

That is just what it was: a lineup. It is a milder form of the third degree. Suspects, without the protection of solicitors, are made to ascend a platform that is brightly illuminated as a stage might be. There the suspect stands in the glare, alone and unsupported. I saw sixteen such suspects stand there, nervous, some of them obviously frightened, some sullen, and answer as best they could an unceasing and often sarcastic list of questions as to their whereabouts at such-and-such a time, what alias they were currently using, what they had been doing so close to the scene of the strangling of so-and-so or the shooting of such-and-such a man or woman.

The questioning was done into a microphone and the police voices were all amplified so that the catechizing could be heard by all. Few answers of any use ever came from the men in the lineup, though they all protested their innocence from first to last. The police would run them on and run them off at a good rate, perhaps five to six minutes being the average. This gave to all the detectives an excellent and unhurried opportunity to study these crooks and suspects; to plant the image of these faces in the individual memory of every detective in the room so that in future mixes with the law, the recognition factor would play its proper part.

I am told the New York police are uncanny in their ability to carry face impressions in their memories, even for years. This is where it begins—here at the morning lineup. If the New York police are positive they have something on a "hot" suspect and cannot draw this forth by the conventional means of ordinary questioning, they told me in some detail of the efficacy of the third degree and asked if I would care to accompany them to see this system in physical application upon a recalcitrant suspect—a "tough guy." I know most of the methods of torture in our present-day world and all those of the past. I said I did not think justice would be any the better served by my watching the process of positive force directed against an unwilling respondent. Any man alive—unless his tormentors are watching his suffering for nothing save the bestial enjoyment they extract from it—will sooner or later say what his interrogators want him to say; or say what he thinks they want him to. And it can have much or nothing to do with guilt, degree of guilt, or total innocence.

The New York police told me that I was quite mistaken about this; that unless the criminal element respected the strength and toughness of its enemy—the hard fist of the average police officer—crime in America would be out of hand all the time. They reminded me of the case of the killer Lipschitz. I remembered most of the details. And he was indeed a cool one. Lipschitz was indicted for first-degree murder, then tried, convicted, sentenced, and finally electrocuted in Sing Sing. And he had never flinched about anything and had not even blanched or batted his eye when he was given the Chair.

"He'll break before he takes the hot seat." This was the guess among all the police officers who had had to deal with him, two of whom were with me now. The American press carried many columns of this and we heard versions at Scotland Yard. Lipschitz had been spectacularly calm.

In the deathhouse itself, after the very realistic skull-shaving ceremony was over, and after Lipschitz was actually seated in the Chair, waiting to be strapped, hooded, and waiting for the sergeant to slice the side of his prison trousers to apply and fasten the electrodes, he was asked if he had anything to say. He smiled impassively but said nothing. Then the sergeant who was doing the slicing of the trousers let the trouser leg slip out of his fingers. He picked it up, but it slipped once more from his light grasp. Lipschitz looked at the guard, crouching on the floor at his side, preparing him for electrocution, and said this: "What's the matter, Sarge, you nervous?" That was all.

The New York police admitted he was really tough. Some are. But when I told them that killings in broad daylight on the streets of London would be unthinkable and they asked me why, I said that from all I could gather, in New York especially, if a killing took place where others could see, the others all fled the scene. In London they'd chase a culprit till they chased him down, many outraged women joining in the pursuit. This seemed to amuse the police officers a great deal.

I was struck by some of the items about those who live in North America that I think have not before been noted by other visitors. The beautiful teeth of the average American and Canadian. I think it may have something to do with the enormous quantity of ice water they consume, though I know this sounds unreasonable. Then, too, most of them had an expected pallor of face, as if their circulation was bad, or as if they never saw the sun, and there were caverns in New York City where this was believable. The intolerable noise wore me out. I could not sleep in American hotels, though they were without exception splendid. The fearful juxtaposition of squalor and elegance disturbed me too. Yet it may be an interesting social commentary, at least on city economics and municipal planning in American cities. The London slum is not only vast but historic. A New York slum can begin in the same square with the finest mansions. It can even be adjacent. The only thing protecting the "high-liver" from the depressed element is the building: his apartment, or flat, never the neighborhood. This seemed particularly true along the city's rivers.

Everything in the States was "100 per cent American" and said so, on the streets, on signs. Worse, even, than we were with "Buy British" and "British, Therefore Best."

Then the awful grind—Albany, Boston, Philadelphia, Cincinnati, Louisville, Buffalo, Detroit, Pittsburgh. I hate to think of it—of three and a half months of it. And people in mobs, never the individual American face, or speech. Always the mass. Mr. Churchill's lectures averaged 4,200 persons and went from lows of three thousand to a few highs of over eight thousand.

It was immensely luctrative for him and he needed the money. He always seemed to need money, but his expenses were quite large. He "lived big."

I had to be continuously on the lookout for danger. Danger was what had brought me. And there was some.

We got about seven hundred threatening letters. These we turned over to the police of whatever city we were in. As you know, Winston had a firm notion about India and this may have been the reason, though a poor one, behind the demonstrations of the natives of India against Churchill. In Detroit these were particularly bad. Churchill never in his life had a "color" sense and the India problem in the Empire and Commonwealth had nothing to do with color, no more so than the Sudan problem or the Kashmir problem. But the Indian people in Detroit execrated Mr. Churchill for the whole time we were there. I think he gave one lecture. Our car was twice stoned, and filth was dumped in our hotel once. I became more and more watchful and resentful.

Chicago was worse than Detroit. At the end of a lecture —perhaps in Orchestra Hall—near the handsome boulevard in any case—Mr. Churchill was speaking privately to some admirers just before stepping outside and into our rented limousine. The group stood in the great lobby of the auditorium, near the glass entrance doors. I am always close by. There were many Chicago detectives located in various spots throughout (the police cooperation on this whole tour was magnificent). A very correctly dressed Indian (East Indian, not American) suddenly hurried through these doors. His intention was to kill my man and you could see this in his eye. But I was ahead of him with my gun out. I did not fire, but merely walked forward to grab him. He spun round like a top, and crashed into the glass door behind, actually striking it with such force as to pass clear through the shattered frame. And right into the arms of two American detectives standing between the supporting columns of the forecourt of this building. All of us got cut up a bit. The Indian's companion fled down the street.

We were entertained in a beautiful suburb by the celebrated editor McCormick, of the Chicago *Tribune*, America's "tough" newspaperman. He was trying to smash up hoodlumism in his city. There was no fear in the Colonel anywhere. While in Chicago Winston and I rode almost everywhere in Colonel McCormick's armored car. Chicago police urged this upon the Colonel during his campaign to clean up his city. The car was impregnable. And it brought comfort to me.

Gangster law was the law of Chicago. Quite by accident, while seated in a hotel overlooking one of Chicago's busiest streets waiting for Mr. Churchill to come out from a meeting, I witnessed one of these typical Chicago killings. I heard the rat-a-tat of a machine gun, a sound made universally recognizable by American motion pictures. A man fell over dead not twenty-five feet from the very table at which I sat. The inevitable black sedan swept past, the inevitable grinning face leaning out. The victim twitched once on the sidewalk, then became still. There would have been quite a commotion in London. What followed had nothing at all to do with courage—courage being a universal quality, not national. I think it had something to do with civic attitude or community respect. What did the hundreds of passersby do? They ran. They just ran. Of fright? I would think not. I saw little fear in America, none in the American face. I believe they just didn't want to get mixed up in it. I am told this is even true in American cities right now, New York especially, where beatings in broad daylight can actually occur on subway platforms without interference from the average American who is innocently on the scene. This to me is appalling. In England it is positively unthinkable. It sickened me.

The killing outside the hotel window and the public reaction gave me an ill feeling toward municipal conduct that I have never been able either to understand or to erase. It was a poor trip for me, anyhow, the sheer speed and pressure of it, but this episode ruined it.

On our second visit to Chicago, I recounted this item to some police officers with whom I was talking. In the group was a gangster whom the police didn't "have anything on" at the time. This gangster was a friend of the police and he was actually a member of the infamous mob that committed the St. Valentine's massacre. I can name him, if it is required. This kind of fraternizing did not seem amusing to the police of Chicago. It was routine. They did not introduce me to the gangster as anything put on. The two groups, the criminal and the police, associated, lived side by side, even intermarried.

I was glad we could leave when we did. Before we returned to New York, a reporter secured access to Winston's bedroom while I was in my own room. Winston could not get rid of this importunate man. He called me, but when I ran in Winston had already thrown the reporter out of the room.

I do not know what newspaper he worked for but when he landed at the other end of the hotel corridor, I feel sure he was in poor shape to report anything save his contusions. I cannot forgive America her newsmen's manners; at least I could not then.

But I was younger. It was my first experience with that side of living, and on that side of the world.

Our trip was over. I was glad of it. Winston had recovered financially. We sent our baggage aboard the White Star liner *Majestic* before going aboard ourselves, then slipped out the servants' entrance of the hotel into a waiting car.

I was most grateful to get away from the twang and slang of American speech. Of course, once aboard the ship, I found that every stateroom in our whole section of the *Majestic* was occupied by nothing but Americans! They were all on their way to attend the Grand National.

Finally I began to understand it. And some years later, to love it.

Upon saying farewell to Mr. Churchill, I reported at once to Scotland Yard. For a year or two I again chased Communists, a lot who seldom give you either a thrill or a fight. They merely lurk and mutter. I hated this beyond description. I could understand most of the crooked thinking in the world and was paid to anticipate its plans, but I could never understand why anyone wanted to *be* a Communist. For one thing, they never took baths and you could smell them in the dark. In England, in the early and mid-Thirties, they were a pack of ruffians who were shrill and illiterate, and they represented to me about the same kind of headache the suffragettes had been to us all when I was a junior officer. They were cheap. They were bungling saboteurs. They were Hyde Park bores in the afternoon and they slunk around at night pouring paint down pillar boxes, or defacing fences, or smashing windows. They had no imagination and they had no guts. They let air out of the tires of parked automobiles. They distributed handbills. They catcalled. When caught, they always began their detention period by insulting the officers and always ended by whimpering.

I never encountered a Communist who was a man and communism appears more and more to me as the disease that overtakes any nation when the central force that built the nation begins to lose its manhood. Communism could overtake England, but it would take a long time, for England was a long time building. Its manhood has a weathering and a seasoning and a curing that has taken fifteen centuries.

For awhile, I despaired of ever getting away from the endless tedium of tracking down and bringing in one furtive nobody after another. One morning it occurred to me that in all the years I had served the metropolitan police, of which Scotland Yard is headquarters, I had never asked for anything. Why shouldn't I ask for transfer to other duty? Though my retirement and pension were but a few years ahead of me at this time (I would have served my full twenty-five years by 1936), I did not then have it on my mind. I merely wanted to set about doing something interesting. I had earned it.

Mr. J. H. (Jimmy) Thomas was my first assignment after Churchill. He was tough and self-made. Being His Majesty's Secretary of State for the Dominions he was of course "The Right Honorable," but he was also the greatest cusser I ever heard, including the Americans, and in half a dozen other ways was a most agreeable charge. He loved sports, he was a fine golfer and fisherman, an insatiable football fan. And he loved horse racing, gambling, and card playing. His wife Maggie was a servant girl when he married her (Tommy was an unschooled engine driver himself), and they rose together in English life, noisily and happily, Tommy himself to become a true intimate of King George V. In a way, there was a good deal of the energy and personality of Churchill in Thomas—a rough-hewn column but from the same quarry perhaps. Thomas rose from engine wiper in a railway roundhouse to the British Cabinet with about the same speed that Churchill got there. But what different routes!

I received a promotion and was detached from his service suddenly. England had a rash of visiting royalty, all with problems great or small. Soon after the bloody and shockingly unnecessary assassination of King Alexander of Yugoslavia at Marseilles, I was assigned to his brother Prince Paul, a very decent chap who loved golf and who played it well but preserved the dignity of the Court even on the tee, for he played in patent leather shoes, fawn gloves, stiff collar, striped formal suit, and derby hat. I had also intermittent duties with General Mannerheim, Prince Charles of Sweden, and the Crown Prince of Saudi Arabia (now King Ibn Saud). I believe the Crown Prince knew more about horses than any living man. He picked every winner but one at Royal Ascot, the first time he ever went to a race meeting in England. The Duchess of Kent, being Prince Paul's sister-in-law, was constantly about and the great love which Prince Paul felt toward the Duke and Duchess' son, Prince Edward, brought much happy informality to the royal atmosphere wherever Prince Paul went. He also lost all fear of being followed or hunted. His English was perfect. So were his manners, both democratic and royal. His very first sentence to me, when I had gone to a Channel port to meet his ship, was characteristic of the man: "I hope I shan't be too much trouble." He had shaken hands with me as if I were an old friend.

We were all under a shadow because of the death of King George. Prince Paul was determined to walk in the funeral procession. After it was over, the new King, Edward VIII, and his three brothers went to the Palace of Westminster to do homage to their father. I waited in the great hall. The new King of England and the three princes guarded the four corners of King George's coffin. The Royal Standard and a jeweled sword lay across the top. I remembered fishing in Scotland with Jimmy Thomas and the King only two years before, and the King's concern that I had caught so little.

And I thought of the pomposity of Lord Curzon, the most mean-mannered of titled personages I had ever met, whom I had also briefly served. "I'll have no detective sleeping in my house!" he had roared, sending me off in the dark to seek a bed in Basingstoke, when I was guarding Churchill and Churchill was Curzon's guest. You never know.

King George was great as a man and his love was constant. Marquess Curzon of Kedleston was a boor and is already forgotten.

As I waited for Prince Paul, my mind moved to the remembrance of many others—all simple, all great: Lord Birkenhead (Churchill's best friend), Lord Beatty, and Sir Philip Sassoon. I felt very privileged, even though I was just a cop.

After the long vigil was over and the new King and the princes withdrew, I escorted Prince Paul back to Belgrave Square to the home of the Duke of Kent. I felt sad and old, and even though I wasn't yet forty-five, I decided to retire when my time should come. It was not far ahead. In the autumn of 1936, I took leave of my colleagues, had the customary farewell dinner, received the homage of my brother officers, made the proper acknowledgements for the correct watch, and took leave of Scotland Yard forever.

Or so I thought at the time.

PART TWO

I saw Mr. Churchill from time to time, sometimes on a friendly visit when I happened to be near his country place at Chartwell and sometimes on brief business errands—even though there had been no official relationship since his lecture tour of the United States and Canada had terminated five or six years before.

In April, 1939, I visited him for several hours at Chartwell Manor. We went over the grounds that we had all labored so hard to beautify. It was a labor well spent and though I got not a single "thank you" in remembrance of the thousands of barrowloads of earth, rock and cement I had moved when he first bought the place, I did not care. We talked of kings and their passing; of nations and their collapse. It was exciting to see the man and to hear his voice, his low meditative laugh.

We had a great laugh over the time I dropped a dollop of mud on his pate. When you are digging out a swimming pool for yourself, I am sure it is pleasurable. I felt, on one occasion at Chartwell Manor, that I had had enough for the day. Winston and I had lined the new bottom with bitumen, after much digging and patching. My clothes had become smothered with mud. I decided to have a hot bath, then resume my dignity and my office. I would spend the rest of the day in seeing that no unauthorized person entered the grounds.

A call came for the Old Man from London, and I had to take the message out to the "dig." I put on my rubber boots and walked over the lawn to his pond. Thick, slimy mud was everywhere. Adhesive mud. As I was walking about the top of a bank looking for Winston, I stepped over a hole cut in the bank. In doing so a large blob of mud dropped down into the cutting and plastered the Prime Minister right on top of his ministerial head. He was outraged.

"Dammit!" he screamed, looking up from the deep hole and cursing some more. He had no idea who was above.

"Were you speaking to me, sir?" I asked, sounding a little outraged myself.

"I'm sorry, Thompson. I didn't know it was you. But if you got hit by a clod of mud like this one, you'd swear as well."

"It's the Cabinet, sir. Calling from London."

"The Cabinet? Let the Cabinet convene this time at Chartwell! And send for some more shovels."

He had other things on his mind, too. He could smell war then and said so. He said to me flatly that we would be fighting the Axis within six months. He said that inasmuch as he would probably be offered some sort of Cabinet post and that he would therefore be obliged to have a shadow, he'd like to know what plans I had for myself. I had of course been very busy with many duties, some long, some brief, in the interval. I told him of my retirement but I told him I'd be most honored to come back into his service if he wished me to and if Scotland Yard felt I could be useful in keeping the Germans away from him—if it came to that. Suddenly, in thirty seconds, I wanted to serve Winston Churchill all over again.

The thought of war was sickening to me. I had seen one. But if we faced another, I had three sons who would be serving. In fact, my youngest son, an irrepressible adventurer, had already joined the Air Force. And he was not yet sixteen.

Events moved with silent speed, much faster than English plans. Poland and Czechoslovakia were about to be bitten off and chewed up by the Axis, and this would surely start it. It was the middle of August following my happy visit with Churchill at Chartwell. Churchill had been in France. He'd toured the Maginot Line. There was a cryptic telegram for me to be at Croydon Aerodrome the following day. I could not get anything more than that from his secretary. So I went there.

Driving back to London, after we passed the time of day talking about each other's minor family affairs, Churchill told me that he'd spent a great deal of time with the President and the Premier of France, and with many of their military leaders and that the only thing of interest that he could profitably pass on to me was that the Germans already considered him the most attractive target in England, more so by far than the King, or than the entire Cabinet. He said the French had told him that there were known plans to kill Winston, whether he rose to importance in the coming struggle or not. Mr. Churchill rather enjoyed the implied heroics here as always and when I asked him if he had plans for meeting this dark prospect, he turned most cordially to me and said: "Yes, I have one very good one and it's you, Thompson. You look after me at night and I'll take care of myself in the daytime."

I reminded him that I had retired from the metropolitan police force in 1936. He said my retirement was about as likely as his retirement. He immediately told me then that there was an advanced plan, though he did not know from the French police whether its operatives were in England yet, to assassinate him at the start of the struggle. He would be quite happy to pay me himself, at his own expense, to protect him during the night. I said I would start whenever he asked, but that upon my filing of intention to retire, I had agreed to report for duty in the event of any emergency at all. This is a common practice among all British police officers. He said he would see to it and let me know.

How quickly things happen! That conversation was on the 23rd of August. On the 26th of August, the state of emergency just referred to was declared to be upon us. He called me on the telephone himself. "Thompson, you are remaining with me permanently," he said. His voice carried a big smile of pleasure. "I have just arranged this with your Commissioner, Sir Philip Game."

There followed a furiously busy week, far more domestic than martial. We spent the time lugging stuff back and forth between London and Chartwell. Then suddenly the whole atmosphere of our life in England—and in very real ways life all over the world—changed to something different and,

I truly believe, changed forever. Churchill was taking all his weekends in London, Mrs. Churchill too. Their flat was crowded with people, important ones, even though Winston was "unemployed." He paced around a great deal, anxious to run something, but no one had given him anything to run. Not yet.

Then came the day—September 3, 1939. There was no answer from the ultimatum that had been sent to the German government. We waited for eleven o'clock, grouped in clusters in the Churchills' large, main living room. No one said anything. Members of the Churchill staff, both clerical and domestic, stood in doorways, waiting for the news. An upstairs clock chimed sweetly. There was no traffic noise at all on London streets.

Then, over the BBC, came the news that we were at war. Churchill did not appear in the least disturbed. Almost at once there was an air raid warning. He bolted out of the room and into the street. I learned a good deal more about him then and that put me on guard once more against his impulsiveness. He could no more stay out of a raid than he could sit still in a debate in Parliament. I did not this time get tough with him because I was not familiar with the sound, meaning, or expectable consequences of these warnings.

The "All Clear" sounded. I walked through the streets to the House of Commons where Neville Chamberlain spoke and England's declaration of war became an official instrument. I jotted down some of the things he said in shorthand.

"The House has already been made aware," Mr. Chamberlain said, "of our plans. As I said the other day, we are ready." I looked at Winston after jotting down this sentence. How he squirmed. "This is a sad day for all of us and to none is it a sadder day than to me." I felt most sorry for the man at this moment. He seemed all through with life.

It is cruel to speculate on what would have happened if Chamberlain had been removed from authority a year earlier. Yet it is inevitable that one should do so, for there was hardly an Englishman who was not sick over the beating our prestige had taken when the Italians went into Abyssinia; when Eden's insistence that we invoke sanctions was unheeded. And I'm sure many an Englishman felt we had betrayed the trust of gallant little Czechoslovakia and that Chamberlain had helped in this betrayal. Only a few months before, in this very spot and at the same time of day, he had said: "If I am right as I am confident I am, in saying that the League as constituted today is unable to provide collective security for anybody, then I say that we must not try to delude ourselves, and still more we must not try to delude small and weak nations, into thinking that they will be protected by the League against aggression when we know that nothing of the kind can be expected." And that was only the previous February!

Here he was now, still talking, but looking sick, looking nearly dead. "Everything that I have worked for; everything that I have hoped for; everything that I have believed in during my public life—has crashed in ruins."

I suppose Chamberlain really did believe he had worked for peace his whole life but the tragedy too often in England's modern history is that idealists have had to deal with rogues. Winston at least was a realist and, in his eye, a rogue was a rogue and that merely meant that it was something to be exterminated. It was a horrible day.

I knew that Churchill would publicly support Chamberlain for that was the stripe of his loyalty. And he did so, briefly. When he could have charged every man in England for not heeding the warnings of the times, he rose and quietly said: "In this solemn hour it is a consolation to recall and to dwell upon our repeated efforts for peace. All have been ill-starred, but all have been faithful and sincere."

We stepped out into the street. "We are going to Ten Downing Street, Thompson," he said bluntly. I did not know, nor he, what Cabinet post would be offered.

As you all know, it was the Admiralty. Mrs. Churchill had arranged for a delightful luncheon party of twenty-four. It took place, but I think it took less than ten minutes. So began another long thrash with daily living that had less schedule than a forest fire and less peace than a hurricane. Through the years I have wondered a thousand times how the wives of famous men could endure the almost unvarying smashup of all their pleasant plans for just a little life of their own: just one quiet undisturbed tea party; one unbroken trip to Scotland; one meal without a phone call; even one good-morning kiss not witnessed by waiting couriers. The mere matter of menus must be the most awful madness! But Mrs. Churchill never showed that she was troubled though circumstance and disappointment have slashed her a thousand times and more. The capacity of the British to endure is not the gift of their men but their women. At least the men have the satisfaction of ordering all manner of elaborate escapades like world wars and cheerfully enough getting killed in them. But the women's plans get killed without battle: killed on the stove; killed over the teacups that are waiting to be filled without the expected hands to take them; killed in bedrooms where men are expected to sleep but who call to say they cannot make it that night—and who go off and are never again seen. Some of our reticence comes from this, the reserve of the men, but far more than that, the self-protective circumspection of the women.

Within twenty-four hours of taking over at the Admiralty, German U-boat warfare had its first big trophy. The *Athenia* was torpedoed and sunk, with 1,400 aboard, including some Americans. It was a sad initiation to Churchill's naval duties.

The British press was around all the time. I kept cautioning them about pictures. It is of the greatest importance that men guarding the lives of other men are themselves as little known and little publicized as possible. We arranged that I would seldom be included in any of the shots, that if my picture were to be published by accident, I would always be unidentified or a "passerby," or not mentioned at all. We kept a good mixture of miscellaneous nobodies around him and often made casual but seemingly positive identifications of people whom we did not at all know ourselves. This scattered the risk and kept an important flow of anonymous beings in continuous parade. I do not have any remarkable or memorable physical features except that I am somewhat taller than the average Englishman, so when I found myself identified or characterized as "looking like a schoolmaster" I was pleased enough, for it meant nothing. And that is the way Scotland Yard would prefer it.

From this day through my long years of service to Winston Churchill to the very end, it does not seem I ever for one night had enough sleep. It has been my lot to go through life worrying about another man, losing sleep over it. But it has been Churchill's destiny. And his worry, being for whole continents, was somewhat larger than my own.

We found time, especially at first with the war going, to reacquaint Winston with firearms. He carried his own pistol now and we had a target range in the basements of various buildings as well as one in his own house. Familiarity with weapons is more than half of their protective potential; having the feel of them in one's hand and forearm, the sense of the weight of them and their position on one's person helps make action almost reflexive if their use is required. One seldom has long to deliberate when one is going to shoot. Winston knew all of these things from the past, but there was one thing—now that the man had grown older— that made his own security more difficult. His *sense* of personal safety had largely left him, to the extent that he would tire of carrying his revolver and forget it. He'd lay it down somewhere and leave it if I didn't check it each time. Sometimes when I found him unarmed, I'd have to give him one of my own revolvers. I didn't like to do this, and didn't often have to. I'm very used to the few that I work with, but it was of course absolutely essential that he should not be alone at any time—even in the middle of the night in his own bed—without a revolver in his reach. He knew this but his excitement about danger had changed from the chemical to the intellectual. I had to watch him all the time. He would draw his gun and pop it into sudden view and say roguishly and with delight: "You see, Thompson, they will never take me alive! I will get one or two before they can shoot me down." He hated to be criticized (though he would grudgingly take it sometimes after elaborate thought) and the times I had to fling my body against his or grab him and toss him behind a post or truck or pile of rubble, the protests that went up!

During my previous years of service to him, I had always looked upon Winston Churchill as a man of endless energy and rash courage. How was he now? Eighteen years had passed—it stunned me to make the calculation—since we had first gone through the Mediterranean together. But from all sides the same report came to me: that Winston was physically durable to an unbelievable degree (this from Lord Moran, his physician); that his faculties of hearing and eyesight were of the keenest. His optician told me Winston's eyesight was better by far than the sight of the average man ten years his junior. I was glad for these things, for it improved his own capacity to protect himself from surprise. And his colleagues in the Cabinet, each in his own way, kept referring to his genius, to his electric judgment. It was apparent, according to the British monitor on the German broadcasting stations that Churchill, far more than the full navy of which he was First Lord, was Hitler's enemy, his real bugaboo, his target. Hitler's rages, over and over again, testify to this very thing. It of course delighted Winston and doubled his pleasure in thinking of new names to call this little Nazi. Never to be treated with respect, as heads of government, did more to kindle the psychiatrical hatreds and rages against Churchill that both Hitler and Mussolini felt than did the fear of either one of these dictators, even at the very end of things, that the Axis was going to lose the fight. Their hatred was insensate and progressive, and I would think it had, finally, a truly depleting effect on their powers; sapping energies they could not spare; wasting these men instead of inspiriting them. It showed their fear too. I have been told since the war, by a British agent who was close to Mussolini's Cabinet, that when Churchill's lovely phrase "tattered lackey" was described and explained to the Duce that this very nearly unhinged the man on the spot. Locker-Lampson could do it, too; his taunt that "his heart and his head were both of lard" made Hitler foam at the mouth and chew the carpet.

With typical directness Churchill set about seeing what kind of navy he had been given. Almost before he had installed a working staff in the Admiralty, he set out to inspect the major naval installations of the British Isles, starting with Chatham.

On the docks there, he was instantly recognized and cheered. One happy re-encounter took place when the master machinist, who had been entrusted with the repair of the sabotaged section of the press machinery when Churchill was his own editor-in-chief of England's only newspaper during the General Strike, recalled the incident to Winston. Winston loved this moment of reminiscence. There was never much time for such, however, and as we pulled away with shouts going up to him and enthusiastic cheers of "Good old Winston!" he was already in the chartroom of the cruiser that was hurrying us to Scapa Flow, the main base of the Royal Navy.

The same enthusiasm met us there, and it was somewhat enriched by his being able to report, as we had received it in code going through the Minches, that we had knocked out a pair of U-boats. On arrival at Thurso we embarked on a tribal destroyer for Scapa. Here we had to pass through

the boom defenses, which occasioned a remark from myself
as to whether it would not be possible for a German U-boat
to follow us through the net, herself concealed by our own
bottom, and the sound of her concealed by the turn of our
own screw. (Later we lost the *Royal Oak* here, you will recall.) "I hope they are not able to do so," Churchill told
me. "I am informed the possibility of their entering is very
remote."

Churchill complained about much that he saw here at
Scapa. There was little or no ack-ack to fight off air
raiders momentarily expected from Germany, who punc-
tually arrived while we were there. Of course Winston knew
that at such an early stage of such a grievous war everything
cannot be ready at once. But what a position for a man of
his calibre to be in charge of the finest and largest navy in
the world—knowing too bitterly how he had advocated
through the years that this country should arm and that
these very guns should be part of her weaponing—to find
this huge naval base practically undefended from the air!

Over and over again, all through the years with Winston
Churchill, he has turned his head over toward me, looked
up and growled: "If they had only taken the warning when
they got it!" Or "I pointed this out four times to the Prime
Minister!" Or "One gets tired having to reiterate such a
simple thing to the Ministry." He was furious here. He
fumed and semaphored but ten days later the guns were
there.

Before the end of that same month the First Lord had
visited the other big installations at Portsmouth and Plymouth. At this latter place I met for the first time Admiral
Sir William James, K.C.B., an unforgettable navy man.
Americans may be able to place him quickly when I say
that this is the jovial and enthusiastic naval officer who is
the original of the famous painting *Bubbles*. Here we
boarded H.M.S. *Victory* as well as H.M.S. *Queen Elizabeth*
of Dardanelles fame, which was being rebuilt internally.
There were some appalling wrecks tied up and supported
by pontoons and a few laid bare in drydock that were surviving victims of the Germans' effective campaign against
our shipping. We were getting cruelly hurt every day all
over the Atlantic and throughout the Mediterranean.

We had an overwhelming advantage in terms of floating
tonnage in our merchant marine fleet but Churchill never

let anyone sit still in comfort on this statistic, insisting that it became less meaningful with the passing of very hour. I shall not burden the reader with anything but the swiftest of figures in this book, but our advantage (Great Britain's alone) in merchant tonnage was twenty-one million plus over a tonnage of thirteen million plus for Japan, Germany and Italy combined. Later, the participating of other merchant fleets from our Allies, as we drew them, doubled our original total. But we never had enough. However, without this early margin we could not have won, and of course we almost *did* lose. More than half of the *world's* tonnage was destroyed before the horror ended, most of it by submarine or air attack, and in less than five years.

We were on way to Scapa Flow, going through storm clouds near the Orkneys when we got the sad word that we had just lost the *Courageous* with six hundred dead. Churchill thereupon began making notes that would soon be heard in the House of Commons upon the British public's need to be ready for bitter news, and much of it, regarding losses of men and ships. By this time there was already a colossal movement of ships. The German High Command was simultaneously laying claim to the sinking of the *Ark Royal* and so certain were they of the truth of this that they had already conferred the Iron Cross upon Lance Corporal Franke, who said he had sunk her, when actually he had never seen her.

We sat down in the water at Scapa Flow. Churchill surveyed the placing of his ack-ack, then fired a round at a target balloon. About the huge anchorage there were mock-ups of battle wagons, big as the ships themselves and so true to the illusion of the real thing that not only could they not be taken for fakes from a height of a thousand feet, they could not even be taken for fakes when one was right on them.

Yet here I had another dramatic demonstration of the uncanny eyesight of Winston Churchill, and the speed and practicality of his brain. He pointed to the impressive fake battleship that was on the far end of the northern string and told one of the warrant officers that it would be spotted by German pilots as a dummy and that they would not waste a bomb on her. "But she's not even been spotted by our own reconnaissance, sir," he was told. "Then they need spectacles!" "How so, sir?" "No gulls about her!" he snapped. "No seagulls. You'll always find gulls about a living ship. But not around a dummy. Not unless you drop garbage for the dummy too. Keep garbage in the water day and night, bow and stern, of all these dummies! Feed the gulls and fool the Germans!" And they did.

What other man in the British Navy would see this and fix it with such speed?

It is noteworthy, in view of the attack made by the Germans on Russia in 1941, to recall the words of V. M. Molotov. Addressing the Supreme Council of the Soviet Union, he accused Great Britain and France of waging ideological war on Germany, saying that after the collapse of Poland the democracies found new excuses for continuing the war which, he asserted, Germany was striving to end. However, this speech in the main did not lend itself to help Germany in any way, and because of its tone a considerable amount of disappointment was felt in Berlin.

October opened with a review by the First Lord of the work carried out during the month of September by the Navy. Speaking of Russia, he mentioned that she had pursued a cold policy of self-interest, but in some respects her interests fell into the same channels as those of Britain and France. Continuing, he said: "I cannot forecast to you the action of Russia. It is a riddle wrapt in a mystery inside an enigma: but perhaps there is a key. That key is Russian national interest."

This appears to be of special note, for events proved that when Mr. Churchill said that in some respects the interest of Russia and Great Britain fell into the same channels, he had undoubtedly made a clever forecast. His general survey of world events created worldwide interest, and American reaction described Churchill's speech as being worth more than an Army Corps. In his speech, and in many which followed during the full course of the war, Mr. Churchill coined a phrase which will go down in the annals of history: "Now we have begun. Now we are going on. Now with the help of God, and with the conviction that we are the defenders of civilization and freedom, we are going to persevere to the end."

The horrible and most feared thing of all had happened after we left Scapa Flow. H.M.S. *Royal Oak* was sunk. My mind went back to the question which I put to the First

Lord when we were passing through the boom defenses in early September.

It is a terrible humiliation for an Englishman to take when one of her finest battleships is sunk at her own moorings! It is not at all the kind of outrage and fury and in a sense the healthy revenge-seeking which the Americans, far sooner than they dreamed, were to feel when the Japs slid over the Pacific and bombed the fleet at Pearl Harbor. That will remain forever as the most ignominious action in naval warfare, ancient or modern. But England was at war against Germany, and the *Royal Oak* was a ship of war. All we could feel was a sickening sense of carelessness, something monumentally un-British and unprofessional in our own handling of an instrument in the superior use of which we had proved our skill to the whole world for three hundred years and more—nay, even from the day King Henry VIII designed and built the first fighting fleet and put men aboard who knew how to fight.

But the terrible truth was that a German U-boat, commanded by a young captain named Prien, had penetrated the defenses of Scapa and torpedoed this great battleship. How much easier to bear it would have been if we could have found that she had been blown up internally, or even from the air since our ack-ack was so newly installed. But we had been magnificently outwitted and unbelievably scuttled in our own dock and without a shot by a great skipper.

Winston now had to go back to London and tell the House of Commons that what they most dreaded to hear was true. He spent hours talking to men who were aboard the *Oak* when she was hit and he spent hours looking at the ruin of her. Then he turned his back on the whole thing and we returned to London. Here he warned Parliament that this was only the start of an unending number of casualties, that many of them would be worse; that some would be catastrophes in the most awful magnitude. And he ordered the main part of the Royal Navy out of Scapa, not chancing further losses till defenses could be overhauled. The fleet accordingly was scattered, much of it going to Greenock.

On the train going back to London, he had drafted what was presently to be made public, the mutual assistance pact signed soon after by Great Britain, France and Turkey. This instantly aroused unexpectedly savage comment from Hitler who hated to have anything happen that threatened to slow down the flow of good news hourly being reported to the German people. But Churchill, while a nimble enough improvisor, was and is a longterm planner. He knew then that we would *almost* lose the war before winning it; that we'd hang on till we did win. He wished he knew how long the period of most critical suspense was going to last so that he could prepare the necessary words and examples to encourage the British people, that they might the better endure the period once they were in it.

We visited the fleet at Greenock. He boarded H.M.S. *Nelson*. He stayed aboard for four days. While there the plans for strengthening the defenses of Scapa were completed. I enjoyed the rest and the relief, and spent some happy hours in the W.O.'s mess with a group of fine young warrant officers.

This completed, we drove back to London. H.M.S. *Nelson* had steamed off immediately after, and even before we ourselves were at our desks and stations, we got word that the *Nelson* had struck a mine and was badly damaged, killing a great number of the crew and officers including four of the young officers with whom I had just been drinking beer and playing cards.

The third week in October Churchill became a seven day a week man with an average weekly total of 120 working hours. His peacetime average is about ninety-five.

Events moved forward. Warsaw had surrendered. An invading force estimated at more than a million and a half Germans, supported by overwhelming air power, had blitzed this agonized nation during the first ten days of attack, though Warsaw resisted to the last grenade and trench knife. The incredible speed of the German convergence alarmed the Russians, who invaded Poland from the East. The two governments now divided this ruined and wretched nation. The Baltic countries concluded pacts with Russia. Finland held firm. The American Neutrality Act, which had so disturbed the British government in October, was amended repealing the embargo on arms to belligerents and the sale of weapons and instruments of war was put on a cash-and-carry basis. This heartened all of us, Winston particularly. He beamed and yelled when the news came. He wanted his government to purchase anything that could be thrown at the enemy and that would explode on contact.

Russia was expelled from the League of Nations for going after Finland. It was already a very dirty war.

At this time Mr. Churchill began to commute by air to France. British Headquarters at Amiens were under command of Lord Gort. But it was of course imperative for Churchill to spend much time with the heads of the French Navy. First conferences included innumerable meetings. Some were quite funny, when Mr. Churchill decided to unleash his Harrow and Sandhurst French—at M. Campinchi, Minister of Marine, and Daladier, Darlan, Gamelin, Vuillemin, Champetier de Ribes, Rio and others I can't remember. There were a few snatched moments that were pleasant for Mr. Churchill, since he was a frequent if brief houseguest of the Duke of Windsor then resident in Paris.

At Amiens we were close to the front lines. An air raid warning signal went off suddenly and from the yard of the château which served as headquarters could be seen a mixup in the sky between a whole swarm of Germans engaging an equal number of French and British planes. It fascinated Winston. He lay down in the grass the better to see it. He was therefore overlooked by a cluster of running orderlies whose duty it was to shoo us all inside where it was supposedly safe. Winston saw what they would do to him if they found him, so he stepped around a hedge till they had themselves taken cover. Then he enjoyed the show.

On this trip Churchill became privy to the daring plan (not the first) to assassinate Hitler. I knew somewhat of it. It was ingeniously and coldly put together by British foreign agents, just a pair of them, who had lived for many years in France and Germany and could pass for very nearly any sort of European they wished. They could speak anything and were known to us at Scotland Yard as masters of disguise. Alas, it came to naught, and it is painful in the extreme to consider what the earth might have been spared in waste of treasure and agony of body and spirit had these two succeeded. But they were never again seen when they departed from their starting place in northern France. It was reported much later that they had been arrested and that they died wretchedly after long interrogation.

The Germans have always had their own special brand of courage but it has always seemed to me an individual affair. Captain Prien who sank the *Royal Oak* is a good example. But there is no basic courage to German thought, nor in the pervasive mood of the German people. Their main instinct is servile, hence essentially brutish, and what one man or one nation in war can at times make noble by enobling its purpose, the Germans can only make obscene out of the filth of their motives and the hypocrisy of their dedication. True, they will stand and die the same as any other good soldier, but they do not honor their intelligence in their soldiering, for they die when told to, never knowing why. Germans have been brought up to die without knowing the purpose of life.

Churchill was sixty-three. He looked it too. But right there chronology and performance parted company. Though he walked with a conspicuous stoop and most of his hair had gone; though he had patches of suet about his midriff and his cheeks were pouchy; he was still rock-hard and tireless. And he exhausted the French command with his ceaseless movement, his demanding tours, his perpetual questioning. The French felt an odd safety in all this whirl and flurry, and they should have, for very little was passing unseen.

This was evident upon our return to London in early November. He made a statement on the war at sea. It was at once terrifying, yet heartening. It turned attention away from the land war in France which was at this time almost melodramatically hopeless. His speeches had a massiveness, grandeur, defiance and cosmic challenge that rallied the average Britisher and scalded Hitler. Has anyone ever used a simple word with greater effectiveness than Churchill? Did he calumniate Hitler? No, he never did. He called him "that wicked man" and left him there, exhibited for the whole world to see.

And he was showing more and more foresight, in his conception of things to come, and the way they might arrive. He was a tonic to England in this early breakup. More than any other man by action, speech, spirit, and proof of purpose, he prevented people from surrendering to the contagion of bad news, which was constantly deteriorating. Without question, he was the number one propagandist for England's cause, and France's too.

In a radio broadcast over the BBC, he said that the Soviet government, embodied in the formidable figure of Stalin, had barred once and forever all Nazi attempts of an advance in the East. He foreshadowed the coming attacks on Belgium and Holland and predicted them within a week of their occurrence. When his prediction was later challenged on grounds that the Nazis had given solemn guarantees to Holland and Belgium, he said at once: "That explains why the anxiety in these countries is so great." In the main burden of his formal address that night, and speaking for the Dutch and the Belgians, he had this word for them: "Let them take courage, amid the perplexities and perils, for it may well be that the final extinction of a baleful domination will pave the way to a broader solidarity of all the men in all lands than ever we could have planned if we had not marched together through the fire."

At the end of this, I walked with him to his car and prepared to take my usual place beside the driver. He had no companion with him that night and asked me to sit with him, as he had some instruction for me. He is wonderful company right after a speech (he's hell when one's on the way), and he had heard earlier that same evening that Mussolini's intention to "colonize" Libya was resulting in the arrival there of large contingents of peasants, all of whom seemed remarkably suitable for military service in at least three of their attributes: age, sex, and physical condition.

"Thompson, you were with me when we heard that Badoglio was in Libya."

"Indeed, sir. It was on a balcony of the Semiramis Hotel that you received the information."

"It looks like we may have to go back."

"Go back, sir?"

"Yes. The Italians like the place. We'll soon be fighting in North Africa."

"What with, sir?"

"I don't know yet, Thompson. I'll have to take inventory first thing in the morning!" And he laughed!

England was in a gray mood. The six o'clock news every night was listened to as if by royal proclamation, and the driblets of favorable items were never blown up to be more than the driblets they really were. The Admiralty was embarrassed not only by continuous losses but by threats of new ones that could not be prevented. One of these threats was from mines. The Germans were dropping them from planes, and they were at first bobbing about and dotting entrances to harbors and rivers. Then there came the magnetic mines which lay on the ocean's floor, not deep (all the water about England's south and east coasts are shallow), and popped up against any hull that was passing. This was an uncommonly effective weapon and hurt as badly.

It therefore became the first duty of the Admirality to capture a magnetic mine intact, in order to study it and figure a remedy, perhaps even a way to inactivate it as it lay on the bottom. Or a way to keep it from rising.

Fortunately for us, on November 23, a mine was dropped by Nazi parachute into the Thames Estuary, but wind drift carried the chute to the shore and the mine landed harmlessly on the beach in the mud. Naval experts carrying their lives in their hands, Winston carrying his authority and all the curiosity of a youngster on a treasure hunt, and finally me, with the revolvers and quite backward about the party, examined this mine, ascertaining its nature. It was with formal tenderness and huge respect deactivated and shipped to Portsmouth for more extensive autopsy. Its internal mechanism, which caused it to rise to the surface under magnetic influence when a steel hull passed above, was satanically clever. The best section of German inventive brainpower had worked on this one. However, the Senior Service quietly came out on top, and found that though they could not come up with anything against the mine itself, they could nullify the target herself. They found that by degaussing the ships, magnetic attraction terminated. The mine merely stayed on forever wherever it had settled.

No sooner was this good news permitted to be enjoyed by the public than some American newspaper of more enterprise than circumspection printed our discovery in the greatest detail for the whole world to look at. And we were, of course, thereby obliged to publish the details ourselves. This was a most wasteful and regrettable leakage. One is less cautious, to be sure, when the war is so far away, especially if it is being fought by others.

Somewhat the same sort of advantage that the noncombatant has over the combatant came up on a larger scale at this same time. While Russia invaded Finland, Germany remained an interested spectator. But President Roosevelt condemned in the most scathing terms this cannibal action of Joe Stalin's. Churchill had to content himself by expressing his "regret" at the action. However, the aftermath came when Finland allied herself with Germany in her attack on Russia in 1941. It would now appear that Russia's various

moves were well thought out; for by this attack on Finland
and other bites into Poland and the Baltic states, Russia was
building around herself buffer states which would be of
great advantage when she was later attacked by Germany.
Following President Roosevelt's denunciation, the U.S.A.
ceased to supply Russia with aircraft. However, by 1941
and 1942, America made a huge effort to supply Russia with
all the aircraft she desired.

In late November we had news that an armed liner, the
Rawalpindi, had sighted and instantly joined battle with the
German warship *Deutschland.* It was probably the hope of
the *'Pindi's* skipper to draw the *Deutschland* a bit nearer to
a strong British force where more serviceable salvos might
be aimed at the German, but he failed in this maneuver and
took such a beating as to be nearly blown out of the sea.
However, the British public was so starved for something
good for a change that it had to take solace in the dash and
daring of the *Rawalpindi's* captain since without armor and
with light guns he still did not hesitate to go after anything
in the German navy.

The U-boat menace was worse than ominous. Churchill
realized he once more had to stiffen the mind of his country
and spoke in the House: "I must again repeat the warning
which I have given to the House last month that a steady
flow of losses must be expected, that occasional disaster will
occur, and any failure on our part to act up to the level
of circumstances would immediately be attended by grave
danger."

We bitterly needed help of every kind; of almost any kind.
It was almost smothering therefore to the average Englishman when he read in his paper what the American Ambassador to Britain had just said about the war. Speaking to his
own countrymen in the city of Boston on December 10th,
Mr. Joseph Kennedy had said and was quoted in all the
British papers as saying: "This is not our fight. There is no
place in the fight for us."

This was far more shattering to us in England than it can
ever be made known to Americans and there is no reason to
dwell upon it now, but for the fact that Kennedy was loved
by England and taken to its heart by the great mass of our
population as an ardent supporter of our cause—more
deeply so than any other American I can name. There have
been Americans, Baruch, for example, who have been greatly

loved by England's leaders, but few have been loved by the multitudes. We all thought, and felt we had a right to think, that anything Kennedy could do to help our country would surely be done. What he said in Boston nearly crushed us. Affection and illusions of affection that were lost then have never returned. Ambassadors have strange powers—often with the power of personality being far more important than protocol or portfolio.

Then quite suddenly, an unexpectedly good thing happened to us. And very dramatic it was. Winston ran around the Admiralty as if he were running the war all alone and we started putting out releases on the naval action in the Atlantic in which the *Exeter, Achilles* and *Ajax* had hunted down and brought to shooting range the sleek and slippery German pocket battleship *Graf Spee*. The *Graf Spee* had been cruising about in the North and South Atlantic in the guise of a commerce raider, sinking a heartbreaking tonnage in merchant ships. Winston's office had spent hundreds of hours in plotting, tracking and outthinking the fast-minded skipper of this amazing killer, but so far from being found and cornered, she was almost never even seen. But there was a flat standing order to find and destroy her. It was a bit like a flat order to harness the sun but such orders are not unknown in wartime and with Churchill around are quite expectable.

News of the fight was received in England with acclamation. When it became known that three small cruisers had been able to throw enough stuff into the *Spee* to damage her and slow her up, it was obvious to our Navy-conscious island that careful plans had been put into operation. It subsequently came out that Commodore (now Admiral) Sir Henry Harwood had drawn up these plans with the captains of the other two ships so that they were able, by concerted action, to unify their separate powers in a concerted succession of telling licks. The *Exeter* took the brunt of this attack, but the three cruisers chased the *Spee*, popping shells at her clear up to the neutral line of Montevideo harbor. It was not possible to tell just what damage had been inflicted, but severe damage could be assumed since if she had been able to stand and fight, she could have blown the cruisers to pieces.

Our own ships were badly hurt. The *Ajax* had two out of her four turrets knocked clear out. The *Exeter*, which took most, had been hit more than fifty times, had three of her eight-inch guns smashed, and had suffered over one hundred casualties. But they felt they weren't through with the *Graf Spee* and stayed on like hostile dogs in an unfriendly yard waiting for the scrap to resume.

You all remember what happened. I met and talked with the officers and crews of all these cruisers after their return to England (except for V-E Day the most gratifying, spontaneous and moving celebration I have ever seen in England) and their disappointment in not being able to finish the *Graf Spee* themselves was still very much in their hearts. But you never know how these things are going to come out. The subsequent scuttling seemed an ignominious end but Captain Langsdorff had no other choice than to sink his ship and shoot himself after Hitler by radioed orders forbade him to surrender the vessel.

Because our own casualties were heavy, there were many heavy hearts in England. But even while some of these grieved, there was wonderful news for many others, for when the *Graf Spee* tied up at Montevideo harbor she released a large number of prisoners they'd captured from ships the *Graf* had sunk.

Hitler's order did not recognize the existence of the third alternative: to fight it out. German navies have always had some great skippers, and here and there a great admiral, but Hitler did not know clearly what a navy was for. So Captain Langsdorff, faraway and not able to argue a point even if his ship could put out and fight, carried out his orders. The *Graf Spee* struggled out of the harbor, a scuttling crew boarded her, fused her magazine, pulled her seacocks, and was on the way back to the river's mouth when she exploded mournfully, shuddered, rolled and went down. Unable to stand up to the disgrace, Langsdorff wrote his report of the last days of the *Spee*, shook hands with his officers and left. He went to the naval arsenal in Buenos Aires and there in dress uniform, with his medals removed and placed in a box on a ward table, he shot himself. There were people in England who could forgive this man a good deal for he had saved the crews of many ships and had immediately released his prisoners in good condition—six captains among them—the moment the *Graf Spee* touched land.

It was pleasant to listen to the BBC giving digests of what the Germans were saying about the action. Naturally

Goebbels, speaking for the German government, had to find someone to blame. But there was no visible culprit, so he blamed the Uruguayan government for not giving the *Graf Spee* enough time to make repairs. When this was exploded by wide publication of the extent of damage that had been inflicted on her, Goebbels changed his story and said that the British had used mustard gas shells when firing on the *Graf Spee* and that her captain had put into harbor for fresh food, his own stock having been contaminated by mustard gas.

The whole world rang with the news of this battle. Great Britain was able a few weeks afterward to honor the crews of the *Ajax* and *Exeter*, the First Lord being among those present at Plymouth when the *Exeter* steamed into port. She was brought in by sirens and cheers the like of which I hadn't heard since 1918. Vast crowds lined the docksides.

These are bad hours for me. All I can do in these situations is stand near the Old Man and miss all the fun. That he should be so idolized here among his own people at war meant that there was equivalent fear and hatred of the same man among his enemies. So I turned my back upon him, as I had in times past in Cairo and Berwick Street when he stood for Westminster.

I was relieved when the launch came alongside and we put out to the *Exeter*. Once aboard her and away from the mob, guard duty would be simple. And so it was. The *Exeter* was in sad shape. How she had struggled across the Atlantic I could not guess, being no mariner, but she looked battered and drunken even where repairs had started.

The crew of the *Exeter*, once their First Lord was aboard, went crazy; at least as far as they are allowed to do so during wartime and under the eyes of their officers. Churchill made a speech. It does not matter what he said. I doubt if anyone heard. He'd utter a sentence and they'd all go crazy again. Liquor of all kinds appeared magically and was passed about, Winston plowing about the decks and the smashed turrets in a rash of excitement, quaffing from an enormous ale pot of some sort—laughing, grinning, his shoulders shaking, his head bobbing, his cap jaunty, his energy shooting forth in all directions, great noises and Admiralty gestures rising and exploding.

It was the same thing all over again when we boarded

the *Ajax* which was anchored in another part of the harbor.

Later that winter a large proportion of the crews of the *Exeter* and *Ajax* came to London and marched from Waterloo Station to the Horse Guards Parade. The streets were lined with a grateful and dramatic crowd, thirsting for something to celebrate. Now they had it. On the Horse Guards Parade there were His Majesty King George VI, the First Lord and the inevitable complement of Cabinet members, visiting celebrities from other nations and people of uncertain origin. Meanwhile Her Majesty the Queen, accompanied by Mrs. Winston Churchill, watched the proceedings from the window of the First Lord's room in the Admiralty. On the parade itself was the biggest crowd I'd ever seen, cheering itself into frenzy as the crews of the cruisers, led by the Royal Marines band, marched to the ground. There could be no doubt as to what England thought of the naval fight in the South Atlantic; and of the men who did it.

The crews were lined up. Mr. Churchill presented Captain C. M. L. Woodhouse of the *Ajax* and Captain F. S. Bell of the *Exeter* to His Majesty, after which those who had been singled out for honors were decorated by the King. (The *Achilles* was already out again on sea duty, having been refitted, fueled and reloaded.)

The most moving part of the whole spectacle was the moment when, in complete silence, the widow of Marine Wilfred A. Russell of the *Exeter* came before His Majesty to receive the Medal for Conspicuous Gallantry, which had been posthumously awarded to her husband. Following this, Their Majesties, the First Lord and Mrs. Churchill went to the saluting base where the men marched past to the ringing cheers of the city. Then the group proceeded to a quiet corner of the parade where stood the relatives of those who had lost their lives. King George and Queen Elizabeth stopped and spoke a word of praise and comfort to each one.

The second half of the ceremony took place at the Guildhall, at that time still undamaged. Four of the six captains who had been released by the *Graf Spee* in Montevideo were there and spoke. Most of England's famous men were in that hall that day, but none received the ovations that were poured out upon the sailors. When Churchill rose to say something, it was many moments before he could be heard. Never again after that moment did I have any doubt we would lose the war, no matter how close to it we might get.

Churchill said: "It was not for nothing that Admiral Harwood, as he instantly at full speed attacked an enemy which might have sunk any one of his ships by a single successful salvo from its far heavier guns, flew Nelson's immortal signal, of which neither the new occasion nor the conduct of all ranks and ratings, nor the final result, were found unworthy." Then his final words rang out, and the noise that followed split the Guildhall: "England expects that this day every man will do his duty!"

At the conclusion of the luncheon, when Churchill left the hall, there was such a press of people that there was difficulty getting him into his car; or in getting the car to him. Half the population of the British Isles seemed to pour out of that building and gush down upon the Old Man. I saw it all coming and put myself between him and the avalanche. But they overwhelmed me in their determination to shake hands with Winston. Sailors were in the majority. Flashbulbs were going off, photographers everywhere. Saving Churchill from his own friends was far harder than saving him from the nation's enemies!

They wanted to pat him on the back and to pummel the poor man, but at his age, even though his condition was so splendid, no man can stand more than a certain amount of such good-hearted thuds and thwackings and he winced repeatedly under their enthusiasm. He was badly bruised from it, and I finally had to use my elbows and knock about a bit to clear the path to his car. I was cursed roundly for my roughness by all those who received a piece of it, while two feet beyond the cheering was undiminished. However, they'd done their duty long before in disposing of the *Graf Spee* and now I had mine to do, getting their First Lord out of this riot while he was still upright. We just made it. Both of us were badly bruised and I had two dirty cuts, from the equipment that we permit our men to wear in full dress. I wish, when we are so severe about everything else, we weren't so elaborate about dress uniforms.

Office routine the next day was suddenly jolted when Churchill found, on talking with one of the six captains released in Uruguay by the *Graf Spee*, that perhaps as many as three hundred of their crews were prisoners on board a German ship, the *Altmark*. This same ship had been known for a long time in the British press as a "hellship." Churchill said two words: "Find her."

Every ship, plane and submarine was ordered to assist in the hunt. Because there were reports that these prisoners were being cruelly treated by their German captors, there was much tension in the Admiralty. It was urgently flashed that the *Altmark*, if found, be prevented by any means from reaching German waters.

A Lancaster plane found her a day later, hugging Norway and well inside Norwegian territorial waters.

Our Intelligence reported that the presence of the vessel was known to the Norwegian government, as was the fact that she carried British prisoners. We expected therefore that she would be boarded and searched by the Norwegians. She was boarded, but no proper search was made of her hold and she was permitted to proceed. We lost her for a few hours, then picked her up again farther down the Norwegian coast close to the headland of Josing Fjord. Because the *Altmark* had no right to the protection of these waters, Winston ordered H.M.S. *Cossack* to enter the fjord. Captain Vian of the *Cossack* notified the Norwegian naval commander that if he received no cooperation from the Norwegian government or navy, he would go after the *Altmark* alone. He invited the commander to assist in a second search for the British prisoners. And he was refused. He proceeded alone therefore.

When the skipper of the *Altmark* saw that the British destroyer was going to engage him, he turned sharply and tried to ram the *Cossack*. The ships indeed did strike, the *Altmark* being boarded in the old-fashioned method, with sidearms very much in use and a great deal of hand-to-hand fighting. The British are severe and methodical in such situations. They stabbed, shot, whacked and bayoneted their way to the hold.

The British prisoners, as reported, were there. The report was accurate both as to the number of men and the probable condition in which they would be found. They'd been in a stinking hold for over three months. But there was an impromptu celebration the instant they came up the ladders and companionways, and the cry "THE NAVY IS HERE!" brought them aboard the *Cossack*. Two hundred and ninety-nine of them.

How Germany screamed and howled! Hitler was going to

burn Churchill, burn his capital. There was no awfulness big enough or cruel enough to be visited on the Old Man. Hitler's voice was hysterical. And his terror of Churchill, not England but the *man* Churchill, was insensate and often quite incoherent. Churchill often tuned him in and grunted in expanding satisfaction, loosening his garments, unconsciously chewing away on a long-dead cigar. Hitler afforded huge emotional gratification to Churchill by being such a comical, spluttering, screaming ape—and like any other primate showing off to a big crowd, most accommodating in the frequency of his appearances.

Goebbels of course called Captain Vian's action "an unexampled act of piracy." "This boarding of a peaceful German merchantman." No German heard, of course, that there were almost three hundred British prisoners on board. And the *Altmark*'s captain, Heinrich Dau, was as big a liar as any other German including Goebbels, for he swore on landing that the British boarding parties opened fire on his unarmed and defenseless German crew. The *Altmark* was registered as a warship.

The end of 1939 and Christmas was little different for Mr. Churchill. The Old Man, after the despairs and then the sudden exhilarations, looked spent. Maybe he was. Surely I was. His secretarial staff was worn out, including the charming little Miss Shearburn, whom I from time to time managed to see briefly, though never when the First Lord might know of it, for he hated attachments of any sort that might dilute the quality and amount of work he wrung from his staffs! So when his doctor gave him an order to have a Christmas dinner with his own family, even if the Germans were on their way to London from landings at the Cinque Ports, we all felt relieved.

We did somewhat recover too, and well it was, for Churchill was up and off to Weymouth, the only naval installation he had not got round to. He spent three days there, seeing the whole of it and being deeply shaken all over again at the losses our shipping was taking from German U-boats. We drove from there to Caene Abbey where he remained for two days as the guest of Lord and Lady Digby, the parents of his son Randolph's first wife. This was truly his first day off in a long time. I think he enjoyed this. I surely did. After finding out that no one was expected and that he was well-shielded, I myself went to sleep without that dreadful feeling that the bliss of rest will soon be broken. I slept for ten hours. I had not done so in some years. Was I getting a bit older?

The next day could have been a very sad one for me. I made a bad mistake. In the evening, when we left the beautiful country place of Lord and Lady Digby, we went to the station by car. I felt fit, frisky and completely refreshed, as if I could take charge of anything. I was in charge of little more than Winston's two official boxes. I kept these in my possession until we reached the station, when Mr. Churchill moved to the other end of the platform. The baggage, with the other boxes, was at the other end and with these I placed my two official ones. As there were a number of people on the platform—most of them, but not all, known to me—my duty was to stand close to the First Lord and not leave his immediate presence until we had boarded the train and were in motion. I left the boxes where the remainder of the party would have them under their eyes. When the train came in, the baggage was put aboard and I accompanied Mr. Churchill to his compartment. I asked one of the party if the boxes had been put aboard and being assured this was so, I got into the train. Passing Mr. Churchill's compartment I saw he had one official box at his side. A special messenger had awaited us at the station with a box he had brought from London. I went to him to obtain it. On finding that the messenger had already given the box to Mr. Churchill, the sudden thought shot through my mind: Where were the two boxes of mine which I had laid down with the other baggage? I asked the messenger, the valet, and then Mr. Churchill's secretary. All were sure the boxes were aboard. However, I entered his compartment and found to my horror that they were not there. They were missing! There is no more awful feeling than this.

Something had to be done at once, even to backing the train to the platform we'd just left. I informed the First Lord, telling him flatly of the mistake and that I was going to have the train stopped and reversed. I saw the railway inspector at once and told him what had happened and that he had to stop. He said it was quite impossible as we had just crossed the points and were on the main line, with traffic feeding in upon us and between us and the station we had left. We could not halt here.

I did arrange for a stop at the next station. I expected to take a terrible reprimand from Churchill for I knew how important the contents of the first box were, having been in attendance when it was discussed.

Before the train stopped, I had jumped off and was at the telephone in the stationmaster's office. It was an unscheduled stop and I got volcanic service the instant our predicament was known to local authority.

The stationmaster at our departure point had realized, thank God, the possible value of anything left behind by the First Lord of the Admiralty and partly due to the local importance to the community of Lord and Lady Digby, special protection was given the boxes until they should be reclaimed.

I informed Churchill. He was coldly relieved. But I got a severe reproof from him which I thoroughly deserved. However, so great was my own relief that I would have taken it ten times without protest. Miss Shearburn was present taking dictation. Churchill scattered his criticism on the matter to include her as well, pointing out the unthinkable dangers if the contents of either box had got into the wrong hands. I of course immediately absolved the young lady but she would not have it so, insisting on assuming her portion of responsibility for the care of the general baggage on such a trip. I think now that Mr. Churchill realized we were trying to shield each other, since there was no logical reason why she should implicate herself. In a humorous way he told us to be more careful in the future. I said it was definitely and exclusively my error and would never be repeated.

It never was. But to this day I hate baggage of all kinds. In my particular job, there was an extra risk to Mr. Churchill due to my being so handicapped in my physical movement and mentally preoccupied with tending gear and boxes. I would change these responsibilities; it would improve security.

We were soon in rough water going across the Channel again, bound for another of the uncountable conferences which Winston held with what seemed half the population of Europe. It was in January. Mr. Churchill's personal private secretary, Miss Mary T. G. Shearburn, told me she was going to Paris with us this time and said she would be aboard the same destroyer that was taking the First Lord. I told her this was a pleasant and romantic idea that would surely please the crew but that such a thing had never happened in the history of the British Navy. At least during wartime.

I was of course no end pleased to find her aboard, and thereafter not at all surprised at the stir she caused. It's a wonder we made land. Miss Shearburn, it being known instantly somehow that she was "Miss," was escorted to one place after another, from bridge to gun turrets to the torpedo room to the wardroom and back. Her name had been included in the list of the party to the destroyer (H.M.S. *Codrington*) and one of the officers recognized the name and greeted Miss Shearburn with the news that he was a friend of her brother, a naval commander. She was not only given every possible attention, she was given more than she needed, every man outdoing the other in forcing hospitality upon her. She loved it too. A whole walking flotilla escorted her to the gangway on arrival at the French coast.

While still some miles away and no land in sight, we saw a number of mines floating in the water. Winston became very excited by this spectacle and was immediately into the fun, taking off his coat and cranking the gun down for sightings and firings. He familiarized himself with the firing mechanisms in a few minutes (though I'm sure the crew found errors there) and he began to fire at them. Six were blown up in this short run, making hollow and fearful sounds that shook the chest and that sent plumes of water hundreds of feet up. These mines, because they were floating, were of a different type from those that attacked by stealth: the magnetic variety that we were only just now learning to deal with.

Miss Shearburn made her graceful departure from the destroyer and within minutes the party was on its way to Metz. Here I encountered one of the disappointments that is the lot of Scotland Yard. While Churchill took off for a comprehensive tour of the Maginot Line, something that had thrilled my own imagination since construction of this "impassable barrier," I was ordered to stay in my hotel room. I had to guard a secret model of something or other "with my life." Churchill saw my disappointment and promised me a look at everything "the next time." In war there is seldom a next time. I never saw the Maginot Line. A few days later, at Vincennes, after a special dinner where Churchill spoke, the Old Man called me into his room and at considerable length lectured me concerning the important duty I had carried out in guarding the secret model, saying that I had performed a much more important duty than in guarding him. I demurred. Around him it does no good to demur.

Early the next morning we were off again, to Rheims, RAF headquarters. An entire champagne cellar was put at the disposal of the party. The French General Gamelin decorated General Ironside and Lord Gort, Churchill made a speech to the 615th Squadron of the RAF of which he is Honorary Commodore, and we were back in England once more. Miss Shearburn seemed aware of me, but in the same way as she might be aware of the greengrocer.

The German U-boat campaign was going forward on an intensive scale. Enemy and neutral ships alike were going down daily. This called for Churchill's appeal to neutrals which he made in a broadcast on January 20th. In the course of the speech, Mr. Churchill said there was a five-hundred-to-one chance of a ship going down in convoy and made a direct appeal to neutral nations to join convoys. Some of the more notable sentences and ideas in his speech were these: "But what would happen if all these neutral nations I have mentioned—and some others I have not mentioned—were with one spontaneous impulse to do their duty in accordance with the Covenant of the League, and were to stand together with British and French Empires against oppression and wrong? At present their plight is lamentable; and it will become much worse. There is no chance of a speedy end except through united action." He had this message of hope at the close: "Let the great cities of Warsaw, of Prague, of Vienna banish despair even in the midst of their agony. Their liberation is sure. The day will come when the joy-bells will ring again throughout Europe, and when victorious nations, masters not only of their foes but of themselves, will plan and build in justice, in tradition, and in freedom, a house of many mansions where there will be room for all."

His warning that neutral nations would be overrun was sadly borne out almost at once. The speech caused much uneasiness in Holland, where his suggestion was considered "unreasonable" by the press.

One cold morning we drove to Manchester, a factory city, where he made a public speech in the Free Trade Hall in the heart of the city. This was the speech in which he appealed for a million women workers. As usual he was way ahead of everyone else in seeing what would be needed and in finding sources that might be used to fill the need. (Over half of England's total female population was finally working in some war job before V-E Day.) It was a long speech and much of it was quoted in newspapers all over the world. You will remember snatches of it: "Come then: let us to the task, to the battle, to the toil—each to our part, each to our station. Fill the armies, rule the air, pour out the munitions, strangle the U-boats, sweep the mines, plough the land, build the ships, guard the streets, succor the wounded, uplift the downcast and honor the brave. Let us go forward together in all parts of the Island. There is not a week, not a day, not an hour to lose. Every minute we let down, the enemy picks up."

Things worsened. There was another quick journey to Paris, Winston's fifth meeting with the Supreme War Council. Because his own responsibility was so limited and his own ability so great, the difference between what he could do and what he was allowed to do was truly enormous. I could see, in the faces of the French, this projected but unspoken disappointment. The waste of Winston in the face of our present reverses was known to them all to be crucially unwise. Today the whole world knows it was evidence of myopic, timid thinking. Much of the fault lies with Chamberlain. He was nominally the central member of the party, but even as Prime Minister he was never the actual center of it—or of anything if Churchill was about. Lord Halifax was along too, a bony aloof man, formerly Viceroy to India. I did not know what tragedy he was bearing at this time for he had kept the death of his son from us all. (I did not of course know that the death of one of my own sons was imminent.)

French crowds in Paris were overjoyed to see the English party and shouts of "Sham-bur-lain" rang out to us from the sidewalks and the crowded cafés and from windows up and down the steep houses. I got no sleep on this tour and merely stretched out on a cot, fully dressed, before the door of whatever room Mr. Churchill occupied on any night.

M. Daladier, at the meeting's eventual conclusion, said it was the most productive and satisfactory War Council meeting he'd ever attended. The whole group of delegates was asked to form itself outside the main building where photographs were taken. As usual I was not in the picture, being to Winston's right and between him and the only exposed corridor. On our return Mr. Churchill asked me if I had had my photograph taken with the group. I said that I had not. He said it was unfortunate.

"I am certain that the people in that group will never again meet in similar circumstances, and the same group will never meet intact under any circumstances." It was another of his quick but disturbingly accurate forecasts. Daladier soon after was no longer France's number one man, and poor Chamberlain, as you all know, was shortly out of office and then died.

Back in England there was increased public agitation over the way the Germans were treating crews of torpedoed ships. Many sailors had been abandoned and many more fired upon while swimming or struggling in the water. They had been fired on while trying to get away in ships' boats, they had even been fired on when loaded lifeboats were being slung to the ocean's surface. The Admiralty was full of eyewitness stories and of the most shocking and heartbreaking photographs I had up to that time ever looked at. Yet the German concentration camps were worse because the brutalities there were so prolonged and so conscientiously planned. The shame of these is a shame that will outlast the end of the Germans, no matter when that end may come and irrespective of the manner of its coming.

Terrible pressures were being brought upon Winston to treat German crews in like manner. He would not do so. He said it was contrary to the dictates of the Royal Navy in treatment of captive nationals and sailors. But here insult was added to injury. The German radio, in its unceasing attack on Winston Churchill, his Navy and his people, gave out the news that all British merchantmen would be treated as ships of war because they were all armed or about to be armed. This was a typical hypocrisy, the Germans as usual whining over something they could not control or insult into extinction. They were crying because by arming our vessels we were able to hit back; many U-boats were sent to the bottom by the deck guns of British merchant ships carrying war materials. This was another of Churchill's ideas that went right at the heart of the matter and worked from the beginning.

Late in February, Churchill had several concentrated conferences on board the *Warspite* at Greenock. They were convened in a great hurry. In fact, I was summoned from my bed in my own little home at two o'clock one morning when I had just lain down after being on my feet continuously for over thirty hours.

"Get to Euston for a trip north on a special train." That's all I was told. I am always packed. I went into the target gallery in my own basement, fired a hundred rounds, freshened my ammunition, then drove through black icy rain on my motorcyle to Euston. After joining Mr. Churchill again this time, we seemed to be in continuous motion. After Greenock, we drove in a fleet of cars to Glasgow, where the First Lord was for a day in the company of Their Majesties and where the launching of the *Duke of York* took place.

This might have been any other launching except that, unknown to me at this time, on her maiden trip this was the vessel which was to carry Winston Churchill for his first conference with President Roosevelt in December, 1941.

Whilst on the *Clyde*, Mr. Churchill and the small party with him had a grandstand view of another mighty vessel— the new liner *Queen Elizabeth*. At that very instant she was sliding down the river on what proved to be a secret voyage to the United States. This was a beautifully kept secret and was not revealed until her physical arrival at the other side.

We returned to London. Papers were put aboard the plane and Winston set about reading all of them at once. He was soon engulfed in a snowdrift of them, and once had to reach up to receive a glass of beer the steward wished to pass down to him.

The papers contained translations of what was being said about the British and the war by the Italian press. It was a long sequence of anti-British outbursts. Italy was most obviously preparing for war.

We again returned to Greenock where Churchill boarded the *Rodney*. Accompanied by the *Renown*, *Repulse* (we lost the *Repulse* off Singapore later) and a group of destroyers, we sailed again for Scapa. Winston had secured it, but on our approach to its mouth, word was flashed to us that the Germans had within the hour dropped a great number of mines at the entrance. The Captain of the *Rodney* considered it unnecessary to enter the main harbor before minesweepers had cleared the channel and it was decided that the First Lord, who had immediate business at Scapa, should be lowered over the side and rowed to a destroyer. This was done. I went too.

There was much activity among the destroyers. They kept circling the big ships. There was a good possibility there were U-boats in the region, and there were some beautiful prizes waiting there if that were true. There is nothing so irresistible to a hostile submarine as a stationary battleship. We rowed through a hundred yards of rough water, then scrambled up a ladder to the jolting deck of another destroyer. Even this ship, which was in a sense pressed into service to ferry the First Lord to the base, kept making continuous sharp circles and quick turns, doubling back without warning and cutting right through her own wake. She kicked up a mighty fuss.

Soon we were alongside the *Hood*. My impressions of her were always the same: the most concentrated unit of destruction ever afloat. What irony! We were soon to lose her in the North Atlantic, in what I am sure is the most amazing single shot in the history of ocean fighting, a shell fired from eighteen miles away not only striking her but penetrating and detonating her magazine!

His conference aboard the *Hood* at an end, we reboarded the *Rodney* and again went through the Minches and down the coast to Plymouth. On our way I was most perturbed to read in ship's news broadcast that another assassination had occurred. It was Sir Michael O'Dwyer. He'd been shot through the heart while attending a public meeting at the Caxton Hall—murdered by a Sikh named Singh Azad. In the same attack Lord Zetland, Secretary of State for India, had been wounded. I have noticed that when there is one attack on a public official, there is often an attempt on another one. Accordingly I was relieved when after arriving in London, we were soon off by plane for Paris again.

Hitler and Mussolini were meeting in what the press of both their countries called a "peace drive." The French Cabinet was nervous. Members of our party, as well as the French, kept offering each other suggestions for a pact between France and Great Britain not to sign separate peace articles. Things were that bad. In fact, while we were there M. Daladier resigned, Reynaud took over, and the German press blared its front page rages, calling Reynaud a pro-British "French Churchill." Winston was pleased to hear this.

The British public was kept openly informed of our ocean losses, but neither they nor our enemies were informed about new launchings. These of course were going on all the time. It was a pity we could not tell our own people. Inside, all the British were bleeding. Near the close of March I accompanied Mr. and Mrs. Churchill to Furness Abbey. This is the home of Sir Charles Craven, chairman of Vickers. Sir Charles is not known to Americans, being one of those quiet, "behind-the-scenes" Englishmen. His name appeared infrequently even in the British press. Our purpose here was to attend the launching of the aircraft carrier *Illustrious*. It would have picked up the morale of every man and woman in England if they could have been along.

Coming back to London, Mr. Churchill handed a news bulletin to his wife. Ley, the leader of the Nazi Labor Front, broadcasting from Rotterdam, was advertising the fact that he was planning cruises for German workers to spend their holidays at the most popular seaside resorts on the south coast of England! It was to take place during the late months of the oncoming summer.

Mrs. Churchill turned to her husband: "Do you think the Nazis can get aboard the Island?"

"No," he said at once. "But they'll make a mighty try. At least I would if I were Hitler." He then opened his coat and his own revolver was briefly in view. "If they do try," he told her, "I'll get a few before they take me." He grinned and growled and looked across the water.

Winston spoke over the air. Before leaving his office, I asked him if he had remembered to bring his reading glasses. I had reminded him many times before and was forever doing it, especially when we got to the United States, where his memory for this one detail abandoned him entirely. He thanked me, went back, picked them up, and we arrived a few moments before his scheduled broadcast. It was the 30th of March.

More and more the public was looking forward to the words of Winston, for though they always told in harshest truth where we stood, they also lifted our whole population. Tonight, as he had many times before, he had to tell England of still more hardships which lay ahead of her. To those who were constantly asking, "What are we fighting for?" he had this curt reply: "If we left off fighting you would soon find out." To those who doubted the rightness of our self-imposed task, he said: "Few there are tonight who, looking back on these last seven months, would doubt that the British and French peoples were right to draw the sword of justice and retribution. Fewer still there are who would wish to sheath it till its somber, righteous work is done." He pointed out that the British had no quarrel with the Italian or the Japanese peoples; that we could still at least try to live on good terms with them. Then he made another true forecast. He said that over a million German soldiers in many armored divisions were at the frontiers of Luxembourg, Belgium, and Holland, about to invade those neutral and almost defenseless nations.

His prediction of invasion was repeated a day later by Prime Minister Chamberlain. It served more to increase the public demand for a Defense Minister than to anneal the public's confidence in Chamberlain. Winston's appointment came (he was named Defense Minister in the Cabinet) a few weeks later. It was received joyfully throughout England. But Hitler nearly had apoplexy. "Bloodthirsty amateur strategist" came roaring over the German radio, as soon as the appointment was confirmed. "Drunkard," "gabbler," "hypocrite," and the one that amused Mr. Churchill the most: "Lazybones."

Winston and I flew across-Channel to France where the now multi-portfolioed Minister met with Lord Gort at British Headquarters. In England Chamberlain, addressing the Central Council of the Conservative and Unionist Association, said he was ten times as confident of victory as he was when war began, and added the sentence that has since been ridiculed a million times: "Hitler missed the bus."

Political comment is not my field but no man in England —irrespective of his insight, degree of education, courage or basic intelligence—could by that time have any other notion about Chamberlain than that he had very little conception of war itself. And I do not today have any doubt that had Chamberlain continued in power for another six months we would have been defeated. I never heard Winston mention any of this, and you will of course recall that upon his own accession to power, Winston retained Chamberlain in his own Cabinet. But I think he did it to keep the old gentleman, who was very ill by then, from dying a few weeks prematurely from a broken heart. Winston never said anything unkind about Chamberlain though I know there were many times when it was nothing but nobility of self-control that kept Churchill from exploding and foaming at his colleague's exacerbating lack of realism. Chamberlain went to his grave still believing that people—even the Germans—would stop behaving like apes; that they would because they should. Churchill knew better. It must have been a persistent, even infantile, naïveté that kept Chamberlain optimistic when there was nothing on hand but the most dreadful amount of bad news.

In Paris, Winston being most fearful the French would make a separate peace, a declaration was prepared by him and M. Reynaud. "The government of the French Republic and His Majesty's Government of Great Britain and Northern Ireland mutually undertake that during the present war they will neither negotiate nor conclude an armistice or treaty of peace except by mutual agreement. They undertake not to discuss peace terms before reaching complete agreement on the conditions necessary to ensure to each of them an effective and lasting guarantee of their security. Finally they undertake to maintain after the conclusion of peace, a community of action in all spheres for so long as may be necessary to safeguard their security, and to effect the reconstruction, with the assistance of other nations, of an international order which will ensure the liberty of people, respect for law, and the maintenance of peace in Europe."

This soon became just another scrap of paper.

Upon his return to England a few hours after publication of the above, he was asked to describe England's position in regard to Russia. He said at once that what had necessarily been a condition of estrangement between us, owing to the signing of the treaty between Germany and Russia, was now looking more hopeful since, to their credit, the Russian government was offering to resume trade talks with us. The offer had just been made by Mr. Maisky, Soviet Ambassador to London, a most conspicuous Russian in that he was the first representative ever sent to us by the Kremlin in many years. All the others were bully boys and stooges, unconscionably rude and unimaginably dull, but Maisky was funny, bright and alive and made many English friends.

The mutual declaration, plus a possible improvement in Russian relations, made Mr. Churchill a target of the press. Photographers haunted us. This made it most difficult for me. All the press, and the photographers included, are quite a fine group of men, just doing their jobs as they see fit. But it was hell on me. I had to discourage them as much as I could. I had to be sure that nothing was going to be allowed in the published picture that would reveal the actual geographical location of the First Lord. I had to stay out of the pictures, not always easy when they were taking shots with silent shutters, shooting from odd angles, or sneaking the pictures. At the same time I had to honor the rightful desires of the nation's press, and of future readers of history who were entitled to see what England's leaders had looked like.

What it meant was this: If you honored the one, you put the other in jeopardy.

Rarely did photographers appear at the back garden gate of Number Ten Downing Street. Security measures had considerably cramped their style, but here they were again. Mr. Churchill and I had just walked from the Admiralty to the garden gate. One very persistent, smiling photographer seemed determined to snap the First Lord. I tried to prevent him from taking the picture at that particular spot. Mr. Churchill went up to the man and in the friendliest tone said to him: "Do you want to take a photograph?"

The man, with evident delight, answered at once: "Oh, yes, please, sir."

"They are forbidden, here, sir," I cautioned him, knowing he full knew it himself.

"So they are, Thompson." And he stood there smiling at the lens and at the photographer. "But how are they to return to their editors with pictures unless they take them?"

"True, but not here, sir."

The photographer continued snapping, Winston continued to agree with me and to accommodate the cameraman at the same time, and nothing could be done about it. On the way in to Number Ten he turned to me softly, knowing I was vexed and that he'd broken the rules, and said they had their own real values and one had to use one's discretion in these matters. "They have to come in with copy, Thompson, or they don't get paid."

That night, in several of London's papers, I was exasperated to find many smiling poses of the First Lord in the garden of Number Ten, with myself making gestures of reproof—an angry scowl on my face—in the immediate background. The caption saved me a light reprimand at headquarters: OVER THE PROTEST OF SCOTLAND YARD, OUR FIRST LORD RETURNS FROM FRANCE AND SMILES AT PRESS CAMERA.

That Churchill could always smile, and do so without

forcing it, must have helped save England by encouraging others to hang on when there seemed so little reason. We were all in a terrible situation. Our Prime Minister was weak and ill. We were being mauled in France. No one could stand up against the Germans. Russia had breached the Mannerheim Line. German armed forces moved north, and things could not get much worse without snapping. Most Englishmen expected the invasion attempt within a month.

Norway had been very much in the minds of the government. Enemy vessels were violating Norwegian neutral waters and passing inside her territorial limits, thence either returning to Germany or passing from that country and escaping into the Atlantic. Churchill of course knew it. By this simple means a number of ships had eluded the vigilance of the British fleet. I knew Churchill had wished for many weeks to take the strong step of mining the various parts of Norway's coast.

Eventually he had his way, though not before appreciable shipping had been successfully sunk. But on April 8th we began mining the Norwegian coast. What tragedy this might have saved, had it been done before, for as we now know, Germany had been sending ships to many Norwegian ports with German troops on board. These troops remained ready but under cover until the actual invasion of Norway was imminent.

This gallant little country was now doomed. The day following the mining of the coast, the German occupation of Denmark was commenced, as well as the military invasion of Norway herself. Denmark was in no position to resist in any way. She had to submit to the iron heel of Hitler's hordes with no way to hit back. Norway could have put up stubborn resistance but Hitler's agents had done their job, and Quisling had many supporters who sprang up on all sides and betrayed their countrymen everywhere.

The day after the invasion of Norway began, the battle of Narvik took place. It was largely a battle of German and British destroyers. It was a big sea victory for us, for Narvik was an important port at which we later landed and embarked troops. We now had positive information that German troops were already aboard many scores of ships and had been for some time—ships anchored at Trondhjem, Narvik, Oslo, Bergen and Stavanger. The Germans of course denied this and stated that their invasion of Norway was "protective of her sovereignty" because we had mined her seacoast.

In contrast to the invasion of Norway was the landing of a British force in Iceland. It lifted Allied spirits everywhere. It was enthusiastically received in the United States; very shortly after our own landing there, America proved her blessing of the action by supplementing the British force with a force of her own. Icelanders didn't like this at first and Hitler made constant reference to it and to the combined aggression of two powers upon a "weak people." But the landing and occupying troops behaved well and this had a reassuring effect on the population of Iceland. Later when I visited there I saw for myself that the strain of occupation was not severe and indeed the local inhabitants and alien troops had settled down amicably together.

Italy continued to sneer at us. All her news items were increasingly anti-British, at this time in respect to the aid we had given Norway. Italy at this time was also ignoring repeated approaches by France for a bond of friendship between the two nations. The day when Mussolini would declare war was quickly approaching. It would not be long in coming either—when Benito would strike at France when France was in full retreat, before the crush of the German offense.

Affairs in Norway continued to go badly. This created restlessness in the House of Commons. Many Members demanded a debate. Others pressed for an all-party government. Mr. Chamberlain stated his willingness to cooperate with all parties, but the mood of the House was one that would not be satisfied by such a statement. Many Members rose and spoke openly against the government's action in Norway. They hated the botching of it. They hated the military fiasco of it, the cost, the delay. Our War Budget was colossal. It had jumped from eight hundred million pounds to over two and a half billion pounds. No Member was willing to accept Chamberlain's explanation.

Churchill rose. He defended our operations in Norway. He defended Chamberlain. A thrill went through me when he turned savagely upon the full membership and challenged them all to see if one Member could answer why, for five years, Churchill had not been able to persuade them to keep our Air Force on a par with Germany's. Churchill had long dwelt on this problem: that our security could never be guaranteed if our Air Force was inferior to our enemies'.

This stilled them. And he said quietly, after the long and pregnant silence which his direct challenge had created, that what the Chamberlain government had done in Norway was the best possible under existing circumstances against a far more powerful enemy. He kept the government together a few more days. But no man could have kept it together longer—unless by some miracle the land area of Germany were to disappear completely. But this would be too happy a phenomenon!

The debacle of Norway was dramatized further by the arrival in London of Norway's King, Haakon VII. He and his Cabinet escaped and continued a resistance movement of their own in exile. Scotland Yard of course immediately supplied them all with individual protection. For Europe, it looked like the roof was about to collapse. It was too. The Germans crashed into Belgium, Holland, and Luxembourg. The Maginot Line? They walked around its two ends. Chamberlain resigned.

In the years I had served Winston—and those of us who had been around him for a long time began to refer to him affectionately as "The Old Man" (he was sixty-four)—I had seen him in many posts. I had often doubted, however, because of the dilatory state of mind of the average professional politician in England, that he would ever receive and occupy the office he had so long earned and into which England, for her own salvation, now so critically needed to see him installed. I guess I had not got over the treatment he took from Stanley Baldwin. And yet, in this crucial time, this was the moment when Winston was called upon to form a new government.

Why Churchill should have fallen out of favor so often—and for such long periods—no man will ever quite know. He seemed an outcast in the eyes of Baldwin. Perhaps, the man was merely too dazzling, infallible and prescient to be believable. This could explain why he could be only half appreciated by those who so deeply respected and loved him and why, for those who feared him or envied his genius or his bearing of command, it was a pleasure and even a relief to see him shelved from time to time.

It is not, however, flattering to British perspicacity. Our

sporadic use of his gifts—instead of our constant and wor-
shipful enjoyment of them—will always, in my view, be a
shameful page in history. Plain myopia. There never was a
man on this earth like him. Other great men will appear but
never again will we see a man so profoundly endowed with
such telescopic foresight and such massive organizing abilities. And these are of course quite apart from the magnifi-
cence of the man when seen in his human terms. And it is the
human qualities that will enrich the legend of the man. His
military and political decisions have already taken care of
the man historically.

In the afternoon of the 10th of May, with the world exploding and the oceans geysering, I drove behind the Old
Man with indescribable pride. His destination was Buckingham Palace. He was to have an audience with His Majesty the King.

We came back to the Admiralty in silence, as we had
gone. As he stepped out of his car he said: "You know why
I've been to Buckingham Palace." And I of course said, "Yes,
sir" and congratulated him. There was pleasure in his face,
but he was very tense too.

"I am most pleased you have finally attained this position,
sir," I told him—and I meant it from the bottom of my heart
—"but I most deeply wish that it had come your way in far
better times, for you have told them a thousand times that
this very thing will happen, and now it has, and you have
taken on an enormous task."

He shook my hand like a friend then, and before going on
into the Admiralty said to me: "God alone knows how great
it is. . . . All I hope is that it is not too late. I am very much
afraid that it is. But we can only do our best, and give the
rest of what we have—whatever there may be left to us—"

For an instant then he stood entirely still, looking at me,
then on through me and into the distance, oblivious to the
traffic and the sound of planes in the air. Tears came into his
eyes and fell. Still he did not move. I could say nothing.
Tears were now threatening my own, so I looked off and
about, made the instinctive gesture toward my guns—an
invisible reflex by now. We both turned toward the Admiralty now. He moved with ponderous purpose to the stair-
way, muttering low, after which his jaw set, the muscles
about his mouth became hard, and he started up the long
flight and the quiet ascent to final greatness and his own part

in the final saving of the freedoms of civilized man. At a proper distance, I followed.

Everywhere, from all the corridor doorways, the whole of England seemed to rush out to him and seize him. His appointment all over Great Britain was greeted with the same thankfulness that was taking place right here before us now. England rose up in a sudden force and vigor, shook herself and picked herself up. It was as if, to the average workingman in England, a new power had arisen in our midst. And undoubtedly it had. His name was on everyone's lips. The man that Britain needed had arrived. Allies and friendly neutrals alike acclaimed his appointment, just as the Axis powers had dreaded it. No wonder they desired his assassination in 1939.

Mr. Churchill made his first speech to the House of Commons as Prime Minister three days after he took office. He outlined the formation of his government. You remember the great concluding words: "I would say to this House, as I have said to those who have joined the government, I have nothing to offer but blood, toil, tears and sweat. We have before us an ordeal of the most grievous kind. We have before us many very long months of struggle and suffering. . . . Come then, let us go forward together with our united strength."

The vote of confidence which followed was unanimous. It gave the new Prime Minister a stumulus that carried him clear through to the finish.

Inactivity had now become activity. Our forces were gradually getting into positions which would bring them face to face with German troops, something not new to the English. We had a well-equipped army. It had waited many months for the collision. Now it was here. What did the future hold? Would Holland resist? Would the Belgians fight? We learned very quickly that both were offering resistance. The British army moved into Belgium. On every side we received tributes that brought back memories of World War I.

The Germans had concentrated enormous armored units at the pivot on the River Meuse. This was the spot where the British and French forces linked up. The Germans smashed in. Within a very few days they had made frightening headway. On May 15th they crossed the Meuse in great force and appeared behind the French lines. German tanks rolled ahead almost without hindrance.

What had happened? Who was responsible? The question came from all sides. It is still unanswered. You may recall that at the Riom Trials efforts were made to lay the blame on various French ex-Cabinet Ministers and on some of the fighting chiefs themselves. There had been, in any case, a terrible blunder. The bridges over the Meuse had not been blown up. This unbelievable error had allowed German armor of the greatest weight and striking force to pass unimpeded into France. The point of catastrophe was actually held and engaged by French troops, but pilots of the RAF were called upon to bomb the bridges. Four flights were detailed for this. The bridges were destroyed. But not a single British flier returned from this raid.

Much reliance was still being placed on the Maginot Line. In the view of the French who had built it, it was thought impregnable. This was the British view as well. Churchill had been immensely impressed by his inspection of it not too long before. The Germans also decided it was impregnable and made no effort to breach it. They just went around it, as we know.

Further, we had been led to think that the French were well supported by aircraft. And they had some armored divisions of their own, not as tough or disciplined as the *Panzers* but dependable units and land fleets nonetheless. But French planes and French tanks seemed to be missing when their time came.

With the Battle of France going against us all, Mr. Churchill on May 16th decided to make an appeal to Mussolini in the hope that he would keep Italy neutral. Churchill sat at his desk and wrote in longhand. The following message was dispatched to Rome:

"Now that I have taken up my office as Prime Minister and Minister of Defense, I look back to our meetings in Rome and feel a desire to speak words of goodwill to you as chief of the Italian nation, across what seems to be a swiftly widening gulf.

"It is idle to predict the course of the great battles now raging in Europe but I am sure that whatever may happen on the Continent, England will go on to the end, even quite alone, as we have done before, and I believe with some assurance that we shall be aided in increasing measure by the United States and indeed by all the Americas.

"I beg you to believe that it is in no spirit of weakness or of fear that I make this solemn appeal, which will remain on record. Down the ages above all other calls comes the cry that the joint heirs of Latin and Christian civilization must not be ranged against one another in mortal strife. Hearken to it, I beseech you, in all honor and respect before the dread signal is given. It will never be given by us."

Two days later, Churchill got this from Mussolini:

"I reply to the message which you have sent me in order to tell you that you are certainly aware of grave reasons of an historical and contingent character which have ranged our two countries in opposite camps. Without going back very far in time, I remind you of the initiative taken in 1935 by your government to organize at Geneva sanctions against Italy, engaged in securing for herself a small place in the African sun without causing the slightest injury to your interests and territories, or those of others. I remind you also of the real and actual state of servitude in which Italy finds herself in her own sea. If it was to honor your signature that your government declared war on Germany, you will understand that the same sense of honor and of respect for engagements assumed in the Italian-German Treaty guides Italian policy today and tomorrow in the face of any event whatsoever."

Before Parliament, Mr. Churchill referred to his letter and the reply to it. He mentioned the hard choice open to the Italian people. He correctly foreshadowed Greek opposition. He predicted the eventual gangs of ravening soldiery that Germany, with Gestapo ancillaries, would send to Italy to help Mussolini "protect" the Italian people.

In an exterminating air attack upon the heart of Rotterdam, the Germans broke and fired this city. Rotterdam surrendered. Queen Wilhelmina escaped to London, her Cabinet following by a few hours. Four days after Rotterdam was hit, the Dutch army ceased firing. This was a paralyzing blow to us and to the Belgians. German mechanized divisions smashed into northern France, roaring down the valley of the Somme clear to the Channel at Abbeville. This split the British and Belgian forces in Flanders and separated them from the main French armies. Overnight Gamelin succeeded Weygand but could not strengthen these tottering columns. Brussels fell, then Namur, and the Belgians and British were thereby forced back upon Ostend and Dunkirk. On the 26th, Boulogne fell. The Belgian forces fighting without rest for eighteen days could take no more. They were exhausted and unsupplied. Their King, Leopold III, ordered them to capitulate. This left the British exposed altogether. A quarter of a million of them withdrew, principally to Dunkirk's beaches. There was nowhere else to go. On these beaches we lost all equipment and thirty thousand men killed or captured. By a spontaneous rising up of the British people in the coastal towns, all manner of seagoing craft, much of it leaky and of insignificant size, put out to pick up the living who were stranded there.

It was after Dunkirk, and after the Germans were beating back the French in an arc that curved from Sedan to Abbeville, that Mussolini declared war on the French and on us.

Three days later, Paris was evacuated. Two days after this, Verdun fell. With savage irony, the same day that Verdun was captured marked the day that the Russians moved into Lithuania, Latvia and Estonia. Pétain followed Paul Reynaud as head of the French government. His first day as Premier he asked the Germans for an armistice. And five days after asking for it, he got it.

This deluge of calamities all fell upon the head of Churchill before he had been in office five full weeks. By this time most of the population in England was planning what to do when Germans began appearing in our own roads and byways.

Winston told them. It thrilled the world: "We shall defend our Island whatever the cost may be.
We shall fight on the beaches.
We shall fight on the landing grounds.
We shall fight in the fields and in the streets.
We shall fight in the hills; we shall never surrender."

There is one thing I must say for the race that bore me: although we often do amazingly unreasonable things and are quite stupid about responding to a sense of timing, we never tremble. Right now, it was all we had left, a very negative endowment. We expected invasion any night.

Anthony Eden was Secretary of State for War. He made an announcement that immediately created great interest in our country. This interest, and the activity which Mr. Eden's announcement started, stayed with us all right through to the end of the war. He announced the formation of the Local Defense Volunteers. This was a very real thing, although I suppose it is hard for an American to understand just what it meant to the British people. The Volunteers contained a high percentage of ex-soldiers and campaigners. All of the men in this new corps were battle-experienced. Most of them had fought in World War I. Their experience and their resolution gave great confidence to the masses of our people. These were the men who would deal with such invading Germans as reached our shores; such as penetrated our towns and villages; as attacked our women.

The zeal to kill Germans had also begun to infect England's women, and I've seen many a British grandmother flat on her tummy, shooting live ammunition at practice targets set up against a barnside or a stump. The Volunteers were heavily organized and units began to spread out over England with great speed. Three weeks after Mr. Eden created this substantial defense of our accessible island, it had six hundred and forty thousand members. They were all armed and most of them were over fifty. Many were seventy. All were in fine condition and were required to maintain a standard of physical toughness hardly less exacting than that of combat troops. It gave us a new sense of safety. It was surely welcome, for we were getting no comfort at all from what was taking place on the continent.

Lend-Lease from America was a great lift, but more so to those conducting the war than to those fighting it as individual soldiers, or to those who were carrying on at home. To most Englishmen, Lend-Lease was a great but intangible thing whose benefits were appreciated in a statistical sense. It was somewhat as if we had been told that Uncle Sam's shoulder was there and that it was a strong shoulder, but that it had not yet been put to the wheel, for only the members of the War Cabinet, and those in Supply, Transport, and Ordnance were in a position to count the blessings America was letting us have. We knew that it was big. But we didn't know just what it was. Another extension, as it were, of the average Englishman's idea of America and Americans: vast, generous, muscular, but indistinct. (It was soon to become most distinct indeed—not only to us but to the world!)

One day in mid-June, with everything black around us, Winston Churchill had a dirty problem to deal with. The Germans, seeing that the U.S. was showing increasing signs of becoming an important factor in the war, wanted to slow down America's contribution as much as they could. They schemed therefore to cause anti-British feeling in the United States. You will recall that the Germans, at the time of the sinking of the *Athenia*, accused Mr. Churchill of causing this loss. Now they were to repeat this stratagem. The German press proclaimed to the world that German Intelligence had received reliable information to the effect that the American liner *President Roosevelt*, then at Galway, would be sunk on her next voyage across the Atlantic, that she was to be sunk at the instigation of Winston Churchill, and that Churchill would then accuse the Germans of sinking it by U-boat. It was known at the Admiralty and of course at Scotland Yard that a number of extremely prominent Americans were aboard the vessel, and the sinking of the vessel, had it occurred, would have caused a terrific outcry in America. We all knew this. It was ABC psychological warfare.

Churchill dealt with this head-on. The vessel made the run all right, the American people and the American press saw through Hitler's scheme immediately, and the whole matter was treated with the contempt it had earned. But it was another vexation that had come on the top of so many others of such extreme nature that it looked, quite suddenly, as if it might break the Old Man. He looked very tired and I told him so.

I reminded him that now that he was Prime Minister he had the right to the use of Chequers, not only on occasion but just as regularly as he wanted to go down to it. I said this half jokingly, and he took it this way too, but I think when I reminded him that I had been an occupant of it long before he had (when I was guarding Lloyd George) and that I felt he could be made safe there, get some sort of change, get as much done under less distracting, noisy and importunate conditions—he began to pick up. You could see it in his face. True, he had been to Chequers once or twice just to test it out a bit, to see if he might find some advantages there. As the permanent residence of England's impermanent Prime Ministers, Chequers offered advantages that he could not find in his own Chartwell. And Chequers offered no problem of expense or overhead. Churchill's extra income—something he had been able to rely on during peacetime when he was almost always at work on books and

articles and which had paid him enormous fees in the past—
had of course evaporated. Chartwell, though sustained by a
skeleton staff, was expensive. I think the idea of Chequers,
its freehold intact and its maintenance guaranteed in per-
petuity by its donor, was attractive to him in this very material sense. He may have been as affected by that considera-
tion as he was by the equally persuasive one—for a man who
loved title and office and a good observance of Parliamentary punctilio—that it was the acknowledged and accepted
country house of the King's First Minister. Winston liked
everything that had a kingly or a queenly ring to it. There
was still some florid medievalism in him, but far from silly,
it seemed somehow right in its very anachronism for it was
as picturesque as it was unconquerable. He had an affinity
for the flamboyant, provided it wore the respect of centuries. This was such a real part of him that he could have
worn and carried into battle almost any relic that hangs
right now on any castle wall in England.

I learned many interesting things about him, what rested
him, what relieved him, what he enjoyed. In a sense the
weekends at Chequers Court did relax him, perhaps just in
time to escape a breakdown, but it was hard to believe a relaxing process was in force if one was in continuous contact
with the man. He worked all the time—only harder. But
there were interesting differences and astonishing results.

Physically, both for himself and as far as my own duties
of security were concerned, for me too, it was like transfer-
ring Ten Downing Street to the country. I found that when
he was enjoying brief intervals of leisure, his mind went
right on anyhow, one side of it being rested while the other
continued to fashion and invent.

There were very positive signs of this. One of these was
his great love of films. It was his greatest pleasure to have
private showings of films in his house. His next greatest
pleasure was music. It had to have a hummable tune and it
had to have a beat to it. It had to have fixed rhythms. He
liked marching music.

Chequers has a Great Hall. Churchill would turn on the
radio and find something to his liking, then begin marching
up and down the Great Hall in ecstatic disregard of the
household and the guests, shouting imaginary orders sometimes, making sharp parade-ground turns when he came to
the Hall's limits, then marching back. He often did this in a

brilliantly colored dressing gown. He had several such dressing gowns. All were garish and expensive. At this time his favorite songs included "Keep Right On to the End of the Road," "Poor Old Joe," "Home Sweet Home," and "Run Rabbit Run." He would make unusual concessions in his footwork so as not to break rhythm with tunes like "Home Sweet Home" which assuredly could never have been fashioned for marching in the first place, and manage to march to it anyhow.

Being a police officer and supposedly well acquainted with most of Winston's vagaries of mood, costume, and sudden enthusiasm, I could never afford to show surprise of any kind. And to show amusement would have been the crudest sort of disloyalty. There were times though, especially when he started popping about Chequers in a blue siren suit, looking so pneumatic as to suggest he might at any moment rise from the floor and sail around over his own acres, that I had to put brakes on my inner feelings, or just refuse to look. And when he would suddenly realize he had forgotten his teeth and send me running for them before he would be seen without them, I was glad for the exit.

There were times, after the air raids had started in earnest, when I have approached the Great Hall to find Mr. Churchill puffing on a cigar, marching correctly but contemplatively in a zouave-blue siren suit, looking like a big teddy bear after a big meal. Many times it has been hard for me to restrain my laughter at the serious look on Mr. Churchill's face. Suddenly he would become aware of my presence. Then he would look up and smile one of his charming, disarming and completely innocent smiles, the boyish look, the relaxed look that those of us who served him loved so much to see.

The discovery I made, after seeing this same march so many times, was that though he did not know or care what he looked like, his mind was free of its office fixtures and was concentrated most exclusively upon a single aspect of the war's prosecution. This way he engaged his problems one by one, and always had a complete answer for the Cabinet Members who came down each weekend to go over with him our latest emergency.

I made the discovery too that much the same sort of mental liberation was granted him when looking at the cinema, and seemingly the noisier and busier the story and the more compelling its plot, the more it seemed to relax his mind. I do not know how much support I might get from psychologists but I do know that Winston Churchill could sit still for two hours looking at a film, know in some detail what he'd looked at, but come away from the session with a brand-new, full-blown revolutionary war plan in his mind. He would then take it directly to one of his secretaries and set it down in detail while its images were as sharp edged and clean surfaced as shells on a sandbar.

Our visits to Chequers gave rise to many misgivings for the safety of the Prime Minister. Enemy bombers were now beginning to come over this spot in increasing numbers on their way from London to the midlands. I recall one occasion when a German bomber passed over, seemed to recognize the place or at least to want to con it once more, and turned and repassed it, then did the same thing from many different angles for a period of minutes. I now suppose that it was taking photographs of Winston's country house for future reference and possible attack. Not long after, it happened again, this time at night, and I went about the grounds with my gun out and a guarded torchlight in my other hand, poking its ray into hedges. Only this time I was sure the German was preparing for a run in on the target. He was low, his props were feathering, and he had illuminated half the county with slowly descending parachute flares. Their brilliance is startling and unsettling. The spread of illumination is both vast and unexpected and there is an astral and almost chilling quietude about the light itself and the haunted aspect taken on by the countryside when under such malign, impersonal scrutiny. Death is in it, and the ghostly false calm of the moment-just-before-death, the baleful silence, the preternatural ribbon of flight, the subtle sudden winking away, and the intensified silence after the bird of prey has visited, seen and plans its own time for striking.

These visits had of course been noted by many hundreds of people. I spoke to him of the advisability of sleeping from here on in the air raid shelter. All who talked over the matter with him, including his own Air Attaché, felt sure it presaged a series of planned attacks upon him. It was a form of assassination against which I could not protect him. Here he would have to do what he was told. Would he? Well, he said he'd cooperate the moment he felt it wise to do so. This of course meant that he would do what he pleased, which would be to stay outside and watch.

"Let me know when they start dropping the bombs," he said to one of his aides, a young officer of Marines who had attempted to reinforce my own cautions.

The next night the grounds of Chequers got well sprinkled by high raiders, bombs going off like intermittent explosions in a system of steam boilers. Scotland Yard had intercepted an interesting item that made this particular tactic of more than passing concern. The chances of killing Churchill by air bombs were not considered very good; no better than our chances of killing Hitler in the same way. It would be a happy luxury if it happened but nothing that could be counted upon or even hoped for. But a planned attack of dedicated raiders and suicide parachutists, landing in numbers on the grounds of Chequers and advancing to a position known to them and known to contain the person of Churchill at that time, such a plan was well within the cunning of the Germans and it had good chance of success. The bomb attack by high raiders would end, doing its damage, but leave the neighborhood of Chequers and the security about Churchill with a sense that the attack was over, when in actuality it was just about to start. It might be the signal that paratroops were at that precise moment descending upon our premises.

We were ready for this too. Every outbuilding at Chequers was manned and lethal. Every dovecote could spit death in any direction, and put a beam of light into the darkest recesses of shrubs and hedges and trees.

I waited in the dark. I have heard parachutists land in the trees at night, heard them cut their shrouds and climb down to earth. But they were not coming that night. We developed, nonetheless, as a result of that night, a new and secret "All Clear." Every officer assigned to the key job of keeping harm from Churchill was given a plot of earth to scrutinize and, for a given number of seconds at a given signal, this spot was illuminated. It would have been a hard system to crack, for there was no schedule in time. You had to be at your own spot, completely hidden, ready to deal with whatever the sudden brief light might uncover.

When I had been at Chequers before, I was younger not only in years but also in experience and confidence. I did not have quarters within the great house and had never thoroughly explored it. Now, with Winston Churchill in residence, I explored it in detail.

Many of England's old houses have some form of mystery about them. Or they have a mysterious legend. So did Chequers. It had a "room." It was located on the top floor of the house, in the oldest section. Did I mention that the original masonry, all of which is still standing, was set together in 1086? That is old, even in England! It was, and is, known as the Prison Room.

A famous court lady was held captive there for two years. The captive lady was Lady Mary Grey, sister of Lady Jane Grey. She was held here during the latter part of the sixteenth century, toward the end of the reign of Elizabeth. Her imprisonment was ordered by Queen Elizabeth when it appeared that Lady Mary, who was an heiress to the throne, was a threat to the Queen herself. In the Prison Room are still to be seen facsimiles of letters which she wrote, begging for her release. Leading from the Prison Room is a secret staircase which has a door opening on to the floor below and which also leads on down to the ground floor. The paneling of the rooms into which the staircase leads is craftily joined. Unless one knows precisely where to look, the way out cannot be quickly detected.

As the war stiffened and Hitler's hatred of Churchill grew ever more splenetic, we kept improving the safety factors and personnel around him. The small guard of local police officers at Chequers was inadequate. It originally was intended for little more than keeping intruders from the vicinity. This group was not supplanted, but it was supplemented by a continuous and self-relieving military guard. Churchill didn't mind it in London, even in his own various residences there, but he didn't like it at Chequers. It brought the war into his gardens and into his private living. It brought up the continuous minor irritation of passwords, codes, new passwords, identification problems, nervous challenges. It changed the atmosphere. It destroyed charm. It introduced suspicion, short temper, and occasional nonsense. But it was all necessary.

It became almost ludicrously impossible to get into the house. If we got a new sentry, for example, it was difficult sometimes for me to get in. Military security officers are hard men and have to be. One of their special duties is to travel about the country, materializing without warning in critical areas for the specific purpose of testing defenses. They try to outchallenge sentries, bulldoze guards, fool other security officers. They make many enemies but they also uncover dangerous weaknesses. We could not function in wartime without them.

On one occasion a major, by pure bluff, passed the sentry in the checkpoint nearest my own quarters and did so without even being challenged. Since I was in charge of security, I had advance knowledge of a possible attempt, but I was amazed to see it come off so slickly. But then, I had never before met anyone quite so slick as that major either. He was suave and urbane and seemed so instantly right in his surroundings that he was subconsciously catalogued by sentries as being okay. This major tried to enter the house itself and did so. Once having breached the house, he decided to see how many rooms he could enter and how many things he could touch before being challenged by the special guards who maintained security for the interior of the house and its occupants.

Inside the house he was challenged almost at once. His deliberately falsified papers were examined and found specious, but his penetration of the so-called "critical distance" was done with such ease—and he had not been there before to study locations—that greater protective measures were put in force. Police officers from London were deputized to take control with the guards at the entrance gates and passing points. No unclassified person ever escaped their vigilance during the whole of the war.

Guarding, when there is real and constant danger, is a strain on community tempers. During the war I had many opportunities to notice the attitude adopted by officers, and civilians too, toward guards at places all over the map of England. I could understand the state of mind of the sentries. They were always being bullied, by the people they challenged or by their own officers who had received severe complaints about them. On one occasion with Winston, we were traveling by car with the officer commanding a western stretch of English coast when we came to a road control that was under this same officer's command. The cars were stopped by sentries with fixed bayonets. A sergeant approached. The car in which we were riding not only belonged to the O.C. but his own flag was flying from the front of it. The officer jumped out and went after the sergeant, furious at being stopped. He rebuked the sergeant unmercifully for not recognizing the car on sight, then for not recognizing the flag, and finally for not recognizing himself, the Commanding Officer. The sergeant, though hurt by the tongue-whipping, stuck to the point and refused to permit us to pass until he had carefully gone over the credentials he forced us all to show. Mr. Churchill did a gallant thing then. He complimented the sergeant for his stubborn conscientiousness, and did so within the hearing of the O.C. Later, just to make his point sink in, he asked me to remind him to write a note of compliment to the sergeant on official stationery.

It is this kind of thing that has helped keep England together.

Increased security at Chequers changed the appearance of the place in addition to changing the domestic atmosphere of it. Every roof contained a nest of spotters, most of them in telephone or shortwave communication with observation locations from their own position clear on out to the Channel—as far north as Greenock and as close to the continental shelf as the Cinque Ports. We always had some advance warning before the bombs began to come down.

How did Churchill live from day to day at Chequers? Many people have asked me that. His weekends were alike as two peas. Our Friday arrivals, usually about four, were like small invasions of the House. There were always a carload or two of guests, Cabinet Members, Americans, European war leaders. Besides guests he needed three secretaries, two of whom were ladies; his personal assistant Commander C. R. Thompson (no kin of mine); a valet, one detective besides myself, two film operators, three chauffeurs, and extra London police for additional outside protection.

Mr. Churchill, upon arrival, would always first of all have his bath. He was as insistent about this as the famous tenor Caruso was reputed to have been. (He stopped our train in the middle of the Sudanese desert on one occasion and ordered hot water to be brought from the *engine's boiler!* And there, beside the tracks in a huge tub he'd seen in a goods car we were hauling, he'd bathed with half of Africa agape. "You would think they never saw nudity before.")

Bathed and refreshed, he would climb into his half comical and thoroughly practical siren suit. He wore this to dinner. He did not care what anyone else wore either and his dinner table was almost always the ultimate in incongruity of apparel. After dinner he would retire for a moment, then come back dressed in one of his gorgeous oriental dressing gowns. He always wore one of these during the film showings. I never saw an exception to this. At the conclusion of the showing, he would chat briefly with his guests, then separate himself from them and go to work, his London staff going on into the offices with him.

Usually he worked till 3 A.M., often till 4 A.M., sometimes clear through the night. He was awake at 8 A.M., never needing to be called. He barked for the newspapers which were always right outside his door. They were brought at once and curt "Good morning's" were exchanged. He read papers while he ate breakfast in silence. It was very dangerous to interrupt him during this period. Phones were cut off and important people who had made frantic efforts to get to him were sometimes, to their surprise and irritation, kept waiting till he had rung to have his breakfast service taken away. Then he shaved and bathed, but he did not dress yet. Official bulletins were brought in. He moved about from chair to chair, reading them. He lighted his first cigar, which presently went out. He would chew on it for an hour before realizing it was dead. He smoked few cigars, each one requiring relighting seven times on the average. He did not inhale the smoke, but blew it about in meditative balloons, often peering into them as if they were fish pools, or as if he might have dropped something of value into their center and were seeking to locate it.

Breakfast was a main meal to the Prime Minister. It consisted of ham, bacon or chipped beef (when meat was available), small mountains of toast under a cover, a pot of tea and a jug of milk with jam or jelly. He loved fish too and two or three mornings a week would have a good-sized sole. Prowling about, after bathing and shaving, and trying out one chair after another, often perching himself on the windowsill, he would read dispatches and mutter. Often, too, he'd return to bed, leaning against a wall of pillows that he kept plopping into more accommodating shapes. There was a bedtable before him and at each side a sorbo rubber pad for his elbows. Most of the morning he spent right there in bed, working. Here, too, he received his most important callers, and most of his heaviest decisions were taken with these men, under these conditions, in direct personal communication with them.

The news dispatches and communiques were brought to him in the same yellow box each morning. I carried it in one morning and, seeing his hands were occupied with something else, opened it for him and handed it to his bedside in this manner. I received his instant reprimand. "That box must be opened only by me, Thompson!" When he saw my chagrin, he softened matters at once by saying: "It is quite all right this time, since you were trying to help me, seeing my hands full. But you will know in future." He says these things only one time, and these solecisms are not repeated.

After his news reading and before his appointed callers begin to come in, he has his staff of secretaries come by, one by one. He gives each one a large amount of work, which they transcribe and type while he is talking to callers. This continues until about one o'clock. One of his secretaries has usually been kept in the room with him for half an hour or so, and at this time he dictates directly to the typewriter. This is for correspondence that is immediately outgoing. There is always a secretary within call, since his interviews sometimes require the sending of a quick message, reminder, or the re-emphasis of a matter not quickly enough taken care of.

An example of his impatience and his technique for getting work out of others with unparalleled dispatch occurred one morning while I was attending him. He needed some special information from the Admiralty. He asked me to telephone the Admiralty offices and get a Captain So-and-so. The captain was a super-conscientious naval officer, as proud of his four stripes as he was of his meticulousness in office matters. I handed the phone to Mr. Churchill when the captain was on. "Good morning, Captain. This is Winston Churchill. I want you to look up for me—" "I'll call you back first thing this afternoon, Mr. Churchill." "No, I'll wait," said Winston and he left the telephone open, immediately laying it down on the bed before the captain could say anything that Winston could hear. He grinned at me mischievously. While the Prime Minister went on working, the captain began to dig. He was soon back with what Churchill wanted. Three minutes. He thanked him and hung up, then grinned at me again. "They can always find it faster if they have to find it themselves." I never forgot this.

He could always cram into one day what no other man could do; what few other men could do in two days, or even three. He spared no one. Another occasion, comparable to the one above, had to do with Lord Halifax. This little exchange took place in my hearing upon our return from Paris, outside our plane at Hendon Aerodrome. It was dusk. We'd all had a gruelling four days in France, no sleep, and the tension of the trip over the Channel. We were all of us physically worn clear through, Halifax conspicuously so. Even Winston looked as if he was ready to give up, but he turned to the group and said: "We'll have a Cabinet meeting at ten o'clock tonight." Lord Halifax groaned. "We've had a most exhausting time, Winston. Cannot the Cabinet meeting be held tomorrow morning?" "Oh, yes. It has been tiring. To be sure it has. I'll postpone it." "Good," said Lord Halifax. "Till ten-thirty tonight," said Winston. "You may take the half-hour's rest."

Winston Churchill often acted impulsively but it would be wrong to think he ever acted capriciously. On many occasions during the first two years of the war, often right after a film showing, he would come down to the Great Hall locked up in deep thought of his own, then go suddenly and alone to a small table and play bagatelle. He would work seriously at this anything but serious game, trying for the highest possible score, and jotting down each result on a piece of paper with religious bookkeeping exactness. Callers seeing such action for the first time went away thinking it an odd caprice, and no doubt reporting it as such. But it was not. When he walked away quickly from large groups and did something alone with what very often appeared as spectacular and unnecessary brusqueness, it was to be alone with a problem until he could find his own answer to it. He always came back with one and laid it out thoroughly for those involved. And they always expected it. What they did not know was where Winston had got it. He had got it, often, right there over the game of bagatelle, or upstairs in the cinema room, or marching with crazy relentlessness up and down the Great Hall to the whispered consternation of the wife of a new British Cabinet Member on her first visit. Or sometimes, I positively believe, he reached right in and grabbed it raw and alive from the center of a billow of cigar smoke.

The war came out ahead in such meditations. Mrs. Churchill, poor beautiful lady, was secondary, as must be the wife of any famous public servant. I have often seen how little time a Prime Minister can have with his wife. At Ten Downing Street, work and sleep went on from day to day with far less relaxation than it ever did at Chequers or Chartwell. Actually Winston and his serene, beloved wife had precious little time together. I did not envy her her position. If other women in Great Britain did, they thought more of the honor than the price of it. "Clemmie" was of course vastly proud of her husband's achievements. She was sustained in another way too: her pride in his achievements was satisfied by witnessing and sharing the rare experience of seeing a great man fulfill his destiny; she saw it happening in their joint presence, rather than recorded and engraved at monument bases for the generations ahead.

This was going on while they were alive, not just something that was guaranteed to preserve his name after he passed, and she with him, into history. Mrs. Churchill knew this, and such moments and such hours as they did have together, or as they shared with small groups, were the more exquisite to her for this reason. A man can take some comfort in the knowledge that his name and work will survive and have meaning and use long after his death. Not so a woman. She wants all of her living to take place while she is herself alive, partaking of the many courses at the banquet table that can be laden in such plenitude only once. A woman would sooner, the world over, be loved when living than famous when dead. So it was here. One had a magnificent sense of the indestructibility of the immediate present whenever these two appeared together, and they felt it most of all.

While on this subject of Mr. Churchill's private life, many have shown curiosity about how he works out a speech, how he sets about writing it, whether he writes it or dictates it, how much help he gets. I am asked repeatedly: "Does Winston Churchill write his own speeches?" "Does he dictate them to a stenographer?" "Do they go directly into a typewriter?" and so on.

To the question "Does he write his own speeches?" the answer is a decided "Yes." He writes every word of his speeches. He moves about rooms, declaiming, changing sentence structures, asking for lines or whole paragraphs to be read back to him. Often he is looking down at jottings in his hand, thoughts put down previously and mentally studied over till the actual moments of speech creation have arrived. Putting a speech together is a desperately exacting task of composition for him.

From the clerical side of it, he dictates to either of his two personal secretaries using a typewriter. He allows shorthand to be used only when he is traveling by car. Sometimes speeches will take their first form in this way. He answers a great deal of his official mail while in motion, to and from Chequers or Chartwell, to and from the buildings of Parliament, to and from his London flat or residence—he has eight or nine now. Directives on general office matters are usually spun out quickly while he is in motion. All such work is transcribed as soon as the typist comes in contact with a typewriter.

When not in motion, his dictation is taken almost without exception, directly onto a typewriter. Special cases have been made for the type of machine he likes, and these are taken on journeys, long or short; different cases for plane, ship, or train.

He can stand any distraction except one: whistling. It sets up an almost psychiatric disturbance in him—immense, immediate, and irrational. I have seen him expostulate with boys on the street who were whistling as he passed and seen the look of them when they stared after him, wondering, rather sorrowfully, if it indeed could have been the great Winston Churchill who had done such an unexpected and uncalled for thing. I have seen people make whirling motions at their own temple, indicating their notion of the condition of the wheels that were spinning in Winston's head, then seen them catch themselves up in some horror for assigning such derelictions to the Prime Minister.

Working for Churchill, especially when in motion, is not at all easy. The movement of a train, not to mention the noise, does not make for smooth notetaking or smooth typing, and makes more difficult the exact reproduction of what he has said. Winston's delivery, from the secretary's point of view, is good. In cold terms of elocution, his enunciation, with that curiously sibilant pronunciation of some words, is not made any clearer when combined with the noise of a fast-moving train. Winston has a touch of Welsh in his speech too in that sounds formed within the buccal cavity often do not come directly out of the mouth off the end of the tongue, but leak briefly through the cheeks on the way. Anyone who has listened critically to Mr. Churchill in a broadcast has caught this. Any word commencing with a labial sound is likely to result in the Welsh overtone and aftereffect. One hears the same pleasing sound occasionally from the motion picture actor, Ray Milland, whose extractions are Welsh. Perhaps I heard so much of it from David Lloyd George and his friends and Welsh relatives in and around Criccieth that I am more conscious of it than others might be. But it's there. One need not be a phoneticist to pick it up.

Winston is never discourteous but always impatient. He will give an intelligible, if somewhat weary, repetition of words not distinguishable at the first hearing. One has to measure the probability of his impatience by the look and the sound of him. Many times a guess, however wild, is infinitely preferable to asking, "What did you say, sir?" Winston's impatience, without ever showing the least rudeness, can produce the most primitive wrath. It is hard to explain how the one can be so extreme without a suggestion of the presence of the other, but it is true.

He likes work typed, usually with two copies. With the necessary digital mechanics of typing, he has no patience. He is devoid of respect in this area. His secretaries suffer a good deal because of his appalling, almost childish, refusal to look at a typewriter, to see what is going on with it. It comes from his feeling that neither man nor circumstance has a right to impede or interrupt him. For example, anyone with any experience of typing knows that to insert innumerable carbons between sheets of crackling, flimsy paper, to slip them into a machine, wind it, remove them at the end of a page and, without pausing, insert another ordered set, requires a finesse obtained only with experience and foresight. Every English-speaking person knows this except the Prime Minister. He has no patience with the little delays this entails since typewriters have been used in government offices. He'll go to his grave having none either.

"Come on! Come on! What are you waiting for!" He'll fume and pace about between pages, in these trifling pauses, as if battle decisions hung on the interval. Just crackle these flimsies in process of reinsertion and he'll splutter worse than ever; worse than anything save whistling: "Don't fidget so with that paper! Stop it!"

Why does anyone take it? The answer is the same everywhere. Everyone who works for him, loves him. They would literally all die for him without a word. This is the truth.

Winston works himself without cessation. I have seen his secretaries, when waiting in rooms opposite the Cabinet Room, nod for sleep when in the midst of actual dictation his delay over a word or phrase permits them a moment without sound; seen them come to with a great shock to realize the Presence has started again and the secretary has missed the gist or even the whole first half of his resuming sentence. Look out then! He too is weary. He himself will sometimes be unable to keep his eyes open and countless times, on a security tour, I've entered the Cabinet Room or a study in the Ten Downing Annex at two or even three in the morning to find the Prime Minister and one of his secretaries on opposite sides of a table, both with weary eyes closed. My own opening and closing of the door would rouse them and they would shake and resume.

When Mr. Churchill decides to compose a speech, he usually gives his secretary good notice of it. She clears away all other work and settles before the typewriter. Sometimes Winston forges ahead with little apparent effort for many pages before inspiration seems to run out. On other occasions he will pace up and down the room, murmuring words and phrases over and over, trying them out on himself, before he is satisfied that the exact meaning has been put into words which cannot be misunderstood or misinterpreted. Warming to his subject, Mr. Churchill will even enter so completely into what he is dictating that tears will sometimes literally stream down his solemn face during the evolving of a particularly dramatic passage. All of Churchill's writings have measurable emotional content. Similarly, when composing some of his famous epigrams—the humorous ones—a wholly delighted expression will come over his face and he will chuckle at his own invention and look gleefully at his secretary to see if he is being adequately appreciated.

Churchill misses almost nothing. On one occasion early in the war, while still First Lord of the Admiralty, he was dictating a paper in a train concerning the *Scharnhorst* and *Gneisnau*. His unfortunate secretary, not being on familiar terms with these names, hesitated before typing them and gave the First Sea Lord, Sir Dudley Pound, a beseeching look. She omitted the names and went on with the following sentences, until the First Sea Lord stealthily slipped her a scrap of paper on which he had printed the two names. With a look of fervent gratitude she turned back the paper to insert them, but the action attracted the attention of Mr. Churchill who immediately wanted to know what was happening. Out it had to come! It called forth some scathing comments on her lack of spelling ability, very much undeserved at that time as the ships in question had only begun to steam into the picture.

When a speech has been dictated and typed in its first draft, Winston takes the typed sheets and goes over them carefully, word for word, erasing here and substituting there, until he can see no further cause for complaint. The whole is then retyped. This process is repeated two or three times. Finally it is put into what is known as "speech form." This consists of arranging the matter on octavo sheets of paper in what looks like a form of blank verse. Paragraphs, sentences and even phrases are separated to facilitate delivery when the time comes. And when it does come, he deviates hardly at all from the finished script.

Broadcasts are treated rather differently. The preparing of the subject matter takes much the same form, but the finished article is typed on quarto paper—though with similar "verses" and inset lines. He gives himself a few marginal stage directions, indicating where pauses and special emphases are to fall.

A habit of Mr. Churchill's which might well be the undoing of a secretary new to his work is that of asking at the end of each page of dictation for the number of words which have been written. This involves keeping a mental note of the number of lines to a page, with an approximate idea of the number of words to fill a line. As each page is finished, he will say: "How many?" and he will expect to be given an immediate answer.

Nothing is allowed to interrupt his train of thought when he is dictating. One summer evening in the country when he had opened wide the windows to let in the cool night air, a bat flew in. The room was large and it would be reasonable to suppose it could accommodate Mr. Churchill, his secretary and the invading bat. The secretary, however, found it difficult to concentrate on typing with a large bat diving about over her head. She was terribly afraid of bats anyhow, as are most women. Continued instinctive ducking on her part caused Mr. Churchill to ask her what was the matter. On its being explained to him, he said: "Surely you're not afraid of a bat, are you?" On being told bluntly that that was the exact trouble and no other, he replied grandly: "*I'll* protect you! Get on with your work!" She went on ducking while he went on dictating.

At various times during the war, mention has been made of Mr. Churchill's rest hour. He takes one every day. It is usually in the late afternoon or early evening. I have been asked whether he takes a nap in a chair, lies down on a settee or really goes to bed. The latter is the case. He undresses entirely and, contrary to many statements, does not wear pajamas. He gets into bed and, if the room is not completely dark, he covers his eyes with a black satin bandage, at least one of which I keep in my own possession at all times, to hand him wherever we might be. He will slip this bandage on in the back seat of a car and sleep hard for ten minutes or a full hour. He slips it on in planes.

As soon as Mr. Churchill's head touches a pillow, he is asleep. I was later to discover this was also true of President Roosevelt. Both men put all activity out of their minds and at once surrendered. With Winston he could be asleep before his last caller was out of his room. So if he wished for one hour's sleep, he did not need two hours in bed. He needed only the one hour, getting that amount without having to wait to drift off.

He has a special pillow and can at once tell his own if it becomes mixed up with many others. If sleeping in a moving car, after putting on the black band he will curl his head down into his chest like a hen and remain motionless to the journey's end. Many times he has remained asleep in the car for some minutes after arrival. We do not wake him unless something urgent requires his attention.

The Prime Minister has never forgotten how to shoot—either rifle or revolver. We set up an outdoor range at Chequers and to this he would frequently repair and fire a hundred rounds or so with his Mannlicher rifle, fifty rounds from his Colt .45, or an equal number from his .32 Webley Scott. He gets well on to the target with all three, but with the Colt Automatic he is absolutely deadly. In 1945, when he was seventy, Mr. Churchill took frequent target practice with me, or with both my colleague and me. There would be little chance for anyone who came within range of his gun. A gun is something he understands entirely. It never thinks back at you as does, for example, the rudderbar or stick of a plane in flight. A gun has one duty and does it at once. It is as dependable as the man firing it and gives instant and sensible answer to pressures properly applied. It never argues. But all other machinery argues and he is in constant warfare with it.

He distinguished himself many times during the war when he tested weapons. I have mentioned somewhere his accuracy with a U.S.A. carbine (a fine weapon), in company with General Eisenhower. Near the war's end, while practicing with me at outdoor targets, with officers of the guard in competition and firing an old Colt .45, only one of Churchill's bullets was on the fringe of the bullseye, the other nine being dead center. This target was taken down and marked by me and noted by those who were with him then. Later I had it officially entered and dated and it is now in the Chequers library.

But any sequence of movement requiring coordination was outside his skills. He was the worst driver in England and would have been its worst pilot. People stayed out of his way on the dance floor. But shooting and painting—occupations that took expertness of eye and steadiness of muscle but that were never at the mercy of timing and that never needed integrating with human or mechanical factors—at these he excelled.

One day, soon after taking over the rooms provided for him at Number Ten Annex, he issued an order to the whole British government against whistling in the corridors. Many times, in the midst of meetings, upon hearing whistling after the posting of his order, he has dispatched the person nearest him to fly outside and find and silence the culprit. I was accompanying him early one morning down King Charles Street. We were on our way from the Annex to Downing Street. A boy passed, whistling loudly and not too well. But he was a pleasant enough looking boy, and half saluted Winston by a lift of his eager brows as youngster passed statesman. "Stop that whistling!" Churchill thundered. "Whatever for?" the boy properly challenged. "It's a horrible noise!" "Then shut your ears!" the boy hurled back upon the astonished Prime Minister. The boy returned to his enjoyment full blast. We crossed the road into the Foreign Office Yard. I saw a slow smile break over Winston's face. He repeated the boy's words aloud to himself, and chuckled. Then he looked up at me. "Shut your ears," he said. "Shut your ears!"

Another "whistling" anecdote had to do with the Horse Guards. Every morning at eleven o'clock (ten o'clock on Sundays) to a fanfare of seventeenth century silver clarions, the King's Life Guard is mounted by one of the regiments of the Household Cavalry at the Horse Guards. To us in England it is familiar and expected and rather the right thing at that time. For here Charles II stabled his troop horses, and on the tilting yard behind, the Tudors held their tournaments. It is famous and beautiful. The clarions make a lovely blast, and there is a fine sound of hoofs. Winston was at work in bed, while all the orthodox sounds rose up to his room, leaving him undisturbed. Then some weak little sidewalk whistling also got up to him. This he heard. He began to roar to me and to his personal secretary. "Open that window!" he roared. She did so, trembling. "Now tell that damn fool to stop whistling!" She looked out, saw the majesty of the Horse Guards Parade. "You cannot interfere with a member of the public on the highway," she protested. To her astonishment, apart from some growling, the P.M. said no more.

On May 26, 1940, Boulogne fell to the Germans. Another terrible thing happened. King Leopold ordered his armies to capitulate. They did. Winston wept. Our flank was left exposed to the Germans. The Nazi commander realized he had our army, and part of the French army, in a trap. For some few days the fighting became extremely fierce. We flew over the agonies that were taking place below us at Calais. You could see hand-to-hand engagements. Though in this circumscribed single scrap only about four thousand troops were involved, including one thousand French, their defense of the town against four times that many Germans has become a short paragraph in that war's history. The Nazi commander demanded the surrender of the garrison. This reasonably proper request was treated, however, with unusual contempt. In continuing so stubbornly there, assistance was being indirectly given to our main army in their retreat toward the coast. Of the gallant defenders of Calais, only thirty survivors got away—twenty-one Britishers and nine French. The Navy got a boat in for them. The others died shooting.

At the end of May, the resistance of our main army cracked. It did not crack altogether or all in one place. That would be un-British. But we were doomed there. We knew it. They knew it in England. It is a terrible thing to be exhausted, to be thirsty, to be lost. Weariness is the great conqueror.

About a quarter of a million men reached the beaches of Dunkirk. Here they stood or sat or just stared while they were shot up and shot at by understandably gloating Germans. Germans always gloat over their winnings—and beg and bawl when they get hurt.

England knew in some detail the tragedy that was forming here. Most Englishmen, even though they had never been across the Channel themselves, could see the place where their countrymen stood; could hear the unspoken cry across the water. Then over the wireless, the call came. The call for ships of every sort, size and seaworthiness. To go to Dunkirk. There was not that night one man or woman in all England who would not willingly have given all he had or held dear for this chance to help or to perish trying. Most Englishmen live in a lifelong state of active skepticism and well-controlled irritability but they die well. Many were dying now.

By day and by night craft of every conceivable description set sail, with no protection from German divebombers, and put out for the Continent's coast. You know the story. There have been rescues before but there was never one like this. In four days we got off alive two hundred and fifteen thousand British and one hundred and twenty thousand French. But the Channel, for weeks, was choked with corpses—not infrequently the body of an English girl. Everybody did something for Dunkirk. Thirty thousand never found their way back. But among the fighting troops who did reach England, all who were unhurt or recovered from their wounds were rested, refitted, and back fighting within six weeks or less. Fliers who engaged the strafing Germans during those four days and five nights have told me they estimated there were seventeen thousand craft of one sort or another that got into the water. Many of them of course were in salt water for the first time.

While the story of Dunkirk was being engraved in history, we had to fly to Paris for emergency talks. The Germans had now formed an unbroken arc from Sedan to Abbeville. From the plane window, we looked down upon the masses of struggling French humanity: refugees hurrying away before the Germans with their sad possessions piled in carts, prams and on the backs of old men. It all seemed even more horrible than Dunkirk. It was the most pitiable spectacle I have ever seen of the living.

Winston turned to me: "How many do you think we have evacuated from Dunkirk?"

"I do not even know the number of troops we had in Belgium," I answered him. (Dunkirk's count was still untabulated.) Winston would never let a man go if he merely said he knew nothing; he'd make the man guess. He did this to me. And I guessed. "Fifty thousand," I said.

"Do you know, Thompson," he said, "I would have answered yesterday that we would be lucky if we got away safely twenty or thirty thousand."

"I hope it will be substantially more than that when we know the whole of it," I said.

He grinned then. "It is now ninety thousand." He sat back against the seat. "Back in England." He looked at the ceiling, then leaned out and peered down into France again. "And more landing every hour." We began to come down to land, in a very steep descent.

For the day and night we were in France, Winston did not sleep. He kept getting bulletins on Dunkirk. About four-fifths of the original British Expeditionary Force got back. The last to leave the coast was Lord Gort, the Commander-in-Chief. "The next time victory will be ours," he said. But the Germans were pouring through the rip they'd made after crossing the Meuse.

Our land army here was now smashed. It had lost all its equipment. The Germans were flying ahead, taking every French town in their way. They now controlled all the Channel ports. This is a terrible situation in a war, when you live on an island and try to fight on a mainland.

It was impossible to meet in Paris because of the proximity of the German army. The Supreme War Council met in a place called La Miguel. There were the usual exchanges of greeting and the now almost comical announcement to the press that we were all resolved to pursue a policy of the closest possible concord, hold to it through the present struggle and emerge with a complete victory behind us. I did not believe they meant it then. They did not look it. They looked licked and sick: Marshal Pétain, General Weygand, Reynaud, and Admiral Darlan (who was to be assassinated on the Christmas Eve coming).

The meeting was held in a large château, quite pretty. Germans had been parachuting into the territory. My orders were to stand within touching distance of Churchill. He would occasionally get fearfully sick of me—who can blame him?—but we had to bear each other. And I can firmly tell you that there was many a moment when I could have celebrated being away from the Old Man, the dignity of time and my own gathering years now permitting this revelation.

I was struck by the fact that Pétain sat in a side room far from the others, a long distance from the room being used as the Council Chamber. Mostly, too, Pétain walked in the grounds during discussions, paying no attention to them. From time to time M. Reynaud would come from the Council Chamber and converse very earnestly with the Marshal, then rush back into the meeting again. Pétain appeared to me an unwilling participant in the talks. I was surprised, later, to read that he had been present during all the talks when he had really been absent.

Late that afternoon word came that Italy had chosen that day and hour—when our defeat seemed assured—to declare war on Great Britain and France. We were indeed beset by difficulties everywhere. The evacuation of Norway was in progress and not going well. France wanted to get out of the war, and who could blame her bleeding men, lost children and worn-out women? France has borne a lot. Too much.

Yet Mr. Churchill was hourly putting all he had in ingenuity, human speech, exhortation, in one meeting after another of increasing tension and expanding despair, to keep France in the war. He searched every means of his mind and experience that would enable them to carry on.

We flew back and forth often these days. On the 13th of June we flew to Tours, and came down in the descent that now invariably brought the haunted faces of refugees fleeing south, south—forever south. How they hated everything upon this earth and the slime of the German most of all! You could see hatred everywhere. It was so raw then and there that I knew it would never heal. It won't either.

The hatred in the face of a French duchess seemed both articulate and lethal. We had landed, and somehow a meal had been procured in a local restaurant. I could not eat any food at all. Refugee faces peered in at us. I put down my spoon and stood near Churchill, waiting for the others. They had no more appetite than I. Torrential rain was falling outside. It was not cold but it was unbearably depressing. Then I saw the face. She was standing, waiting in the courtyard. She had no gun (though we found a knife on her person later). You could look into her eyes and tell two things: that she was a killer and that she was after Churchill. I stood where I could watch her but where she would never notice me. I drew my gun and nonchalantly moved down upon her in the courtyard. All she realized was that I was not Churchill. She ignored me. Churchill did not know he was in danger. He never knows from us—almost never. For a duchess she could surely move. She seemed to go through the air after him. I caught her and silenced her hysterics. She was certain this was the Englishman who was responsible for the present condition of France. I have never been so rough with a woman since the suffragettes in World War I.

We got to the aerodrome and took off again for England. There was a sea mist very close to the surface but it was bright above. We felt alone and safe, but a moment after I had relaxed we went into a steep dive that flung Winston into the back of the seat. A German Heinkel had swept in near us. Our pilot dove, a terribly dangerous maneuver but the only one possible. The Heinkel dove with us, shooting. We got down into the sea mist. This was worst of all. Twice through the fog I saw the spars and slatting sails of fishing boats. The Heinkel let go a burst at two fishing boats as we flattened out together, then we lost each other in the ground fog that had blown to sea. The steep dive and the gamble that we wouldn't crack up, though we kept kissing the wave-tops, was all that saved us on that trip. It was an odd feeling. Then I knew if we hit something we'd never know it anyhow, and out of an almost passionate exhaustion and a deep, accumulated fury at our total circumstance, I went sound asleep right there in all that roar and mess.

That night, back in London, Churchill was to get a great and sudden lift over the flashed words of President Roosevelt accusing Italy of "striking the dagger into the back of his neighbor."

This lift of spirit lasted less than two days. The most dreaded thing of all then, inexorably, happened. Winston kept in constant touch with Reynaud. And Reynaud flew often to England where they would meet at Admiralty House. But his position with the French government was at an end. On the 16th of June he quit. Marshal Pétain took over.

That day was fateful for France. Disaster was now inevitable. Churchill told me to arm well; told me he was well armed. We were to take a very special and secret journey. We were to travel by destroyer, by submarine, and by airplane. Our takeoff point was conventional enough: Waterloo Station. I had been in it over a thousand times.

Our train was waiting. It looked innocent enough. I went into our compartment, poking about its meager accommodations, and then declared it secure for him. He came in. He sat down immediately and took a deep breath. He would sleep now for a few moments. I stood in the doorway. A courier rushed up. He had a small folding dispatch case. He showed his identifications, including new signals and password. He answered challenge correctly. I took him in to Churchill who opened the message.

This tireless, exhausted, unbelievable man wept for a moment—as if it were the one disappointment too many or the one final, destroying blow—then summoned me off the train with a jerk of his head.

Pétain was at that very instant asking the Germans for an armistice. This was the blow beyond bearing.

We drove back to Downing Street. He flashed word to the French government that there was no release from treaty obligations sacredly drawn with us and that the French fleet had to be sent to a British port. During the night we got sputtering and uncertain assurances from the French on this point.

Of course it was hard for the French to surrender their fleet to the British, or to anchor it suddenly in waters safe to us, then face the wrath of the Germans when laying down their arms to them.

The period of waiting which followed this was a cruel strain on Churchill, a strain on all. You will now recall that Winston Churchill had a plan then (and to this day insists it is sensible—if not the only ultimate scheme of salvation that mankind has left), a plan whereby Frenchmen and Englishmen would become as *one nation*, and in which the French army, navy and air force should make their way with all possible speed to North Africa and there carry on the fight. These were more than frantic jugglings and desperate improvisations churned up when the cauldron started to boil over. They were revolutionary ideas that had great practical sense, and they were generated in his mind many months before the first shot. Long before Poland in fact.

What an immense idea it would have been! Just one example of what it would have salvaged: if the Churchill plan had been put into operation, we should never have lost control of the Mediterranean.

France fell. On June 18th, Mr. Churchill dealt with this catastrophe in the House of Commons. He also laid the British Empire on the line before all the world. He said the Empire would come what may, continue the fight to the end; to the last drop of blood and to the last shilling. He repeated that if final victory should reward these efforts and these risks, the French people would share in this victory and their full freedom would be restored to them. He included also all the countries that had been overrun by the Nazis.

He reminded his listeners that now that the battle of France was over, the battle of Britain was about to commence, and he finished with these words:

"Let us therefore brace ourselves to our duties, and so bear ourselves that if the British Empire and its Commonwealth last for a thousand years, men will say: 'This was their finest hour.'"

This shook and thrilled the Island. Every Englishman knew that we now stood alone against the might of Germany. It gave us all a composed confidence, and a dreadfully fatalistic acceptance of attack, invasion, and death.

On June 21 the French plenipotentiaries were received by the Fuhrer in the same railway carriage in which Marshal Foch had dictated terms of armistice to the Germans in 1918. It is simple to imagine the humiliation of the French, that day in the forest of Compiegne, sitting in this railway carriage.

This was Hitler's greatest instant of triumph. It was well photographed, as you remember—even to the exultant detail of Hitler dancing his little jig when he could repress his jubilation no longer. It was very close to funny, except for the dead behind him and those yet to die—and the pervasive insanity this gesture memorialized.

France was broken. The terms had to be accepted. By July 24, when Italy also signed an armistice with France, the war in the West was proclaimed by Hitler to be at an end.

If this was Hitler's greatest triumph of the war, it was also the forerunner of one of his many mistakes. Out of the debris arose General de Gaulle (whom Churchill could never endure) with his Free French Movement to band together loyal Frenchmen everywhere. I do not believe anyone could stand de Gaulle but I am also very certain that he was a real man.

There remained the enigma of the French fleet. We got no satisfactory answer from the French government. Very much against our will and tradition we were forced to take steps in various ports—Oran especially—to prevent parts of the French fleet falling into the hands of the enemy. To me, this is still the one great dilemma. France knew we had to do it yet never forgave us. It makes me ill to think of it. It is most painful to write it. Churchill and I were there at the site of this wreckage only a few weeks after we had shelled and destroyed some of the finest units in the French navy. Many died. I expected repeated attempts on Churchill's life and we were heavily prepared for it.

I shall not angle this to what might be construed as the British side, but the instance of Bordeaux is worth citing here. Before we shelled the French fleet, it was clear to all military and naval leaders in Britain that the French, to gain favor with their German masters, were assisting the latter much to our disadvantage. In Bordeaux there were four hundred German pilots—prisoners of war. They had been shot down by the Royal Air Force, picked up and interned. Because they were our rightful prisoners, their being returned to us was part of the agreement between Churchill and the French government. Following the change in this government, these German fliers were returned to Germany, not to us. All of them were absorbed into the Goering arm that within a few days began to knock down our cities.

No professional warrior would object to the Germans' interest in securing a great fleet—and the French fleet was in every sense a great one—from a captured nation and using it against an enemy. Hitler would have turned French naval guns on the British Isles. He'd have held pistols to the heads of the French if he couldn't get the guns fired any other way. Everyone knew this. There was only one thing to do when the French refused to surrender their fleet or to take it out of Hitler's reach and scuttle it: immobilize the ships. Decommission them. Silence their guns. Sink them. Burn them. Deactiveate them by whatever means there were.

The French returned our fire. (We, I am sure, under the same conditions, would have returned theirs.) So we steamed in close and did a thorough job.

But there was no shame in any of this action, only an unutterable pity.

There were many instances like Bordeaux that fed our fears, examples that made it evident that the French nationals were interpreting their obedience to Marshal Pètain in an actively anti-British way. Corsica was another, not unlike Bordeaux. So was the token opposition in Madagascar.

Germany was feeling its first real pinch through the loss of many of her experienced pilots, so France's action in regard to the prisoner pilots in Bordeaux was of enormous benefit to Hitler. Hitler's invasion barges were appearing in rapidly growing cluster across the Channel from the Cinque Ports. We knew we were in for it. Russia jumped in here, demanding Roumania return Bessarabia and Bukovina and the territory was ceded without bloodshed, almost without protest.

I went with Churchill to Harwich on June 26 to guard him during his inspecton of our defenses against German invasion. A week later, July 4 in my notebook, Mr. Churchill announced with sincere regret, and without any mitigation, the true facts in regard to our shelling of the various French men-o'-war. He detailed to the ton the damage we had inflicted. There was grief everywhere. We had never before been called upon to fire on our own Allies. Pètain of course broke with us in consequence.

The one great irony of the Battle of Oran was that the biggest ship we destroyed there was the twenty-six-thousand-ton *Dunkirk*.

At the end of Churchill's report of all this sad news to his Cabinet and to the House of Commons, we came back in the darkness. It was quite hot. There were planes up. Churchill said nothing. My mind went over the crush of events through which we had just now passed. The list was staggering:

German armies had invaded Belgium and Holland. They had fired Rotterdam. Queen Wilhelmina had fled her throne. The Dutch army had capitulated. The Germans had reached the English Channel at Abbeville. Brussels and Boulogne had fallen. Four hundred thousand British and French had been stranded helpless at Dunkirk. Italy had declared war on us. Verdun had been captured. Paris had been evacuated by the French, then occupied by Nazis. Pétain had replaced Reynaud and asked the Germans for an armistice. General de Gaulle represented the only resistance France had to offer. The French scuttled some of their ships at Toulon. We ruined most of the rest of her navy in North Africa. Pétain set up a government at Vichy that broke with us. England had no allies and no sign of allies. We were standing by, expecting invasion and not ready for it. Laval was designated as Pétain's deputy.

All these staggering blows had struck Churchill when he had not yet been Prime Minister for eight weeks.

Hitler began to bomb England severely in the early part of August. London was getting hit harder and oftener. What was the British reaction to all this? I think it was astonishment, first of all. Then, in turn, apprehension, bitterness, and anger. We thought, somewhat naïvely, that service establishments would be hard hit, and factories of all kinds. But it was hard for the British mind to get used to the German purpose: that this was to be very indiscriminate going from the start. We had fewer planes and fewer pilots, but the quality we had of both was better than the Germans. You could stand in a city square and merely look into the sky and watch the relative skills of battling fliers in performance. We were inflicting devastating losses upon their planes and their flying personnel.

Meantime they were smashing up England.

The damage being done upon our homes and places of business and means of domestic transport brought a sharp focus upon that force still called the Local Defense Volunteers. Soon they were called the Home Guard.

This body of men now numbered one million. There were many veterans of World War I among them. There was a temptation to scoff at them. Nothing infuriated Winston more. He would lash anyone who raised a voice against this guard, grotesque and ancient though some of its elements surely looked. "Do not scoff at the Home Guard!" he would snarl. "They may be the means of saving this country!"

One day, reports came to us that scores of hundreds of dead bodies of uniformed Germans, some of them badly burned, were washing up on beaches up and down our eastern coast and clear down to the Cinque Ports. I am certain their barges took off on many more occasions than this. And we had a system that was devised to convert, without warning, great areas of the Channel waters to fire by floating huge stores of gasoline to the surface and igniting these areas by remote electric contact if the Germans, in large numbers, penetrated this far in an invasion attempt. Much of this is still secret.

Under heavy guard we took Winston Churchill to a secret aerodrome in the southwest of England where he was shown the Stirling bomber and the Typhoon and Whirlwind fighters. They performed wonderfully, and from that day production went ahead. They since have more than proved their worth. My son Fred made forty-two successful flights in a Stirling as a Pathfinder, over German or enemy-occupied territory. He did not come back from the forty-third.

Germany kept us informed, day and night, of what we were in for: that London would be wiped out, ports and harbors blasted and rendered useless. It looked not only as if they *might* do it; it looked as if they *were* doing it. The damage from daylight attacks on the London docks was awful to see. The attack on this dock area was of course a legitimate war target but it hit us in our shipping at a time when it seemed about all we had left. Great damage to foodstuffs was caused. The fires were often enormous, but what was even more arresting and defeating was that they were so numerous. There were just too many to put out. They would go on burning for days. Then another smash would start them all again. Picture for yourself the firemen, many of whom had never fought fires before, spraying water on buildings while the fumes of pepper, rum, paint, and burning grain filled their nostrils.

Winston would stand with them, cursing and sweating and looking into the sky.

Hitler made a mistake in failing to reckon with the RAF. Goering kept bragging that the German planes and pilots were not only more numerous than ours, which was true, but that they were superior to ours, which was untrue. Incoming records began to show this statistically.

The Battle of Britain lasted from August, 1940 to October. In that time our pilots destroyed over 2,300 German planes. We lost three hundred pilots killed in the same period and the same number wounded.

Almost daily, in ever-increasing numbers, dive bombers and bombers, escorted by fighters, attacked this country, with London the prime target. They were met each time, usually well out over the Channel, by intercepting fighters who engaged them with the utmost vigor. Often they would fight to their last round, then land and refuel quickly and resume the battle.

An air attack over your own city is a most dramatic thing. And in a strange way, it is also spiritually moving to a high degree. Owing to the frequent approach of hostile aircraft at all times now, watchers were posted on building tops to give warning. Churchill named these watchers "Jim Crows." The name stuck throughout the war.

At the beginning of the Battle of Britain, on hearing the Alert, the Prime Minister would carry on his work and even when the bell was rung he ignored every request to go into the air raid shelter.

He hated to be shut in. Often with the guns going and the enemy overhead, he would walk into the garden at Number Ten, wearing his steel helmet. Sometimes, when it would slide over his eyes as he was trying to watch the sky, he would send the thing scaling into a hedge. He also ignored the cigar rule. In fact, the Prime Minister ignored anything that he wanted to ignore.

However, he was typical of thousands of English men and women, whose interest and excitement in what was going on was infinitely greater than their fear of what might happen to them as individuals. I am sure Churchill would never have entered a shelter at any time during the whole war but for the fact that those around him, sharing his dislike for confinement, could hardly be expected to take shelter when the Prime Minister felt it to be so poor an idea as not to bother about it. Yet he very much enjoyed herding masses of people into the underground entrances. It satisfied his patriarchal feelings of responsibility to them, although they just wanted to watch too—and so much the better the fun if they could do so alongside the Old Man. And if he insisted on their going down to safety, they did so with reluctance, no more deceived by his boyish method than they were grateful for protection they didn't want.

As time went on, his contempt for the bombing became extreme. It grew quickly, in fact it grew till it became absolute. Then he was most difficult indeed. He is a heavy man and hard to throw around, though this was many times necessary. He and his staff would carry on, working either in his bedroom or in the Cabinet Room on the ground floor.

During the days of the colossal air battle, Mr. Churchill did not refrain from visiting the dangerous areas or those that had been plastered with bombs. Sometimes in standing at the edge of a crater, surrounded by the intense devastation of a whole block or cluster of homes and shops, he would stare and talk, chatting with survivors, listening to their recounting of what had happened to them. And he would silently and without any shame or embarrassment weep without speaking and for many minutes.

We went to Dover and Ramsgate. While at Dover Castle an Alert sounded and from the cliffside we could see the approach of the German bombers and the resulting clash when our fighters attacked. The battle went on over our heads for several moments. During the fighting, dodging and shooting, two German planes came down into the sea, perhaps half a mile from where we stood and watched. It thrilled us all to see the enemy in flames, hurtling down at terrific speed, to meet the rock-hard sea with a splash, a roar, a hiss and a fountain of exploding waters.

Within a matter of seconds, three small RAF sea rescue launches put to sea and darted out of the harbor to pick up the pilots who had bailed out. They could be seen drifting away from the land, toward rougher water far from shore. Contrary to our methods of sea rescue work of bailed out pilots, the Germans used rafts supplied with all kinds of food and first aid material, the pilot having to reach the raft by his own effort, although German rescue planes, painted white with Red Cross markings on them, patrolled up and down, supposedly to assist the pilots to find these rafts.

One would wish to be able to record a single fine strain of nobility or humanity in the Germans. I cannot do so. It is not there. It is commonly known that the Germans have no respect for such emblems as the Red Cross. During the course of this same tour with Churchill in the southeast, we were able to examine one of these planes which had been captured by us while patrolling the Channel. It was fitted with radio and was in actual fact acting as a reconnaissance aircraft, the logbook, found intact, showing her duty.

Driving from Dover to Ramsgate, we saw a fighter plane shot down and Churchill immediately asked our driver to take us as close to the point where it would crash as we could get. We arrived at the spot. Churchill jumped out and proceeded on foot, with me at his side. This was an unnecessary risk, as the Germans did a great deal of strafing and always shot off whatever they still had aboard before scooting for home again. Firemen had arrived just before us. Flames were shooting up. We had not been able to determine whether it was a German fighter or one of our own.

"I hope to God it isn't a British plane!" Churchill remarked. He walked right up to the blazing craft. To the relief of us all, we found it was a German and that the pilot had bailed out.

We went on to Ramsgate. The raiders had done a good job there. It was badly smashed up. A restaurant had been one of the places hit. Mr. Churchill, accompanied by Sir Kingsley Wood, Chancellor of the Exchequer, entered the premises. The Prime Minister spoke for some time to the proprietor, who was not badly hurt. But he told Winston that he had lost everything when his place of business had been destroyed. On leaving the scene Mr. Churchill turned to Sir Kingsley, saying: "We must arrange for compensation for shopkeepers in cases like this. Will you work out a scheme? We must help them. We must help them all. This man has lost his livelihood." This was later done upon our return to London.

An Alert sounded as we stood there. The major of Ramsgate urged the party to descend into Ramsgate's famous air raid shelter. It is huge and unbelievable—cool, and a bit eerie. It is cut into the chalk under the town.

Before we entered the tunnel, Mr. Churchill lighted a cigar and hung his steel helmet on his hip. He was told at the entrance he might not smoke in the shelter. A number of men were waiting to go into the shelter and one of them, on hearing the request that the Prime Minister not carry in a lighted cigar, asked for and was given the cigar much to his delight. The raid continued but the man stood happily above, puffing a fine cigar.

The Ramsgate population seemed familiar with its situation. Some were standing in groups chatting; others reading under fair light. A local newsboy, who did not consider that the Alert should seriously interfere with his job in life, went along the tunnel shouting "Paper!" The boy recognized Mr. Churchill and nudged the famous man in the flank. Churchill turned, a bit surprised at such familiarity. Then he saw a newsboy with a fresh paper. Winston cannot resist newspapers. He gave the boy a two-shilling piece.

From Ramsgate we went on to Manston Aerodrome. Great damage had been done there. Our planes could still take off and descend here but all about was the litter of crashed Germans. It was comforting to see the evidence of the toll our men had taken of the invader.

The conversations which Winston had here indicated that in the judgment of those in command of our defenses against air attack in the Battle of Britain, the Germans were now very close to their peak efficiency and that if we could hang on, even a few days more, they would pass this peak and the climb down would begin, whereas we in turn would begin to improve our own position. The crisis was just ahead.

The days of air battle continued with our Air Force unceasingly taking toll of the enemy all over the south of England. One day we traveled to Fighter Command where we were to follow an air attack which was expected to be made that day.

Shortly after we arrived, a large force of German aircraft commenced their journey from the Continent toward England. We were able to follow on animated maps with mechanically operated plane models the approaching bombers and their escort; we could see too our own fighters going in for the attack. The fight started in the Channel, continued on to and over London, then back to the French coast. Mrs. Churchill was present with us on this occasion. She was able to listen to our pilots—to hear their actual voices—as they went in to attack. This day was our greatest, from the point of view of destruction of Germans. We shot down 185 in a single day. We never knocked down that many again. But we never quite had opportunity, for this day, as predicted, marked the high point of German daylight raiding. We hadn't won the Battle of Britain. But we had survived it. And as we had weakened the Germans in the air, we had been getting stronger day by day.

Churchill's tribute to British fliers followed soon after we got back:

"The gratitude of every home in our Island, in our Empire, and indeed throughout the world, except in the abodes of the guilty, goes out to the British airmen who, undaunted by odds, unwearied in their constant challenge and mortal danger, are turning the tide of the world war by their prowess and by their devotion.

"Never in the field of human conflict was so much owed by so many to so few."

It was August 20, 1940.

Germany's failure to crush us by daring daylight raids prompted Hitler's nighttime blitz. It was a gambler's last throw to smash the main cities and towns of this country, preparatory to invasion. It nearly worked, too.

For some nights before the actual night bombing commenced, enemy planes had flown over London for reconnaissance purposes and began to establish a certain value as nuisance raiders. I do not believe we were prepared, however, for the intensity of the bombing of London proper. Early in September the bombing schedule got very heavy. It put a terrible burden upon our population and of course just that much more increased the load of the Prime Minister. As for myself, it multiplied my hours of duty while reducing my periods of rest. I always had to be on hand. I had absolutely no life of my own from then on, not even a game of darts if I could have found the time to spare.

Mr. Churchill did not alter his mode of living in any way. He carried on until early morning every night despite the continual raiding. From a security point of view my presence was as mandatory as it would be at any other time for a Prime Minister, but I also had to have ready all his gear —helmet and the more or less complex but neatly boxed respirator apparatus—in case of emergency. He hated all this fuss but it was a Scotland Yard order as well as a government order. I caught him making faces at these instruments of mercy and survival one time, when he pretended to be familiarizing himself with their values.

I announced to the authorities that in my opinion Number Ten was a deathtrap. If it were to take a direct hit, all within would likely perish. On two occasions bombs hit close enough to emphasize my estimate. One hit the Treasury, just at the back of Ten Downing Street. The house shook like a struck toy. The walls split open clear up the east side. Glass flew. Furniture toppled. Cupboards flew open and dishes flew out. Beds rolled about. Highboys crashed over on their faces.

One of these hits occurred when the Prime Minister was dining in a basement room with Sir Archibald Sinclair, Mr. Oliver Lyttelton, and Lord Brabazon. During the dinner another bomb fell near by. Mr. Churchill left his guests. He went out to the kitchen and ordered the staff there to go to the shelter. Shortly another hit occurred between the Treasury and Number Ten. This destroyed the kitchen only fifteen or twenty seconds after he had cleared it. It lifted the kitchen floor and flattened it against the kitchen wall. It crushed everything in between, including the stoves and pantry boxes. It smashed an army hut next to us, but fortunately no one was in the hut.

Because my opinion of Number Ten Downing Street as a bad security risk for the Prime Minister prevailed, it was thought wise he should repair each night at the sound of sirens to a safer building. But I could never get him to move until the guns had started to fire. Then with the utmost disregard for his personal safety, he'd walk round part of St. James Park until he reached the spot we were headed for. It was not a long trek, but after all, one step forward in the wrong place at the wrong time might have meant the end of him.

On one occasion we had only been in the building a few seconds when we were startled by the terrific explosion of a bomb dropping close by. This hit was as close as the one that had demolished the Prime Minister's kitchen but the bomb was of greater destructive force. The concussion sent us both reeling against the wall, myself continuing to whirl until I crashed into a clothes locker. On going outside it was seen that a bomb—a thousand-pounder—had been dropped on the exact spot over which we had passed as we turned to make entrance to the building.

This building was then being used both as an office and sleeping quarters by the Prime Minister.

Persistent attempts were made after this to get Winston to do his night work in the shelter. He eventually accepted the offer of the railway authorities to use their offices, more than one hundred feet below the surface in the Down Street Tube Station.

There was a raid every night. Many nights there were two raids. Sometimes the attacks would be so sustained or would come with such rapid succession that we would withstand a whole night of attack without letup. Fires burned everywhere. The sound of screaming splitting a sudden, strange silence was a sound that never left me after those nights; of children burning; the piteous crying of the trapped and choking; the loud, inspiriting cry of the rescuers as they hurried to haul away and clear away. And there was much quiet death everywhere and citizens blown or burned into dust as if they had never been. Fourteen thousand civilian residents of the city of London died that fall in the German raids, most of them crushed or burned to death.

The plan to break us was a well-worked-out plan. Although the people of London stood up to it magnificently, there was always the possibility that, with the day bombings following the night raids, the increasing difficulties in obtaining food and pure drinking water, the nearly unbearable discomfort of broken sleep, English morale might crack. Anybody would crack sooner or later under what we were compelled to take.

But there were enough good things happening and enough gratifying retaliations going on to help us through the worst of it. The Royal Air Force began making raids on all the continental ports we could reach and the knowledge that the most painful distresses were being rained down upon the heads of the Germans in Antwerp, Ostend, Calais, and Dunkirk gave the average worker in London a fine lift. We kept burning quantities of expensive equipment which Hitler had planned using against us. We ruined many of the German High Command's plans and points of embarkation. There were unmistakable signs that the cross-Channel invasion was just about ready to be launched when our Air Force began to strike the congested center of its apparatus.

This news was put on the wireless of course. And the British had the priceless advantage of knowing that what they were listening to was the truth. They had stood up under some shattering truths of the conditions against them. Now, this was better. We could somewhat turn around.

The fall weather began to favor us, as we knew it would, and as the Germans had not sufficiently gauged. Another lift came from the visible presence on corner after corner all about the London area of large numbers of guns. They were of course constantly manned, and always at first warning, their muzzles were cranked to the enemy. Once the Germans appeared, a terrific barrage was put up against the raiders. The din was appalling, but there is nothing Churchill loves like a din. This had a heartening effect upon the whole people.

We had yet to go through the worst but I think now we knew this and somehow felt we could survive it. The United States was paying attention to what was going on and though her help seemed far away, it was assurance of strength. The Stimson-Layton Agreement was of great physical assistance to the technical directors of our war effort, the agreement providing for standardization of military weapons and equipment of all kinds, as well as a general policy of pooling our secrets with those of the American military powers and exchanging proven working formulas for arms production.

Wherever they saw him, people cheered the Prime Minister spontaneously. On leaving London by train one morning from Holborn Viaduct Station, people rushed to his side. "Thank God for the guns!" "Give 'em hell!" We had been hit. Now we were hitting back.

I have mentioned Mr. Churchill's disregard for danger. In walking through the streets of London, when raids were at their very height, it was surely bad. I am very hard to frighten and was this way before my training at Scotland Yard made it altogether illegal, but Winston skipped me about into some of the awfulest nightmares that man's ingenuity for noise and destruction could fashion. One evening in October I received an order from the Old Man to go visit gun sites in and around London. For journeys such as this an armored car had been put at his disposal. He hated this car and the cumbersomeness of it. But he was requested to use it.

On this particular night we started off toward Hammer-smith. Bombs began to come down. Shrapnel fell. Fragments peppered our car. One of them smashed in our bonnet. On reaching the bridge at Hammersmith flares could be seen coming down ahead of us. Flares disturb me for bombs follow flares. A string of them floated down into the road in front of us. "Carry on," said Churchill as the driver half turned. The driver didn't want his own head blown off either. Somehow I knew then that we were going to en-counter serious trouble. The bombs that we expected after the flares came down in one of the most generous showers I can recall, an almost profligate display. They knocked out the Barnes Railway Station. In a moment we passed this sta-tion, burning hard. We got on to Richmond Park, which was to be our first call. A number of staff officers with their cars awaited us there. The Germans appeared in greater numbers in the sky. While we watched, one of the Germans was hit by one of the guns before us. We watched it break up, a wing snapping clear of the fuselage, and saw it streak to earth.

Watching the city burn that night put the images in Win-ston's mind which England heard only a few days later in these phrases, when he took personal notice of Hitler:

"This wicked man, the repository and embodiment of many forms of soul-destroying hatred; this monstrous prod-uct of former wrongs and shame, has now resolved to try and break our famous island race by a process of indiscrimi-nate slaughter and destruction.

"What he has done is to kindle a fire in British hearts, here and all over the world, which will grow long after all traces of the conflagration he has caused in London have been re-moved."

It was September 11.

Churchill was fascinated at the sight of the gun crews in action. On leaving, seeing that the other officials who were to accompany him were traveling in ordinary cars, he re-fused to get back in his armored car. "I will take the same chance as the rest." Then he put on his stubborn look. But he had tempted Providence.

Our nest gun site was Caterham. A bomb fell in a field we were passing. It lifted all four wheels of the car from the road surface and we ran on two wheels for many yards be-fore rocking back. No one seemed bothered. Winston said,

"That was a near one, Thompson. It must have been my beef that kept the car down." We got to the Number Ten Annex uneventfully. The Prime Minister was standing watching the explosion of shells and bombs, while he and the Sir John Anderson discussed how to improve the technical use of searchlights. There are double doors here at the Annex entrance. One of them was closed. Mr. Churchill was standing in front of Sir John in the open part when I heard something coming through the air toward us that sounded like Lucifer's chariots. In such circumstances I disregard protocol. One does not ask if one may have this dance, as it were. It was a huge bomb and its premonitory whistling was truly frightening. It seemed to be coming dead on us. And of course you cannot see.

Mr. Churchill was also interested in this auditory phenomenon and at that moment it struck the railings opposite. At the same moment I grabbed Churchill with all my strength and swung him round behind the door. He was absolutely furious. His fury did not rise above the blast that struck us then. It knocked us every which way in the lobby. "Don't do that!" he screamed at me. I think he would have hit out at me with his cane but it was fortunately well lost in the commotion. Then he swore, shook and stamped about and poked his jaw right into my face; a whole gush of ugly sounds accompanied the reverberations of the explosion in front. I have quite a bit of jaw myself and I poked it right back into his face. Besides, my colleague was bleeding with shrapnel and in much pain. "See there!" I shouted back at the Prime Minister, as if it was his stubborn stupidity that had hurt one of his own security officers.

Winston hates to be grabbed suddenly but there are times when it had to be done, and I never for a minute hesitated to grab him and send him spinning behind some protecting wall. Or to pin him against a wall and hold him there with my own arms. He could curse like the devil. And he would glare at me long afterward.

But I refused to let this worry me. It was my duty to keep death away from this man. When death was near, I had to forget that he was famous and dignified. I had to remember that death had no rules. So I had none. I couldn't. Mostly he hated to lose his hat. And when my occasionally roughing him also knocked his hat away, what he would say while searching for it was a sin against the language.

He had another form of daring which I considered reckless and foolhardy. This had to do with his actions when on top of high buildings at the height of the blitz. He often rushed to them on hearing the sirens. Sometimes he'd run about first, hunting for his fieldglasses. Then he would stand and watch the effects of the bombing and gunfire. He'd count the fires. And he'd time explosions by their flashes, then count the interval to judge their distance—five seconds per mile. No persuasion of any kind would stop him. Mrs. Churchill had tried her best. Finally she gave up any idea of altering him.

He had given instructions to be notified immediately when an air raid was pending. With his thick siren suit, Air Force overcoat and cap, his gas mask and with his steel helmet on his head, he'd go to the roof and there stand out in the open, smoking a cigar and watching. This was the ancient Marlborough burning within. Whenever he was the least bit polite to me, I knew he was feeling most wretchedly guilty. It might be thus:

"I'm sorry to take you into danger, Thompson. I would not do it, only I know how much *you* like it." (The Americans had a word for it, as I found out next year: "The hell you say.")

I would answer, with malicious politeness, equally insincere: "I am not so sure about that, sir. I am mostly concerned with your safety."

Then sensing how provoked I was and how bad he was and knowing what a sham the whole show was, he would give me his weak defense: "When my time is due, it will come."

One night during a heavy bombing Mrs. Churchill said, "Inspector, I have asked Mr. Churchill to come downstairs to bed in the shelter. He has promised to come down—will you see that he does?" I replied, "I will do my best, madame," knowing full well how difficult this would be. To my surprise, about 2:30 (A.M. Winston came along the corridor and announced he was going downstairs to bed. I went to my own room and stayed alert, for I had noticed a mischievous grin on his face. Shortly after, my bell rang. I went to his room. He was standing beside his bed in his dressing gown. Smiling, he said, "Pick up my clothes, Thompson, I have kept my promise. I have been down here to bed; now I am going upstairs to sleep."

I always had to be available to take him to the top floor in the lift. When it reached the top of its shaft, he would step out and start up the winding staircase that went to the roof vents. He would not get there without much exertion. He was a poor climber. And in his middle and later years, I found he winded easily. How could it be otherwise, considering his pressures and his confinements?

To the end he ignored the possibility of being hit. Falling shrapnel did not even distract him, though pieces often fell large enough and with sufficient velocity to penetrate the skull or rip off a hand completely.

Did his going to the roofs ever stop? Yes, it finally did. But this did not come about because of fear or from his having had his fill. His excursions ended with the coming of the flying bomb. And he would have still made these ascents except for one thing: no sufficient warning of their approach could be given him. The flying bomb was a swift and stealthy thing. The flying bomb was the first thing ever to enter our life from Germany that I was thankful to see. Keeping Winston Churchill downstairs brought order back into my life.

Churchill's daily routine during the early bombings would be to go to Down Street Underground after the blitz commenced, to dine and hold meetings of the Chiefs of Staff. He went to bed, as he had in previous years, usually between two and three in the morning. Often he would return to Downing Street while the raid was still on, and before it was quite daylight. As a usual thing he would remain at Ten Downing Street during the day even when raids occurred.

Officials around the Prime Minister were extremely relieved when he used the Down Street Station, but from various remarks which he passed from time to time it was obvious that he did not feel happy at being underground. Presently he decided to use the Number Ten Downing Street Annex, which had meanwhile been strengthened. At the Annex powerful rooms had been constructed deep underground. These were for himself, his Ministers and Chiefs of Staff. Later a suite was provided on the floor above for his wife and family. Numerous raids took place after the Prime Minister took over the occupation of the rooms above the security area but only on one occasion could he be persuaded to use the downstairs rooms. My most important duty was to obtain for him the latest information of the approach of hostile aircraft, so that he could go to the roof to watch. On my own authority I later had a sandbag shelter put there for him.

Winston was alone much on the roof (except for security officers such as myself) but I would like to point out that during the whole period of the day and night raids on London, he and his Ministers and the Chiefs of Staff went about at all hours in the London area, during its very worst periods and they did so right up to the dawn hours night after night. It was not bravado. There is very little in us, none in Churchill. But there was a reason for all this; there was a vast amount of work to be done and one walked through the streets no matter what was happening in them because one had to get from one place to another at a certain time. It had to be done.

To be assigned to Churchill is a strain. He will move at a moment's notice. He will move without notice. He is an animal. In war he is particularly feral. Tensions increase around him. And they increase within the men assigned to protect him. Often these tensions are present without the fact being known to the man so plagued. I was under terrible tension. I made a quick move once and shot myself painfully through both legs. It happened like this:

We had instructions that Churchill would be leaving that night for Chequers. One hour. Time enough for a bite of supper. I hurried around to the room I occasionally used, a small room having a direct telephone connection to Number Ten. I was laying out some fresh cartridges. The telephone rang quickly, two rings. This always meant instant action. In a hurry to reach it, I leaned over a settee. A frayed ribband in the upholstery caught my automatic and pulled it forth from its holster, as I stood in crouching position, my hand outstretched for the telephone. I stood up. The weapon fell inside my trousers. I followed it down with my hand, tenderly. Knowing that the safety catch was on, I let it fall a few inches. Unfortunately it dropped on the hammer, the safety catch being released by a thread inside my trouser leg, and the automatic went off.

The bullet hit the calf of my left leg, and there slightly diverted entered my right thigh. It went through flesh and muscle until it plowed up to the top of the thigh and hit the bone. My right leg collapsed. I began to bleed severely but though deeply penetrated, I was not much injured. While I had the telephone in my hand, I asked for aid.

Presently it came. Scotland Yard had an ambulance for me in seven minutes. My two wounds were dressed as I lay there in the small room. I remember worrying over what Churchill would say. "Do you think he'll let me handle his armory after this?" I asked the young surgeon who was probing me.

I had been handling and firing guns of every kind every day for more than twenty years. This was my first and only accident. Pain set in, but it was little to my anxiety over what I would hear.

News traveled fast. The Germans used the story to the full, setting forth that: we were behind in the war; Churchill was unpopular; everyone was sick to death of war; there were demonstrations for peace all over the country. The story got through censorship, we knew not how. But the Nazi press stated that public sentiment against Churchill had reached such a point that an assassination attempt *by his own people* had only been thwarted at the last minute by my having interposed my body. They faked photographs of Churchill lying down in a crowd, an ambulance behind; a man being toted off on a stretcher; guns, police, women wailing, tear gas, etc. These press pictures are the easiest thing in the world to fake and look very real.

In time I mended. Then I presented myself to the Prime Minister. I asked him directly: "Do you feel, sir, that I can still handle your guns with safety?" He greeted me warmly, then asked for the details. At the end of the recital, he said: "I have no doubts about you whatever, Thompson. You are a most careful person. Carry on as before."

During these months and as soon as I could take the full load again, I accompanied Mr. Churchill on visits to more than sixty different towns and aerodromes which had been hit by the enemy. At Coventry Churchill's control was nearly shattered. He was unable to speak while examining the havoc here. He walked, silent, between the bare walls of the cathedral, shaking his head, looking about at the blind windows listening to the wind in the frames. There are always sad relics in a smashed cathedral. He picked up one and brought it with him.

In succession we saw Liverpool, Sheffield, Portsmouth, Southampton, Plymouth and Devonport—all flattened at the core. In England one home in every five was either destroyed or damaged too severely to be habitable.

I believe it was Hitler's plan to crush our people when he could not crush our war machine or slaughter our armies. This was another error. In all parts of England, wherever bombs fell, the organization was such that relief in all forms followed immediately after the "All Clear." At the time of Coventry's worst raid, for example, the Prime Minister was at a certain country house from which a number of mobile canteens were dispatched with necessities on the road to Coventry, a hundred miles distant. These canteens were in motion, on their way to Coventry, while Coventry herself was in process of being blitzed.

There was another fine service. It was known as the American Food Flying Squads. These were very much to the fore following heavy raids, yeoman service being done by all those attached to the vans.

Bristol was another place we visited. This poor place was really razed. Yet from the ash and the standing chimneys there rose a morale and a spirit stronger and surer than in those places that had been passed over by the Luftwaffe. We heard everywhere: "We can take it! But give it to 'em back!" We got there in the early hours of the morning. It was but an hour after an overnight raid. Mr. Churchill went to a hotel. After asking about the extent of the damage, he asked for the impossible, a bath. He received an immediate "Yes, sir" from the manager. It did not sound convincing to me. This hotel had escaped what the others had taken the night before but it had not recovered from half a dozen hits in previous months. It had a sense of lean to it, as if it needed shoring up in order to stay in business. Of course there was no hot water.

But somehow, somewhere, in but a few minutes, an amused procession of guests, clerks, cooks, maids, soldiers, and walking wounded materialized out of some mystery in the back part of the building, and went up the stairs with hot water in all types of containers, including a garden sprinkler, and filled the tub in the Prime Minister's room.

After his bath there was breakfast. Then we made a tour of the previous night's disasters. They were indeed terrible On arriving at a badly damaged block of buildings, an elderly woman, covered from head to foot in dust, came toward Mr. and Mrs. Churchill. They were told that she had just been dug out of a bombed house. They wanted to meet her, for she had said one of the mightiest lines ever uttered under fire, just before the ceiling fell in on her little life. She had set aside her broom, shaken her fist at the invisible. Germans somewhere above in the black sky, and shouted: "How I hates that Hitler! He's such a fidget!"

Mr. and Mrs. Churchill shook hands with her. Although she was still shaken by the experience of being trapped, she spoke up, apologizing for her dirty hands. And she seemed to be in a hurry. With nowhere to go this was unusual, until she said directly: "I am sorry I can't talk to you any longer. I must go and clean up my house." And off she went. We were all quite suddenly in the presence of greatness. And I think we all knew it.

During this visit, Mr. Churchill, as Chancellor of the University of Bristol, conferred upon Mr. John G. Winant, United States Ambassador to Great Britain, Mr. R. G. Menzies, then Prime Minister of Australia, and Dr. J. B. Conant, President of Harvard, the honorary degree of Doctor of Law.

Winant was a favorite with Winston. They talked for hours at a time. Winston was always inquiring where the man was, or making special efforts to attend something the American was also attending. It was a different sort of friendship from the one Churchill had with Baruch. He loved Baruch in a good deal the same way he loved General Smuts. He loved their wisdom and sought their advice. In Winant there was poetry, philosophical profundity, vast pity. His self-destruction, not much later, was something Winston could not understand. He never got over it. Winant had the most beautiful face I ever saw in a man. Great sad eyes too. He had the Lincoln look.

We came back to London. We were very tired. Hitler realized his efforts to break us had aborted. It was too late to try a cross-Channel invasion. That would have to wait till spring. As the losses which we could inflict on his night raiders increased, his mass night bombing diminished. There were times when it appeared as if Hitler and the Luftwaffe were pounding away at the same town night after night. Perhaps he succeeded in completely destroying some towns in this way. Then he turned to other targets. Towns just hit could recover.

What Hitler did achieve, however, in a year of air raids

was the killing of over forty-four thousand civilians, and the injuring of fifty-two thousand. Coming back after Bristol we saw that the Chamber of the House of Commons was destroyed. Churchill had spoken there before our last tour of visits, receiving a vote of confidence, with a majority of four hundred and forty-four.

We were still very much alone in this war. It showed in the increasing irritability of the Prime Minister. One could see it in many ways, large and small. He would turn on any handy person and let off steam. Because I was *always* handy, I got a good many of these scaldings. Nothing I seemed to do appeared correct in his eyes. I bored him. The necessity of my job bored him. My everlasting ubiquity must have bored him to death. It even bored me. I asked Scotland Yard if a temporary shift might be advisable. At times I felt thoroughly disheartened with the work. I felt I was falling down. I kept wishing somebody would attack him so I could shoot the attacker.

On one occasion General Sir Hastings Ismay, secretary to the War Cabinet, was present during one of these outbursts. I asked him if he could explain why I had been told off so harshly. General Sir Hastings came forward from his customary remoteness and smiled with a sudden flash of intimate understanding: "I get it just the same, Thompson. If it lightens the load, it is worth it."

I realized things were all right again when I listened to Churchill, shortly after this, make a public reply to a speech by President Roosevelt. "Put your confidence in us," said our Prime Minister to the President of the United States and to the world at large. "Give us your faith and your blessing, and under Providence all will be well. We shall not fail or falter. We shall not weaken or tire. Neither the sudden shock of battle nor the long-drawn trials of vigilance and exertion will wear us down. Give us the tools and we will finish the job."

The war took a new turn. The struggle in the air subsided. Under the sea it intensified. On November 5 the Prime Minister declared the German U-boat to be our greatest enemy; that its destructive power had overtaken the destructive power of the bombing plane. Our own Navy was active everywhere. Weeks earlier the *Ajax*, of *Graf Spee* fame, sunk three Italian destroyers. We followed this quickly with the Battle of Taranto. Here we blew up two Italian battleships, and sank six more units by aircraft attack from the fleet air arm.

General de Gaulle, in a bid to liberate the port of Dakar in French West Africa, approached the port with a small fleet, thinking he would be unopposed by the Vichy government representatives. He was very mistaken. Nearing the port in a small boat, swung off from his warship, he was fired upon by the French garrison before reaching the landing stage. His attempts to parley with the officials ashore also failed. De Gaulle's arrangements for taking Dakar had gone wrong. From that time until the latter part of 1942 Dakar resisted all efforts to capture it. Mr. Churchill refused to deal with de Gaulle's attempt. He never made a full statement, saying it was entirely a French affair.

Bad things were happening to our land forces. General Wavell had opened a strong attack in Libya and had pressed back the Axis forces to Benghazi. But our troops were desperately needed in Greece. Wavell's work was lost. He had to pull his forces out and retire them almost to their old positions.

President Roosevelt was re-elected for the third time and announced a Lend-Lease plan. It was implemented in record time by the Congress and we began almost immediately to receive its benefits. We had only recently received the fifty "overage" destroyers from the United States, and these were already in service, combating the submarine menace. For the destoyers the United States received a ninety-nine-year lease of naval and air bases from Newfoundland clear down to British Guiana and including Bermuda, Trinidad and Jamaica. But the announcement of Lend-Lease was the most gratifying statement we had received so far from the Americans. "You share our purpose, you will share our dangers, you will share our anxieties, you shall share our secrets, and the day will come when the British Empire and the United States will share together the solemn but splendid duties which are the crown of victory."

It came just in time. We could not use the treaty ports on Ireland's western coast. Mr. de Valera declared that Eire would not hand over the ports of Britain because such action would involve her in war. Of course we could not do so without violating Irish neutrality. There was much public pressure on the Prime Minister that we just move in and seize the ports. We were losing lives all up and down the west coast of Ireland by U-boat sinkings that we could prevent if we had the ports. When Churchill was challenged directly with the question: "For God's sake, why don't you go in and take them?" he remarked instantly and with equal force: "No! That is the very thing we are fighting against! I will not do it!"

By this time Wavell's troops had arrived in Greece from Libya. Within a month, however, the Axis, smashing through Yugoslavia, forced our withdrawal, forty-eight thousand of the original sixty thousand getting away safely. They went to Crete. Here they were again overwhelmed by the Axis and once more forced to pull out. It was humiliating, discouraging and desperate.

Churchill was extraordinarily interested in a rocket apparatus. He made numerous trips to Shoeburyness. There his own son-in-law, Duncan Sandys, M.P., a completely excellent and enchanting fellow, very brilliant of mind and especially so with the mechanical rig he was assembling there, was hard at work with a number of troops and rocket experts, perfecting this invention for antiaircraft work. They completed it in a few months from this time, but it came at a frightful cost to the Churchill family. As one visit followed another, we gradually saw the progress that was being made on the whole complex assembly. One of the last places visited was a town in Wales. For the purpose of this journey I rose early in the morning to go meet the Prime Minister by railroad coach. Meanwhile Major Sandys, who had been in London, preceded us by car. He became involved in a most serious and painful motor accident which then and there ended his military career. This was a terrible blow to Winston, to Duncan's young wife and to all of us who knew the man. His injuries were indeed quite awful and he is, while recovered somewhat, not able today to walk without canes. However, he is as plucky as the rest and this has not held him back from his political career. But it was a deep tragedy and a deeper emotional setback to those about him, the group beginning to achieve secret success with the rocket.

The Prime Minister was delighted by the return to his capital of Emperor Haile Selassie of Abyssinia. Hitler never failed to delight Churchill too. He had translations of the speeches played on the gramophone for himself, and never allowed the technician to cut out any of the cheers and screams. He loved to listen to the German hordes dismembering him (Churchill) and would lean forward in his seat, rich in the images that fled past. Hitler was now threatening, in his frequent spiels in the Reichstag, to drop one hundred bombs for each British bomb dropped on the Reich, until Britain got rid of Churchill. The Prime Minister liked to play back the parts where Hitler mentioned him by name. There were other Cabinet Members who did not think this entirely dignified. Winston did not consider it so either, no more so than his madly meditative marching about the Great Hall at Chequers with the BBC wireless blaring. But it released something. And that was good.

We lost the *Hood*. It had been chasing the *Bismarck* and the cruiser *Prinz Eugen* all over the Atlantic. The *Hood* took a salvo that detonated her magazines and she blew up in a million directions. We lost nearly her whole complement. Churchill went around in a daze. From the instant we lost the *Hood* it became a serious game of hide and seek— the *Bismarck* trying in every conceivable way to avoid contact with our forces. The Germans of course wanted to be able to enjoy their immense victory and could not very well do so unless the victorious *Bismarck* returned safely, for supplies and refueling. It was presumed she would try to get to Brest. The British Navy never hung on so hard, even though we couldn't find the mighty German. Aircraft were taken from other assignments to locate her. Ships began closing in from all directions. Then we suddenly did see her; through a crack in the clouds she was sighted by a slow-flying plane and her position fixed, her identity established. We hit her with a torpedo and damaged her steering gear. She traveled in circles, ever going slower. Then we moved in and sank the unsinkable. Two days after her own death the *Hood* was somewhat avenged when we sent the *Bismarck* to the bottom.

But it was a cheerless winter nonetheless. "Not only great dangers, but many more misfortunes, many shortcomings, many mistakes, many disappointments will surely be our lot. Death and sorrow will be the companions of our journey; hardship our garment; constancy and valor our only shield."

The months were rushing by. A year had gone by since France had been defeated. We still remained alone. Winston always seemed to feel the need of reports and photographs on all phases of the war. H'd peer at photos of German submarine pens and improvise methods to slide bombs into them, as he sat there watching and studying, when told the concrete roofing was too tough for any bomb yet built. He did not create the "skip" bomb that was used to break up this construction at Saint-Nazaire but he instantly saw that it would work.

There were formidable gatherings of invasion barges below us. Thousands of them. They looked ominous, even though empty. For one could see them glistening with fire and glinting with blade, carrying their lethal congeries of cunning Germans, slipping over the water to stab us in the dark. Churchill ordered a concentrated attack on all those spots where these clusters of barges were known to be under camouflage.

This attack coincided with a record output of heavy bombers by English factories.

Hitler's air blitz had failed. It had burned us and torn us and sorrowfully disfigured us, but it hadn't broken our bones and we could still therefore fight.

Hitler's preparations for invasion seemed also to be slowing down and sloughing off. He had a huge war machine but he seemed uncertain how to use it. Churchill knew that Hitler did not long stand still in such dilemmas; that he would presently take action and probably not the classic or professional one. Any amateur in war can look intuitive if his physical power is initially vast, his authority absolute, and his method unexpected.

Information from flights over the Channel and up and down the coasts of Belgium and France indicated to Churchill (though he did not for a long time say so to the English people) that Hitler's instinct, somewhat instructed no doubt by the punishment his barges had taken, was rapidly suggesting he abandon any idea of invading Britain. It would not seem possible that any man—even a crazy one—would think of giving up the fight for the Island and taking on Russia. Yet Churchill not only suddenly suspected Hitler might do this, he suddenly saw that it was exactly what Hitler was going to do next. Churchill apprehended this before there was any movement at all toward concentration of German troops on the Eastern Front.

Churchill warned Stalin Hitler planned to take him on. Nobody in the world believed it. Yet all of a sudden, there were the Germans, athwart the Russian border, pouring over it without warning or declaration of war and in direct defiance of military plausibility.

We were in the imposing gloom of Chequers. It was a Sunday, a day greatly favored by the Germans for their acts of treachery. Though the aspect of Chequers has a baronial chill to it that deadens the appetite, the day itself was beautiful in the extreme. Churchill got word there that the Germans had crossed over into Joe Stalin's back yard and the implications of this were indeed most joyous to us all.

It was difficult for Americans to understand the exquisite relief, the sudden release from pressure. The Canadians could understand it better through their kinship to us and the bond of the Commonwealth. But the knowledge that we could have a few moments to repair our own war machine, with the striking power of Hitler concentrated upon great stretches of ground in an area so many miles away, was surely something to set the heart humming and lift the mind.

That very day, from Chequers, Winston Churchill broadcast to all the world promises of aid to Russia, aligned the British Commonwealth with Russia as Allies and said with brief eloquence and majestic summary: "We are no longer alone."

Also the United States had stepped in by sending American troops to Iceland to join British troops already there. Iceland in German hands would have constituted a terrible menace. I don't know if Americans, reading this today, remember that their great country had American troops joining up with British troops in Iceland, to strengthen the Atlantic lifeline, a full six months before Pearl Harbor, but that is the historical fact. Although the United States was not at war with anyone, it was obvious President Roosevelt was determined that supplies to our own country, and now to Russia, were going to get through. And they did.

Concurrently, the forces of liberation were at work in France. Inspeakable stories of torture kept coming through to us, describing what the Nazis were doing to those they caught. Germany will never be forgiven for this. But even so—and in tribute to the spirit of the French—their movement gained momentum day by day. We heard the word *Victoire* was chalked up everywhere, from which the "V" sign ultimately emerged and became universally recognized.

Churchill went about happily flashing the V at the whole world. In a broadcast to all occupied countries he described it in these words: "The V sign is a symbol of the unconquerable will of the occupied territories, and a portent of the fate awaiting the Nazi tyranny. So long as the people of Europe continue to refuse all collaboration with the invader, it is sure that his cause will perish, and that Europe will be liberated."

People everywhere flashed the same right back at him whenever he held up his hand and spread his fingers.

We had been through some awful months. We all knew we still had many more—and many more years of awful months too—with death at the end perhaps. But anything that made things look as if the struggle might finally begin to even out and turn into a fair exchange made the present supportable.

Churchill's "We are no longer alone" captured this mood and it swept over England. We felt strong again and ready for another round.

Then a subtle but electric thing happened. It was on the second of August. A "secret journey." Frankly, I always loved these things. Winston Churchill probably had never shown so much exuberance and excitement since Harrow. He bumped over the grass of his country place like a balloon dragged by a hurrying child. He was all smiles and mystic gestures, quick lurches of the head, whispers. His hands were never still. Something big. No doubt of it.

It was all doubly delightful to me, for not only had I had a few days' leave, my first in fourteen months, but I was permitted to know it was to be a sea voyage. This meant I could get still a bit more rest, for Winston is happiest aboard ship. If this could also, by some happy chance or wise precaution, be a huge battleship besides, I knew it would be an experience to remember the rest of my life.

I cannot tell you how, but I had ascertained we were to visit President Roosevelt at sea.

Churchill rushed about Chequers, being in favor of everything and approving of everyone. Very unusual for him. On the day we were due to leave, his keenness to be off grew more and more intense—actually boyish—as the hour came. He very well knew the hour, yet he kept asking me it. He seemed to like to hear me say it. At one o'clock, for the third time, he once more asked me if everything was ready and *exactly* when we were to depart.

"About a quarter of an hour," I answered him, amused at his suspense. I felt some myself, of course, but I am a cop and this is not an authorized part of our equipment.

Today, I do truly believe, if I had studied my wrist watch for a second or two and then said with quiet positiveness: "We leave in exactly thirteen minutes and eleven seconds" he would have stood it out. (And we were only going to the station to catch a train!) But he couldn't stand it. At 1:05 he jumped into the waiting car and instructed the driver to take us to the station at once. He was grinning at all and flashing his most bewitching smile on even unknown persons.

Of course he had to wait, as would any other schoolboy far ahead of his schedule when embarking on his first holiday in the country. There was nothing to do but stand around. Finally the train came. It already had quite a supply of some of the most important Englishmen alive. And a lot of champagne too.

Everyone was in a fine mood. Professor Frederick Lindemann, now Lord Cherwell and considered by Churchill in terms of sheer intellectual accomplishment to be the "brightest" Englishman alive today, was happy as a vacationist as soon as the Prime Minister was safely aboard and we were in motion.

Sir John Dill, C.I.G.S., was another member of the party. So were Sir Dudley Pound and Sir Alexander Cadogan. Many of my own colleagues from Scotland Yard were along too.

The mood of the group grew happier at dinner before we arrived at our point of embarkation. Churchill not only had his regular pint of champagne, he had a bit more tonight.

He turned to Lord Cherwell, a brilliant mathematician, and asked him to work out in his head how much champagne he had drunk, at the rate of a pint a day, in twenty-four years. He seemed very satisfied with the answer. But when he turned to the professor again and asked him how many railroad coaches it would require to stow and carry all that champagne and was told that one end of one coach would be more than ample, he was very put out and disappointed, feeling himself a very uninteresting imbiber at best. He wanted it to require several trainloads at the least. Then Sir John Dill asked Mr. Churchill how many yards of cigars he'd smoked. The Prime Minister wouldn't get into it, and it also came out that the definitions of smoking would have to be gone into with considerable care, many seeming to know that Winston, while seldom without a cigar in public, was also known to carry it about unlit for long periods of time, so that a single cigar might last half the afternoon, most of the time more ornamental than functional. You can see how significant the dinner conversation had become.

We arrived in the far north of the Island in a cool heavy rain, but nothing would dampen the spirits of the Prime Minister or the pervasive sense of mission that went with this group.

By this time I knew by sight many ships in the Royal Navy, and there before us was the *Prince of Wales*.

We went aboard at once. There the Prime Minister was met by Admiral Tovey. Churchill stepped forward to shake hands with him. He had not noticed yet that a quiet, sickly looking man had also stepped up. Then these two shook hands. I'd seen the picture fifty times but did not at once identify the man.

It was Harry Hopkins. He had just come back from seeing Stalin.

"Hello, Harry!" said Winston jovially. "How is our friend Joe?"

"Joe is looking very well, Winston, and is sorry he didn't take your advice."

"Joe has a lot of work to do now," said Winston.

"I guess he knows it now," said Harry.

"He should have taken my advice. *Everybody* should take my advice," he added good-naturedly. "At all times." They grinned at each other, Harry nervously, his shoulders constantly hunched as if repelling a chill or a shiver. He never looked quite dressed or sufficiently nourished. And he smoked his head off. Except for King Zog, I never saw anyone smoke so much or so continuously.

"The Germans have a way of keeping you busy once they decide to pay you any attention at all," Winston said. They walked down the deck together. Harry Hopkins was to be with us for the trip, then to transfer to the President's ship at the time of rendezvous.

There was a lunch served for the party aboard the *King George V*. I accompanied the Prime Minister, then left him to come back to the *Prince of Wales* and go over the security problem which the voyage represented to me. Churchill is a real fidget on a boat.

I learned that we were to traverse waters that were thick with German submarines. And I was told that although our exact route was at that instant not even known to our own captain, it would be naïve to think the Germans, through their Intelligence, did not know this meeting was taking place. It was hoped they did not know specifically where. But if it was known to the Germans that it was a sea journey and not an air journey, the point of contact could be assumed to be one that would favor the President of the United States, because of his physical impairment, and it might therefore be nearer to the shores of that continent than ours.

I was rehearsed in what to do in case we were hit by a torpedo. I already knew what to do if, through some unlikely mischance, an assassin were aboard ship. I laid out my own stratagems to the proper ship's security officers to take care of this hazard.

I like ships too and feel quite at home on them. Winston had brought a quantity of serviceable clothing for the voyage and several uniforms for such formal appearances as would be required. I had a horrifying thought. He had not brought his own valet! I would get that burden! I sought relief from the Royal Navy and I got some.

Well, I would just have to face up to it. Anticipating his laundry and valet needs, I poked about the vast ship, seeking help, and ascertaining the locations of such critical items as tubs, soap, pressers, and drying space. A policeman's life!

But I had a certain amount of importance, at least by proxy. I could keep people away from the Prime Minister, and I could tell the hundreds of inquirers that I had no idea where we were going, who was to meet us, or what was to be said, then looking wisely and laconically away as if I actually was carrying the plans in my trousers. I enjoyed a great deal of prestige and was well served at mess time. But too often, when in the midst of a cluster of eager questioners and holding them spellbound, there would be the warning buzz of the ship's loudspeaker, then the momentous summons: "Inspector Thompson, lay aft to the laundry to fetch the Prime Minister's fresh linen!" "Inspector Thompson, lay aft to the Prime Minister's cabin to porter his laundry." "Inspector Thompson, the Prime Minister's uniforms are ready!" And off I'd go, the whole Navy sensing my odd humiliation. And enjoying it.

I did not know the exact spot but had a pleasant time trying to guess in my mind where we might arrive. I had hoped we might get very close to America (what a different sort of feeling I was developing for her from the one I had in 1931!), and perhaps, as courtesy escort, go back from the rendezvous and drop anchor at Norfolk, Philadelphia, Brooklyn, Portsmouth or Boston. I knew it would give me at least a momentary lift to stand on the shores of a nation—a strong one—and look into the faces of a free people who were not yet in desperate contest and very much able to fight. I knew this was idle thought, so I put it out of mind.

In and out of the Prime Minister's accommodations many times a day and being in continuous service to him, I of course heard enough to realize his inner attitude was not entirely hopeless; that he had a cogent and well-reasoned list of proposals and direct propositions to offer the President of the United States, and that once offered, they would be well argued.

About 9:00 P.M., the second night out, the captain of the *Prince of Wales* announced over the loudspeaker and to the ship's company that our destination was somewhere near Newfoundland. All my questioners looked knowingly at me and when close enough to speak to me they all, without exception, announced that they'd known from the beginning —though their guesses had ranged from Reykjavik to Jamaica.

It was evident that Winston was putting great faith in the coming conference. But he was unusually guarded in saying anything specific or revealing any of his most secret thoughts and hopes even by an inflection of the voice. He was cheerful. He sang a lot. Thank God it was too rough to paint! He also bathed with gusto and frequency, making up for the train journey by using half the Atlantic. In water, fresh or salt, he's like a seal but without the sleekness. He's more like a whale, I guess.

When we'd been to sea a couple of days Mr. Churchill really did relax. He even read a book. This is a very unusual thing for him to do. Usually he is writing them. I commented on this. He said he was deriving a wonderful benefit from the rest and the fresh air. He admitted that he needed it. Reading rested his brain. It was a light book.

The sea calmed a bit. An escort of destroyers slid in without fuss. Churchill walked for many hours on the quarterdeck. Every man on that ship got a great kick out of just *seeing* him, just knowing he was on their ship. He represented something cosmic and imperishable, something monolithic and good. Something great. Something that would not be seen again. The ship's company knew this. You would sense greatness in him and about him even if you were coming upon him for the first time and knew nothing of him. It is there in the Churchill face.

He liked getting about various parts of the ship. He liked to go about alone. He was poor with ladders and hopeless with a rope. He definitely belongs in a modern navy. Men stepped aside to let him pass. Often they stiffened and saluted. Once permitted, they'd crowd the poor man to death. There was always laughter coming out of the groups he created. And strays and trailers followed him about everywhere, not talking among each other so they'd miss nothing of what he might say to others. He'd stop and chat with anybody. He did this constantly on this trip. If an officer called them smartly to attention, he would normally protest to the officer, with a simple sweetness: "No, no. Carry on. I want to walk about without interfering. Allow the men to be at ease. I want to feel I can have personal contact with them at any time. Nothing could more increase my enjoyment of the hospitality of the *Prince of Wales*."

On Wednesday night, Mr. Churchill was dressing for dinner. I am not much of a valet but I kept passing him things as I felt it was time for them to go on. Winston was an immaculately, almost fanatically, clean person in all his habits. The frequent rakishness of his appearance and the sprawling abandon, even the shocking incongruity of some of his getups was partly due to his not caring what he looked like when appearance had no importance at the moment, partly because he enjoyed certain pieces of raiment and hung on to them even though they might belong to eras fifty years apart. He also had certain things made for himself that no one could ever decipher. But when it was time to dress up, he had the wardrobe. Anthony Eden wears a homburg with easy conviction but somehow as if he expects to be photographed. But when Winston Churchill wears one, which is not often, it immediately becomes a physical part of his inner mood and being.

I casually mentioned to him, while he dressed, that we had been on a number of trips together and I tried to make a guess as to the number of miles.

He thoughtfully looked down at the rug as he shoehorned his feet into evening slippers. "Yes, and I hope it will be a few thousand more, Thompson. If we get back from it."

"I'm sure you'll get back from it, sir," I said easily.

"I suppose we'll get back if we're supposed to get back." That was characteristic of his attitude about all dangers and long endeavors. They would come to their proper ends in their proper time. While living, all he could do was the work before him and derive the satisfaction that went with its accomplishment. I remarked that his meeting with President Roosevelt would make history. At once he replied:

"Yes. And more so, if I get what I want from him."

"I think you will, sir. We all know it cannot be anything but honorable."

"But a pack of villians has broken loose and got in the gunroom," he said.

Then he referred to the occasion in France when he asked if I had been in a photograph of the Supreme War Council, and had added that never again would this same group be seen together. Some would perish, some would be deposed, some would change allegiance, or make a compromise from which there is no return. Some would stay on to the end. He was thinking of this.

In speaking of President Roosevelt, of whom I had no more than an English newspaper notion, I gathered that Winston was rehearsing in detail what he was planning to say, and in what order. He and Harry Hopkins were together much of the time. Winston had a world-sense. It was English, and it was personal, but it was a world-sense nonetheless. He seemed to feel that he held the continents in his right hand and the custody of all their inhabitants, and that in his left hand he held the oceans. I began to feel that Winston viewed President Roosevelt as similar in makeup: that here were two men of prestige and power, mighty accomplishment, elaborate thought, fearless initiative, supported by the impassioned love of the multitudes. Winston felt it likely that this, also, was the way the President of the United States felt about *him*self.

With Hitler preoccupied with Russia, and still to face the Russian nervelessness and fanatical love of land, there might be time to put an end to mankind's most awful dilemma, and the time might be *now*. A world without war is indeed a world to dream of. It seemed almost as if these two men could *will* it so.

But it was only a dream, wasn't it?

The weather held beautiful for two more days, but Saturday dawned dull and wet. The ship shone from stem to stern, however. I was walking about the deck at six, then dropped down to Churchill's cabin to find that he also had risen early and had already had his breakfast. There was an outline of land ahead, then land itself, then the outlines of ships, some carrying sail.

Just ahead now was the U.S.S. *Augusta*, with the President of the United States aboard her.

We steamed up very close, then incredibly drew away again and put out to sea for an hour and a half. We never got an explanation for this. It infuriated Winston. He banged about the decks, hunting a target for his wrath. We never talked about the matter afterward somehow. There must have been a report of an emergency of some kind, yet a submarine warning hardly seemed to explain our separating so quickly when we were in hailing distance. Somewhat later, someone suggested the possibility of an aerial attack though this was at once scouted by others listening, one of whom pointed out that no capital ships had ever been destroyed by aerial bombs. The bitter irony of this of course is that this very ship, the mighty *Prince of Wales*, was to be the first capital ship, to go down under aerial attack—and not much later at Singapore. Winston never recovered from this news, never understanding it.

We approached once more and spirits lifted at once. We soon reached our anchorage in surroundings very similar to Scapa Flow. Around us were numerous units, big and small, from the United States navy. How hungrily Winston looked over their firepower! How we needed it!

As we passed, slowly and majestically between these ships, bands were playing everywhere. It was most beautiful. It was hard to hold back tears. We sailed clear around the *Augusta* playing a number all the Americans love: the

Sousa march, "Stars and Stripes Forever." We received a salute from her and she right away struck up "God Save the King." Winston had forgotten our odd detour out to sea. All was pleasant.

We anchored. An American admiral came aboard to pay his respects. A senior officer from the *Prince of Wales* boarded the *Augusta* for the same purpose. A few minutes later the Prime Minister, looking like a sea lord every inch— accompanied by Lord Cherwell, Sir Dudley Pound, Sir John Dill, Sir Alexander Cadogan, Commander Thompson and myself—went aboard the *Augusta*.

As I reached the head of the gangway, I saw for the first time in my life a United States Marine. I must say I have never seen so colorful nor so smartly set up a fighting man anywhere. He was more than that; he was imposing.

The *Augusta* had a large canvas awning over the quarterdeck and as we arrived, the band played "God Save the King" again. We went to the deck above. The President of the United States was here. So were officers of the U.S. army, navy, and air force.

President Roosevelt was standing by the rail, supported by his son Elliott, an officer in the U. S. army. It was a most impressive moment. The President looked strong and healthy. He did not smile at first. He was a serious man, I found. Character and decision was written into every line of his face. He stood very straight. He had a cape. It gave him an aloof elegance. It did not appear incongruous.

Winston Churchill moved forward. Then President Roosevelt smiled most winningly. I had never seen such a smile. They shook hands warmly, informally. They were mighty glad to see each other. After greeting the President, the Prime Minister presented the various officers who had accompanied him to the *Augusta*, and of course those of the Cabinet and War Council.

At the conclusion of this, Mr. Churchill handed to the President a letter from His Majesty the King. Here, most regrettably and contrarily, the sound camera suddenly ceased to function. What was said then is now lost. I caught only a broken snatch or two. It could not be reconstructed.

Following this, the Admiral's barge moved away from the cruiser. Mr. Churchill gave the V sign to numerous members of the ship's company who were standing at attention all along the rails.

The same party returned later for lunch, but the President and the Prime Minister lunched alone in a separate cabin. Just prior to leaving the *Prince of Wales* for this luncheon meeting with the American President, the Prime Minister had taken a small piece of red leather that he had been using as a placemark for papers he was reading, and on which were engraved the words: "Ask and it shall be given. Seek and ye shall find." At that moment I drew Mr. Churchill's attention to the appropriateness of the words for the situation into which he was advancing, and suggested he regard them as a good omen for the conference just ahead. He smiled beatifically at this. "Yes, Thompson, I hope it is a good omen. For I have much to ask for." Then, as he stepped out of my sight for his private luncheon with the President, he looked up quickly and caught my eye, showing just a little corner of the talisman, knowing I would recognize what it was. I grinned back.

We got back to the *Prince of Wales* after the two warriors had lunched together. At three o'clock a welcome surprise was in store for the crew of our ship and for all her escorting destroyers. Several small boatloads of small cardboard boxes came alongside. We could not imagine what they were. The boats were manned by Marines, all the same height and appearance as the one who had so caught my attention when boarding the *Augusta*. They brought these hundreds and hundreds of boxes on deck. Each box contained two hundred cigarettes, two apples, an orange or other fruit, and half a pound of cheese.

You cannot imagine what a lift this meant. Most of these men hadn't tasted an orange for two years, hadn't even seen one. This was a present from the President of the United States to all crews. And in each box was a printed folder, on the front of which was inscribed: *The Commander-in-Chief, United States navy, sends his compliments and best wishes, Franklin D. Roosevelt, President of the United States, August 9th, 1941.*

As these were being brought aboard and opened, the Prime Minister came on the quarterdeck and asked a British seaman and some of the Marines to show him the contents of the boxes. They were of course delighted to do this. Right off he called for a number of the Americans to gather round him and a picture was taken of this happy group. The gesture was appreciated all over and the picture was the envy of the Marines' comrades back on the *Augusta*.

Churchill took a short nap—he tossed about a good bit during it and may not have slept, though he can usually sleep under any circimstances—then he bathed and slowly and carefully dressed. We did not talk. Sometimes you don't talk around him. It is easy to tell the times. You don't talk if he doesn't.

We went across the short stretch of water between the two ships. Winston was not even talking to his own party. Dinner on the *Augusta* was at seven. I hung about for five hours. I am used to not eating. We returned to the *Prince of Wales* after midnight and the Prime Minister went to bed. He was still silent. There was terrible tension all over the ship.

Sunday morning came. It was beautiful. The shore gleamed. The world seemed happy, the ocean noble, the ships at peace. President Roosevelt was due any minute aboard the *Prince of Wales*. Everyone was excited. At ten-thirty an American destroyer went alongside the *Augusta*. The President, with two of his sons and a large staff, was brought over to us.

On the quarterdeck the Prime Minister, his officials and the ship's officers awaited the President who came on board shortly after.

Drawn up at the after end of the quarterdeck were American, Canadian and British sailors and marines—all mingled together, a neat cluster of color. They were to attend a church parade to be led by the two greatest men of our time.

It was a moving sight. Away off there was music, organ music, though I did not know its source. Everyone seemed solemn and quiet but not at all sad or downcast. Then as the procession advanced and the robed chaplains stood together and opened their books, the feeling of solemnity relaxed somewhat. I believe we all felt in the true presence of God here in this harbor, with the known ordeal of the hard years ahead.

The President came to the end of the deck and he and his sons took their seats. A meeting of this character had never been held before. The circumstances in which it came about will remain forever with those who were present and who took part. All about were ships of war, encircled by the high rocks of the clean coast of Newfoundland. Far off, planes drummed but remained far off. The head chaplain read the service, standing before a rostrum draped with American and British flags. We were all deeply moved. Three hymns were sung, all of them selected by the Prime Minister. He knew the sea and knew the hymns the majority of the sailors would be sure to know. The sound rang richly across these strange waters. There was never such singing.

When the service broke up, the President remained for a long time talking at the ship's rail with the Prime Minister. There was a short tour of the ship later, then lunch, and President Roosevelt left the *Prince of Wales* about three o'clock.

Still you could not read a sign in Churchill's face.

As the presidential destroyer moved away from our ship, Roosevelt waved his hat to us across the water. A terrific cheer broke out. The Prime Minister waved back. Then he suddenly looked down at his feet where a little black and white kitten was rubbing itself against his leg. He is a great lover of cats and on this occasion stooped down and picked up the little animal, and it became part of his departing salute as he waved to the President, to the evident delight of all the crew.

Were the tensions going down? A shore party was arranged, an informal one. Churchill changed clothes; he had brought an easy tourist suit with him. Walking on land, the mere prospect of it, was most pleasurable to me. About six of us went. Winston's manner changed as soon as we were on shore.

The man had had over a year of some of the most crushing disappointments and reverses ever sustained by a single individual. He seemed to put this behind, to let it sink into the deep ocean we had traversed. We climbed a hill and got to the top of it, cool and rocky and silent. People spoke and saluted and took pictures but it was no mob such as on the Continent. Winston kept the party amused by humorous comments upon the trip, the food, the contrast of so many different people trying to find a protection under which they could stand in safety. His heart was growing lighter. He was seeing some way out.

From the top of the hill we could see a small inlet of water on the other side. Although rain clearly threatened, we continued on our way. We came upon several small sailing ships which were turned over upon their sides in the low tide. They seemed to have been hurled far up on the land by gales, but men were working about them with patient industry. Suddenly rain crashed down hard and we got thoroughly drenched in a very few seconds. It disturbed Mr. Churchill not at all. He merely cupped his hand over his cigar and went on talking and pointing and puffing.

We were as soaked as if we had been lifted up and dipped in deep water but no one cared in the least. It was a warm rain and a friendly island.

Back on the *Prince of Wales*, speculation was running high as to the present status of the meeting and its probable outcome. I was questioned continuously. When is America going to realize we can't take this forever? *Is* America coming in? What are we going to get out of all this trouble? *Do* Americans realize how close this awful war is drawing to themselves? What is their attitude? How much had I heard that I could tell?

There was no end to any of it. If I were seen to be standing behind the President's chair, because that would be close to where the Prime Minister might be standing at the time, I would be supposed to know the answer to any riddle put to me and expected to give, at least, a cautious off-the-record summation. But the Chiefs of Staff were in almost continuous consultation.

That evening the President and the Prime Minister dined together. I remained nearby their private supper on the *Augusta*. Several American officers told me they had been watching the Prime Minister's face in hope of being able to see what was going on in his brain, but because of his constantly varying expression they had been puzzled. I told them that I had been in the same predicament more than a thousand times. Even when one knew that the war situation had improved in some detail or other, pleasure was by no means necessarily depicted on the Prime Minister's face. Often, in such circumstances, his expression had been grim and not at all satisfied. The relief of good news seemed to give him license to growl his head off in the belief that the growling, because the news was good, could not demoralize any of those around him.

Gus Gennerich, who was normally the President's private bodyguard, was not aboard the *Augusta*, having taken ill before the departure. But another famous White House regular was on hand, a fine fellow named Mike Reilly. We became attached to each other, so far as our duties permitted. He came over to me and offered to introduce me to the President. I was delighted. I've seen all the famous people in the world—and by and large you can have them, for they are too often the great bores of the planet, their eminence so often resulting from a lifetime attention to their own affairs and to nothing else—but the man Roosevelt was one to capture the imagination. From the instant I had heard his voice on the wireless, I had wanted to behold the man in person, to look at him and listen to him. I must confess I got quite a start when Mike offered to make this very thing possible right here and now.

Mike is like all the other Americans I ever met in one respect at least: suggestions are put into action right away. They are never delayed in committee. We hurried across the deck to the President's cabin. "Isn't there some sort of warning? I mean, some ceremony? Some protocol?" I very much didn't want to be guilty of a breach in punctilio, and didn't at all understand the American system for such things.

"Hell no!" he said cheerfully, rushing me along with a powerful shove across the shoulders. "*Any*body can meet the President if I think they're okay." And he seemed glad to be able to do this for me.

At the very doorway of the presidential suite, I collided with Winston Churchill, just stepping out after a conversation. I immediately told him the purpose of my coming in and the courtesy being shown me by the American Secret Service. Churchill beamed and grabbed us both, one in each hand.

"Oh, no, Thompson! I will perform that introduction myself! It will be a great pleasure for me."

So he came right back into the presence of Roosevelt, not even knocking on the door. I stood at his desk where he was reading and writing. He looked up and smiled most amiably. He seemed relaxed and good-natured, a leaner and sharper edition of Winston himself in some ways, and extended his hand across his desk to me. He had good arms and shoulders and an unexpectedly powerful grip. Winston spoke:

"Inspector Thompson has faithfully guarded me for a period of nearly twenty years. It gives me great pleasure to present him to you." We then chatted for about ten minutes, the President offering me one of his cigarettes from his silver cigarette case.

Churchill slipped out. Roosevelt asked me to stay. Mike went on into the suite somewhere.

Roosevelt asked: "How is he standing up under it, Thompson? How is he *really?*"

"He has marvelous reserve, sir, and fine working habits, including the habit of periodic rest."

"Good. Good. See that he goes on observing that. I do this myself."

"Yes, sir. I understand so."

"Does he sleep at night?"

"When he finally goes to bed, sir, he goes off at once."

"It's useful. I cultivated it many years ago. It's a valuable habit for busy people." He smoked thoughtfully for a moment, leaning back and looking at me, as if measuring me to see how much strength stood between the life of the Prime Minister and the dangers and the terrors about him. "Is he hard to handle?"

"Yes, sir. He's reckless and self-willed. Restraint of any kind is unendurable to him."

"Well, take care of him. He's about the greatest man in the world. In fact he may very likely *be* the greatest. You have a terrible responsibility in safeguarding him. You have the responsibility of four or five hundred million people, Thompson."

He smiled, dismissed me, and was instantly at work. Churchill was this way, too, total attention to the matter under scrutiny.

We then left the *Augusta*, finding Ensign (later Lieutenant) Franklin D. Roosevelt, Jr., waiting for us at the gangway. He and Mr. Churchill spoke together. Young Roosevelt said a most comforting thing, and in my hearing: that a thorough understanding had been reached. It was the first I heard of it. The younger Roosevelt accompanied us to the *Prince of Wales*. On the way Mr. Churchill said to him: "Your father is a great man."

This precipitated one of the most interesting conversations—at least for individual slant—that I have heard. Roosevelt, Jr., immediately thanked the Prime Minister, then amended the observation to: "I think my father is be*coming* a great man."

"Yes," said Winston, seeing the point at once. "He has certainly had much to get through. And to get over."

"That is it. He has been determined to get over his affliction, and he has done so. It hasn't reduced his activity, mental or physical, nor impaired the fairness or clarity of his judgments. My father is a very religious man, Mr. Churchill. I presume you know this."

"I have sensed it."

"He is brainy but if he is great, it is through his determination to set aside obstacles. Setting aside his own was first."

"It is my opinion, and one not arrived at without a considerable range of samplings and comparisons, that your father is one of the greatest men on the earth today."

To this young Roosevelt replied, smiling: "Father was talking to me of you while you were out of the dining room yesterday and said that Churchill——"

Here the Prime Minister interrupted with gruff good humor. "No—no! Never that. 'Winston.' 'Winston.' Your father always calls me 'Winston.' He's never to do anything else!"

"Yes, sir. Correct, sir. So he does. So he will too, I'm sure!" They laughed together here. Roosevelt, Jr., continued. "In any case, he said quite plainly and without reservation that you are the greatest statesman the world has ever known."

Churchill's eyes glistened and a tremble went through him.

"I do not think of myself this way. I hardly think of myself at all. I'm just in the flood of the circumstance."

"But the world thinks of you this way, Mr. Churchill. So does my father. I told him that history would have time to make these evaluations but meantime it was my own evaluation that he—meaning my father—and you, sir, were certainly the greatest *two* men of the age and that together you can bring peace to the world and keep it here."

"Very diplomatic of you, young man. And very challenging. Thank you now, for bringing us across." Our little ferry trip in the launch was over. We shook hands and went aboard the *Prince of Wales*.

The Atlantic Conference was nearing its happy ending. In a few days the world would have news of what has since become known as the Atlantic Charter.

There was a happy little rider to the Atlantic Charter that meant nothing to the world at large then, but much to us. I have said before how much Churchill relied on the Home Guard, even though it was somewhat ridiculed by those whom it was organized to protect. And it was a quaint-looking army, to be sure. One of the reasons, a pretty good one, why this ridicule had some justification was that the Home Guard had little to guard with. It was singularly unarmed. Roosevelt gave Churchill two million rifles for the Home Guard.

It was time for leavetaking. This was done with impressive brevity. Very soon the fleets would separate. At 5 P.M. with the crews lining the sides of the ship, and to the strains of the "Star-Spangled Banner," the *Prince of Wales* commenced her homeward journey. As we passed the *Augusta* where her ship's company also lined the sides, the Prime Minister stood at salute and remained so until we had passed all the U.S.A. ships.

The Old Man was tired, and I was glad of it. He took a rest. I sat down outside his cabin, cleaned my guns, then picked up an American magazine that I had not before chanced to read. It was a magazine called *Newsweek*. It had an astonishing story in it, and it was printed in the magazine as an advertisement, very different from the English system.

It was a ringing appeal by one single American, Russell Birdwell, to all other Americans, setting forth his own attitude toward the war and what the attitude thereto, for the rest of the American nation, ought to be. It shook me all up and thrilled me. Here it is, in part:

WHAT THE HELL CAN WE GET OUT OF THIS WAR?

THE ANSWER: The best bill of goods any nation has ever had; the only bill of goods by which any nation can survive; the only bill of goods by which this nation has ever lived—Decency!

And what is decency?—the right to live and die without fear.

Hitler has spit in the face of every decent man and woman in the world. He has spit in the face of every child, in the faces of men and women who follow God, be they Jew, Protestant or Catholic.

Hitler must be killed and all the others who would be Hitlers must go with him to their graves.

The United States must declare war against Germany and with this declaration add a simple clause condemning to death Hitler and his agents. The international gangland must go.

I have a feeling the world will be decent again and the United States will help its gallant brothers England and China to make it so. If it takes the rest of our days, let's at least bequeath our children a decent world. That's a mighty fine legacy we inherited.

It's close on to midnight . . . another dawn is about to break through.

Mr. President and Congress, we are awaiting your marching orders. Surely there is a job for every man and woman in the United States to do at this zero hour.

RUSSELL BIRDWELL,
New York City, July 10, 1941

In the middle of the Atlantic we suddenly and dramatically changed course by several compass degrees. You could feel the great battleship turn, even if you were not watching the water. A destroyer ahead of us suddenly cut right across our bows. We all thought of U-boats of course. The ship's sirens sounded.

Then the captain announced to the ship's company that we were going to Iceland, and from that island on to Scapa Flow. He particularly emphasized the need for vigilance.

"We are in dangerous waters here," he said coldly.

I immediately rehearsed Mr. Churchill in his first and second duties: the physical mechanics of escape; and his movements from one position to another in the event we were attacked. He added his own plan: if it appeared he would fall into enemy hands he would shoot it out, keeping his last bullet for himself.

We were warned that air attack was far from unlikely and reminded that the Germans by this time had full information about the conferences having taken place. In matters of this kind, the enemy always knows something but how much is the question. Right now, we didn't know whether the Germans knew our exact location and they would have rather known that than any other secret at the moment.

On Friday, August 15, we learned over the speaker system of the ship that a huge convoy was ahead of us. We were told we would more than likely pass very close to it, that its presence might attract a pack of U-boats, and that we were to be ready for attack at any time, wearing life-belts while on deck. The "No Smoking" rule was invoked.

Soon the convoy appeared before us, ten or fifteen miles east. There were over seventy ships in it. Food and supplies and munitions for England! It was an unbelievably gladdening sight and concrete proof of America there at our shoulder.

Apparently a signal had gone out to the convoy from the *Prince of Wales*, for it seemed to open up politely at the center. We passed right through the gap. It was ranged in ranks, about five loaded freighters in fourteen different clusters, with escort vessels fussing about and darting busily back and forth. Hundreds of planes were lashed to decks, and huge cases of unknown contents. Their crews lined the sides and waved. It was a wonderful sight and one which, should it have been witnessed by Hitler, would have made him perspire and jiggle about. Passing the leading ship, we made a circular movement and came back through the lines of the convoy again. Mr. Churchill then sent the whole convoy a message of good luck, flashed to them all in several ways, including winking from the battle tower of the *Prince of Wales*. We received acknowledgment from the Commodore of the convoy fleet in return. We then circled off north and headed up to Iceland.

We anchored the next morning a short distance from Reykjavik, this island's capital, and proceeded to the port by destroyer. On this trip from Newfoundland we had been accompanied by the engaging young Lieutenant Roosevelt who seemed to me in every way a splendid chap, never counting on or referring to the importance of his father or trading on the usefulness of being his son. Very few knew it, except for the brief conversations recorded earlier, and the times when he would be serving as personal companion to his father, assisting his movement.

On the shores of Reykjavik, a bleak place but not at all inhospitable, we were greeted by the Regent, Sveinn Björnsson, and Mr. Hermann Jonasson, the Prime Minister of Iceland.

Winston Churchill went straight to Government House, where he made a short speech from a window. Then we went on a tour of inspection of the British and American troops stationed there. A car was offered Winston, but he seemed to like the looks of the road and the terrain wasn't steep at these places, so we walked. I shouldn't at all like to live in Iceland but all the people seemed extremely happy, goodhearted, and healthy. They had a marvelous direct look in their eyes.

The whole parade seemed to stretch more than a mile and after the inspection, they all marched past the Prime Minister. He took the salute under the flags of all the represented nations.

On the way back to the car that would return us to the dockside half a mile away, a huge crowd had gathered to wave to Winston. He was pleased and impressed. Several children came up to him, one cute little girl with a bouquet for him that was truly a bit bigger than she was. He took it with a great smile and a deep ceremonious bow, then immediately handed the awful thing to me.

Soon we took leave. There was a deafening sound of cheering from every dock and yard. Members of crews waved from mast and rigging, from shroud and ratline, from anchor chain and forepeak.

We reached Scapa Flow without incident, got on the train and rattled on back to London where he was met by his Cabinet, his colleagues and many friends on the station platform. There was a huge crowd of people. He was given a great ovation there. Eight days later in a broadcast he reported the full story of the Atlantic Charter meeting. The broadcast was in many ways just for Hitler. It was in effect a declaration from the democracies to all peoples of the world that the tyrannies overrunning Europe would be brought to military termination by the democracies and that freedoms would everywhere be restored when Hitler was liquidated.

I have many times wondered what we in this country would have been offered as a defeated nation.

The war continued. You know we lost the *Ark Royal*. This sent Churchill into a long depression. The unbelievable statistic in this immediate catastrophe—that only one life out of 1,600 had been lost—lifted his spirit considerably.

Japan was showing her muscles and her grinning impudence. In a speech at the Mansion House, Churchill warned Japan that we should fight at the side of the U.S.A. if they were ever engaged in conflict and that a declaration of war upon Japan would follow within an hour of America's making a similar declaration.

The autumn had brought some interesting results: first, of course, the Atlantic Charter; then, a heartening speech by the American President that the U.S. might be forced to fight the Axis; and a third item, probably now forgotten: in a joint action British and Soviet troops compelled the Iran government to throw German agents out of their country.

Hitler began sinking American ships. In September the President ordered the famous: "Shoot at sight," for a U-boat had just attacked and sunk the U.S.S. destroyer *Greer*. The order did not stop Hitler. He sunk several American ships in a row. At the same time, American assistance to British convoys in the Atlantic improved and continued daily. And the President ordered the U.S. fleet operating in the Atlantic in defense of American waters to destroy Axis forces operating there and to protect all merchant ships in that area.

The months moved on. Air raids lessened over London though they never ended altogether. Invasion of the Island was still a possibility. Mr. Churchill became warden of the Cinque Ports (southeast coast of England, on down to Dover) where the attempt to breach the coast would surely come. Arrangements were made to flood this land and mire down any equipment the Germans might be able to land, and to shell them from the rim or higher ground that fringes this whole stretch. Plans to let in the sea water were carefully made by our army's engineers and the gates for this are still there. Such Germans as might escape or actually pass through the fire would be slowed here behind the littoral and killed by rifle fire or in direct hand-to-hand combat. It would be a very dirty business.

As petrol began to arrive in great quantity and with increasingly dependable regularity, provisions to accelerate its transportation were made. A pipe was laid clear across the waist of England, and a *pliable* pipe that would bend like cable and could be unreeled from cable spool was being designed for later use to lie on the Channel's bottom and feed gasoline for land and air transport when the time for their use would be at hand. Of course it was a long time coming, but it was there when the moment called for it.

The Japanese representatives were in Washington, discussing the differences of their two countries with Cordell

Hull. The bobbing Japs kept "hoping" that war could be averted, all the time knowing what was smoldering at the other end of the fuse.

Then that perfidious thing happened! And with Roosevelt's note actually on its way to Japan's Emperor!

When the Japanese attacked Pearl Harbor, they also landed in half a dozen places on British territory. The circumstance was in some measure foreseen by Churchill, enabling him in advance to warn Japan that we'd fight with the Americans if they had to fight the Japanese and enabling him to back up that warning, and actually within "the very hour" he had threatened. We were shoulder to shoulder with the Americans now in a war that was now a global one.

Having foreseen the possibility of Japanese attack, Churchill had detached the *Prince of Wales* and the *Repulse* from their duty in holding the German main fleet to continental ports and had sent them both to the Far East.

You will remember we lost these two mighty ships together and but a few hours apart.

Never before had a capital ship been sunk by aerial torpedo. Furious blame was laid at Winston's door for this. He was in a daze, hardly believing. Duff Cooper put it succinctly: "The English are more than usually right but sometimes thirty years behind."

Admiral Phillips of the *Prince of Wales*, who had been a fighting captain in the Royal Navy for over forty years, did not believe in air support. No Englishman, for that matter, believed either that Singapore could be taken through her kitchen door. Yet she was.

For days Churchill moped around, sitting and staring. "I don't understand what happened. I don't understand it."

The loss of these two great ships, in the same attack, was a terrible setback to the increase in our naval strength that we had just managed to win by an overwhelming effort.

Winston wept quietly over the disaster in the Far East. I never saw him take a war shock so hard, nor ever saw one prey on him for so long a time.

It was December. The Prime Minister was to go to the United States. We would leave within forty-eight hours. We were to go on the *Duke of York*, the great fighting ship which I had seen launched by Her Majesty the Queen months before.

The journey commenced in terrible Atlantic weather. We were in dangerous waters west of Ireland. We traveled at a considerable speed without escort. Later on we were met by U.S. destroyers, many of which found it difficult to keep up with our flying battleship, the fastest I had ever been on, or Churchill either. At Bermuda, when I stopped to have a glass of ale, I ran into an American sailor who had just disembarked from one of the American destroyers. He was telling a bar friend of the trip. He had a good summary of it: "We were told to escort a battleship," he said. "Not a goddam greyhound!"

The *Duke* was certainly fast, I can testify.

We arrived at Chesapeake Bay. The Prime Minister and his party immediately left the ship and flew to Washington. It was night time. Those in the plane were transfixed with delight to look down from the windows and see the amazing spectacle of a whole city all lighted up. Washington represented something immensely precious. Freedom, hope, strength. We had not seen an illuminated city for two years. My heart filled.

We were driven in a huge convoy of cars to the White House. This was my first experience with the enormous protective measures thrown around the President in Washington. I had never seen or heard of anything like it. Our Prime Minister, with two Scotland Yard men (my Scotland Yard colleague on this trip was a fine fellow, Sergeant Charles Dudgeon), is able to travel freely anywhere in England, while the President not only has to have an armored car wherever he goes but is also protected by a minimum of twelve men—often eighteen—all bristling with guns.

On arrival at the White House, the President went into a large sitting room and received the large group while seated behind a flag bedecked table. One by one, the members of the Churchill party passed by and were introduced. I personally felt quite honored when he looked up brightly at my approaching him and shook hands warmly. "Well, Thompson, I am very glad to see you again! And to see you have taken such good care of the Prime Minister."

I was immediately struck by the obvious sense of easy cordiality between Roosevelt and Churchill. They were instantly *en rapport*.

Several of the men who had accompanied Churchill to Newfoundland were also with him this time but three important additions had been made in the December trip: Lord Beaverbrook, Air Chief Marshal Sir Charles Portal and General L. C. Holliss of the Office of the Ministry of Defense. Altogether there were over eighty of us.

Among the Americans who had made up the core of the President's group for the Atlantic meeting were Mr. Harry Hopkins, General George Catlett Marshall, and Admiral King. Here in this room now were most of the brains that would have to find the solution to the problem of the Axis' destruction. And they looked as if they could do it.

There was the White House Christmas Tree lighting. It is a pretty ceremony. Hymns, robed choruses, and a presidential Christmas greeting to his own nation, that was in turn flashed around the world by radio relay and short wave. I believe we witnessed the nineteenth consecutive year this happy ceremony has been conducted by an American President.

I know that all of the Englishmen watching were struck by the significance of those lights in America; what it meant to us cannot quite be stated. And apart from any symbolic interpretation which might be put upon the proceedings, the scene itself—with a light, picture card fall of snow —was unforgettable. The vast crowd, the voices drifting across the keen night air, the songs and the children's voices —then the fine bracing sound of the U.S. Marine Band— Roosevelt's voice, then Churchill's—I shall remember the spell and the exhilaration of this hour all my life.

The second time you do anything, it is always easier. So it was with this second meeting with President Roosevelt. I was completely staggered by the security arrangements all over Washington. There were even extra officers from Scotland Yard, but to run into Mike Reilly again seemed very good indeed. We had become good friends in the Atlantic Charter talks.

In the White House, though one felt surrounded by guns, a true friendliness came through to us all. The Americans seemed to adjust more easily to the melodrama of "assassination possibility" than the English do.

And it was true that I was to remain in the White House, close by Mr. Churchill's own suite. My first night in the White House I spent in getting acquainted with its security problem and attuning myself to it and to any conceivable demand on my being needed in a hurry. While poking about, sizing up things, determining heights, distances, telephone locations, exposed risks from bed to bath, etc., I was aware that Mr. Churchill was also poking about, opening drawers and getting himself settled. The room was very warm. All rooms in America are always very warm. Mr. Churchill throve on this. I heard him yawn once or twice, and heard ice chinking pleasantly in his drink. There was a knock at the door. Churchill's valet was not about. "See to that, please, Thompson."

I of course went to the door and opened it, only a crack of course. I was somewhat astonished to discover it to be the President of the United States. He was there in a wheelchair all alone. I opened the door wide for him to come in, then saw the President look curiously beyond me, not with fright but with something very unlike approval. I turned. Winston Churchill was stark naked, a drink in one hand, cigar in the other.

The President offered at once to withdraw and began to turn his chair.

"Come on in, Franklin. We're quite alone." He beamed cordially, then looked innocently down at his dramatic nudity. President Roosevelt hesitated, then with an odd shrug that might have meant, "We're all boys together," he moved on in. Churchill posed briefly and ludicrously before the President: "You see, Mr. President, I have nothing to hide," then tossed a Turkish towel over a shoulder. For an hour he strolled about, happy and full of talk, sipping from his glass, twice filling the President's. He might have been a Roman at the baths, relaxing after a successful debate in the Senate. I don't believe Mr. Churchill would have blinked an eye if Mrs. Roosevelt had walked in too. He's the most modest of men, but with him nudity and modesty are unrelated, nudity being man's most natural state.

In Washington, everywhere we went, all the Americans wanted to know what the bombing was like, and what the city of London looked like. It was not hard to tell them. There was an enormous variety and contrast of outlook among the Americans. Some showed greatly informed curiosities about us, many of course had visited England; but many had very odd views indeed which I tried to repair. But I also found that most Americans prefer not to have their present notions of much of anything repaired but would prefer to retain what they have, whatever it may be, and in this respect I cannot find they are much different from the English. In one respect, though, we were all together, and the Americans themselves were closely cemented. They all had the same notion about the perfidy of Pearl Harbor.

Some perfectly delightful Americans took pity on us two rather lonely Scotland Yard officers. Mr. and Mrs. Frank J. Wilson—Mr. Wilson being of the United States Secret Service—invited us to join them for Christmas dinner. Before leaving the White House to keep this happy engagement, a Negro maid came up to me and said: "I have been asked to give you this by Mrs. Roosevelt."

I opened the package and was pleasantly surprised to find a beautiful necktie and a small white envelope enclosing a Christmas card. These words were written on the card: "For Inspector Walter Henry Thompson—Christmas 1941—A Merry Christmas from the President and Mrs. Roosevelt."

I guess my jaw must have hung loosely for a moment, as the Negro girl stood watching me in dubious fascination. I simply could not believe that the President of a nation, with his countrymen preparing to wage the greatest war in their history, could think of giving a necktie to a police officer on Christmas. Sergeant Dudgeon couldn't believe it either.

My instructions were to be ready to accompany Mr. Churchill to the President's and Mrs. Roosevelt's church for worship and I was of course ready.

All my earlier ideas of gangster-ridden Chicago came back to me, with the added incongruity that we were bound for church to worship our Maker. Enormous precautions were taken. Ahead of us were two long lines of uniformed police on motorcycles with sidecars. Directly behind the President's car were two immense, open touring cars, filled with Secret Service men. All traffic stopped as we proceeded to the church. On arrival within the edifice I had thought dimly that the ancient right of sanctuary would have somewhat reduced the size and obviousness of so much armed protection. But it was not so. All the approaches were under guard. Occupants of houses all the way along to the church had been ordered to stay out of sight, off their porches, and to draw their blinds. I did not see a single face looking out of a single window. At the church itself a whole cordon of Secret Service men, with guns drawn, spread out in a semicircle, watched all the windows in the neighborhood, waiting for any emergency. I could not help thinking back over the years at the many occasions when the Prime Minister had visited Westminster Abbey or St. Paul's—or when Their Majesties had done so—and the great difference, the freedom with which they could move.

I walked into the church at my correct distance from Mr. Churchill, my hand quietly holding my gun butt. It all seemed fantastic that fine people had to be so continuously and visibly protected from elements so bestial even though unseen.

Inside the cathedral it was little better. The pews before and behind were occupied by agents and there were many more standing about. I of course cannot condemn these methods and am not doing so. The Americans know their local problems and deal with them. And whatever their methods, they managed to keep harm away from their President as I had thus far been able to do for my own charge.

Coming back from the service was about the same—as if a huge consignment of gold bullion were being moved to a bank down a street where known groups of gangsters with machine guns were waiting for the right moment to strike. Churchill felt this way too, for he gave me a most dramatic look as he stepped from my immediate protection back into that of the Americans—a look that was half deprecatory and ludicrous. Yet that was the temper of the times and those were the precautions considered necessary.

Returning to the White House, Mr. Churchill wanted to be left alone for several hours. It had become known that he had been invited to address both Houses at the Capitol. An air of excitement prevailed. Everyone wanted to know what he was going to say. What could I tell them? I was most relieved that Sergeant Dudgeon and myself had our own dinner invitation to accept. Churchill was greatly relieved that someone had taken us in, and when I told him of it and asked his permission, he said: "Of course you must both go. I shall be enjoying myself with the President for a few hours and writing for many more after that."

We went downstairs in the huge White House and found that our Secret Service host had put a car at our disposal. We were driven to Mr. Wilson's home. On arrival there we met a Mr. A. H. Callaghan of the Secret Service of Chicago, his wife and a Mrs. C. E. Douglas. We had a most enjoyable time. Our hosts had really excelled themselves. I have never seen such a meal.

They also had presents for us and cards, including a card for the Prime Minister.

People, especially in America, seem most interested in Mr. Churchill's smoking habits. Our Christmas hosts were no exception. It is true Churchill usually has a cigar in his mouth. But if you remember the motion pictures of him, you will recall that he does not seem to be *smoking* the cigars. And this is true. He will light a cigar immediately after breakfast, but by lunchtime the same cigar may be only half finished, having been relighted innumerable times and quite as often abandoned soon after. He chews cigars, he doesn't smoke them. And his average of cigars destroyed is about five per day. He hates cigarettes and though he will accept one at a cocktail party or reception and even will accept a proffered light, I have noticed repeatedly that the cigarette will disappear almost at once.

He likes Cuban cigars best by far, for smoking or merely for waving them about as he talks. His special brand is Romeo and Juliet. People are forever giving him cigars by the thousand.

One day a United States soldier came to Number Ten Downing Street and asked if he could see the Prime Minister. After being told by the doorkeeper that it was not possible and upon my seeing how downcast the young chap felt, I went forward to him and asked if I could be of some help. He informed me brightly that he had discovered where Mr. Churchill purchased his cigars and had been to the store and bought two, one of which he was then smoking but the other of which he wanted to hand to the Prime Minister.

It seemed to this young American to be a matter of the greatest moment. I asked him to wait and slipped out to a telephone. I called the store and was informed that the young soldier had indeed just then left the store and had said that he wanted to buy a cigar for "the great man" and "have a puff or two with him."

As it appeared genuine, I informed him that the cigar would be given to Winston Churchill and that he would in time receive a personal letter from the Prime Minister. This was done and the Old Man did actually smoke the cigar the soldier had brought to Downing Street.

But this is very rare. It would be easy to put poison in a cigar. They could be loaded in many ways, even with germs. For security reasons I could never allow Winston to have them unless we knew the sender well.

Insisting upon this precaution was sometimes embarrassing, but on our American visits it was often very close to tragic. At the White House particularly it was most sad, for here each day and from all over North America and South America and from hundreds of West Indies islands came uncountable boxes of the finest cigars ever made. Hundreds of thousands of them went right into the White House incinerator. Others often smoked them or took them home. But never Winston. And none of the White House staff was permitted to smoke them anywhere in the District of Columbia. But I never heard of one exploding.

His cigars, in a real sense, were somewhat as his drinking. He loved good whisky and brandy but drank very little. He *could* drink and I have heard him say he wished he might at one time have had the opportunity to see whether he could carry as much as Oscar Wilde who could drink three bottles of brandy in a day, so it was said. Of course his suggestion was pure imagination and swagger. But probably he could drink the Russians stupid—nearly anyone could do that if he tried, the trick being not to drink fast—but many days could pass in a row and Churchill never touch a drop save his pint of champagne every day. He was religious about the champagne, his only health fetish. People think he drinks and many people think he drinks hard. There are two reasons for this: one is that Churchill thinks people *want* to think this of him so he lets them think so; the other, that when in company of people who are drinking, he always has a drink in his hand. It is usually full up too, but at the end of an hour, when other guests have had two or three or even four, Churchill's glass is often still full up and still the same glass.

Also he drinks a lot of iced soda water without whisky. And further he has a most disarming little trick: he likes to busy himself at the tables or sideboards where the liquor is being decanted. People think he is taking care of himself. And he is.

He hates anything that delays or impedes or blurs his

thought, and though he enjoys Scotch whisky and brandy and may perhaps, in a month's time, consume quite an amount, I have never seen him drunk in his life. When Field Marshal Montgomery was explaining his perfect physical condition to the late King ("I never touch tobacco or spirits and am 100 per cent fit"), Mr. Churchill immediately rejoined that he himself was an enthusiastic user of brandy and cigars "and I am 200 per cent fit." And that is true. But only the appearance of heavy use is there, not the intake. In all things physical, he is moderate.

Churchill is always quiet before a speech. It is dangerous to speak to him. There is one little ritual between us. I must always ask him whether he has remembered to put his speech glasses in his pocket. He is forgetful of then, and has great difficulty reading typed notes without them. He patted his pocket. Yes, he had them. He beamed brightly.

We then started our journey. We were more impressively surrounded by bodyguards than ever before. And all the members of the American Cabinet seemed to have their own guards. We could have taken on quite a squad of armed Japs between us. Mr. Churchill and the President were cheered all the way to the Capitol. I was very proud of my man. Many people along the wide boulevards of Washington gave the V sign and waved and shouted. The Americans let out their feelings a lot better or at least a lot oftener than we do.

Within the Senate Chamber it surely looked like a full house. All present were keyed up and eager to hear Mr. Churchill. Shortly after, Mr. Churchill entered the Chamber, and everyone rose and cheered for many minutes. When Americans cheer they cheer all over. Flashbulbs appeared from all about. Several hundred pictures were taken. For myself, usually cool, I felt such an enormous pride I could not sit still and hated to think how good my aim would have been if I had had to use my revolver. Among those present to hear him were the Duke and Duchess of Windsor.

After he was presented, a great hush fell upon all those in the Senate Chamber. Those in the gallery leaned forward. Winston began to speak with great assurance and, in the early states of his address, with much humor. I should like to recall some of it for you:

Members of the Senate and of the House of Representatives of the United States: I feel greatly honored that you should have thus invited me to enter the United States Senate Chamber and address the representatives of both branches of Congress. The fact that my American forebears have for so many generations played their part in the life of the United States and that here I am, an Englishman, welcomed in your midst, makes this experience one of the most moving and thrilling in my life, which is already long and has not been entirely uneventful.

I wish indeed that my mother, whose memory I cherish across the vale of years, could have been here to see. By the way, I cannot help reflecting that if my father had been an American and my mother British, instead of the other way around, I might have got here on my own.

At this point the happy laughter and affectionate approval broke up his speech for several moments. Afterward he became more personal as to his own purpose and belief, and candidly told the Americans what he felt about the war. I will quote enough of it to bring back this great event to you.

The forces ranged against us are enormous. It is quite true that on our side our resources in manpower and materials are far greater than theirs. But only a portion of your resources are as yet mobilized.

We have indeed to be thankful that so much time has been granted to us. If Germany had tried to invade the British Isles after the French collapse in June, 1940, and if Japan had declared war on the British Empire and the United States at about the same date, no one can say what disaster and agonies might not have been our lot. But now, at the end of December, 1941, our transformation from easygoing peace to total war efficiency has made very great progress.

I think it would be reasonable to hope that the end of 1942 will see us quite definitely in a better position than we are now, and that the year 1943 will enable us to assume the initiative upon an ample scale. Some people may be startled or momentarily depressed when, like your President, I speak of a long, hard war.

Our peoples would rather know the truth, somber though it may be, and after all, when we are doing the most blessed work in the world, not only defending our hearths and homes, but the cause of freedom in every land, the question of whether deliverance comes in 1942 or 1943 or 1944 falls into its proper place in the grand proportions of human history.

Many people have been astonished that Japan, in a single day, has made war on the United States and the British Empire.

Is it possible they do not realize that we shall never cease to persevere against them until they have been taught a lesson which they and the world will never forget?

Members of the Senate and members of the House of Representatives: I'll turn for one moment more from the turmoil and convulsions of the present to the broader spaces of the future. Here we are together, facing a group of mighty foes who seek our ruin.

Five or six years ago, it would have been easy, without shedding a drop of blood, for the United States and Great Britain to have insisted on the fulfillment of the disarmament clauses of the treaties which Germany signed after the great war.

The chance has departed; it is gone. Prodigious hammer strokes have been needed to bring us together today.

It is not given to us to peer into the mysteries of the future; yet, in the days to come, the British and American peoples will, for their own safety and for the good of all, walk together in majesty, in justice, and in peace.

He stood still for a moment at the end, then turned and sat down. There was an instant of dead silence. Then, as the Americans say, "all hell broke loose." Something great for all the English-speaking peoples all over the world had happened in those minutes and it is still going on.

The enthusiasm that flowed with Winston Churchill that day in Washington carried on into Ottawa. He greatly loves Canada and loves to be in Canada. He busied himself, even before leaving the United States, with the address he was preparing for delivery in the Canadian Capitol.

We left Washington on December 28, being accompanied by Mr. Mackenzie King, Prime Minister of Canada. At the Canadian border we were met by numbers of the Royal Canadian Mounted Police. They are most picturesque in their red tunics, blue breeches, highly polished jackboots and stetsons. I have seen many of these men during my visits to Canada and I consider them, not only in terms of physique but also from the point of police officers, to be among the finest in the world. One felt safe at the mere sight of a Royal Mounted Police officer in Canada.

We were met in the Ottawa station by a huge crowd,

well muffled, most of them in furs. We wished the same for ourselves the instant we stepped down. It was fifteen degrees below zero. The ovation Mr. Churchill received was a typical Canadian one, and we had considerable difficulty in getting him to his car.

The journey to Government House had been arranged so that Mr. Churchill could take in many parts of the city, and during his drive he was greeted from every side. The orderliness of the people here, en route, was most noticeable. They remained where the police had suggested they stay—on the sides of the road—very much as London crowds would do. "Good old Winnie!" would ring out, then a cheer. "Good luck, Winston!" Such could be heard constantly.

After luncheon at the world-famous hotel, Château Laurier, with members of the Canadian Cabinet and Chiefs of Staff, he was greeted by Inspector Wilson of the Royal Canadian Mounted Police, and told the Inspector he was honored to be in their charge. The Inspector gave him a large round box and suggested he open it later, at the press conference at Government House. This Winston did. With all the newsmen gathered round, Winston unwrapped the gift and found it to be a Canadian fur hat, a real beauty. He wore it all the time after that and would never allow anyone to touch it, but would stand indefinitely while his picture was taken.

Tuesday, December 30, was the day of his speech in the Canadian House of Commons. Here the preliminary greetings were as noisy, if possible, as they had been in America. When the great room became still, he commenced, very quietly at first, then warming to his subject. Sometimes you can see something coming from Winston for several moments before it arrives. It was evident now, from the humorous smile that began to grow larger and larger on his face. Everyone knew something unusual was on the way. Referring to France, he said: "But their chiefs misled them. When I warned them that Britain would fight on alone, their chiefs told their Prime Minister and his Cabinet that in three weeks England would have her neck wrung like a chicken." Here he paused, took off his glasses, and peered down at the multitudes in front of him, and loudly shouted: "SOME CHICKEN! SOME NECK!"

Never will I forget that day! This comment, hilarious,

defiant, indomitable, brought the whole House to its feet, roaring.

Our journey back to Washington, where we were to spend a few days before the Prime Minister was to have a brief holiday in Palm Beach, carried us out of the old year and into the new. All on board Churchill's train were delighted to receive a message that the Prime Minister wished to see them in the dining saloon. Drinks were passed around, and at midnight Mr. Churchill gave the toast: "Here's to a year of toil, a year of struggle and peril, and a long step forward to Victory!" After this, with hands joined, "Auld Lang Syne" was sung, the Prime Minister holding the hands of Sir Charles Portal and a Royal Air Force sergeant. It was a representative and typical party, including press photographers, newsmen and women, the white and Negro staff of the train, and the private staff of the Prime Minister.

Back in the United States the interest being shown in Churchill's speeches was apparent everywhere. He was constantly being quoted. References in all the journals were being made to him and what he'd said; so were short paragraphs from his speeches, remarks selected at random. One especially that caught the American imagination was this: "We are looking forward to the invasion—So are the fishes!" But the one that stayed with most, that will go on as part of the life and legend of the man, was the following. "We shall not flag or fail. We shall go on to the end. We shall fight on the beaches. We shall fight on the landing grounds. We shall never surrender."

Our stay in Washington was very short. Soon we were in West Palm Beach, having been flown there in General George Marshall's plane. Winston needed this rest very badly.

A beautiful villa had been placed at his disposal at Palm Beach, at a considerable distance from the next nearest property. I had never seen a place quite like it and was having much trouble in forcing myself to believe that we had within less than four days been in temperatures which went down to thirty below zero during the night, and stayed below zero all day.

I don't know whether it was a vacation or not. He went into the ocean practically every day, sometimes more than once, but he refused to take it as a holiday and refused to let his staff take it as one. He worked on until the early hours of the morning just as if he were in London, and on many occasions was on the telephone to London or Washington, sometimes at three and four in the morning.

The day following our arrival, I approached the Prime Minister to find out what kind of a swimsuit he would like me to get for him. I told him I was going to a store in town to get one for myself.

"I don't think I need one," he said blandly, and to my astonishment.

I made the polite sounds implying doubt and just the faintest remonstrance—the kind of noises butlers make in the cinema when they don't use words.

"No," he continued, unimpressed. "It's quite private here. And no one knows I'm staying in this part. It's quite a secret. And I've been promised it's one that'll be well kept."

Both these statements were of course true.

"You see, Thompson," he encouraged, waving toward the villa, "I have only to step out of the back door into the sea."

"But you can be seen through field glasses, sir," I said.

To which he instantly replied: "If they are that much interested, it is their own fault what they see!"

I knew it would be money thrown away to buy him a swimsuit. What did he do about this? Just what you think.

He did carry a large towel "in deference to local propriety," as he said. This covered him from head to toe, but he would abandon this garment as soon as he got close to the ocean itself, and paddle about, puffing and swimming, treading water, floating on his back, rolling, foaming and in general taking complete charge of this portion of the Atlantic —and just as happy and as naked as the day he was born. Then he'd sun himself in the nude. He looked like a huge, well-adjusted and slightly over-bottled baby boy, all grins and natural surrender.

His valet, who would stand by patiently with the towel, waiting for the Prime Minister's eventual beaching, kept darting his glance up and down the long white strip of sand, fearful that this awful secret might somehow get out.

One day it very nearly did, not so much the nude swimming of the King's First Minister as the fact that it was indeed Churchill who was staying at this particular villa. No one but a king or a gangster could command so much attention and curiosity and require so many armed guards. But nothing exasperates or challenges the average American newspaperman so much as a story they can't crack or a place they can't crash. They *knew* somebody interesting was in this villa and that it was not the owner.

On our third day at the villa a car drove up containing two ladies. They alighted and politely wanted to be told who was in residence. The American Secret Service men put them off by saying that someone who had been ill had rented the villa. They hoped the explanation would suffice. I knew it wouldn't.

The women were representatives of the press and no mistake. I thought of the *Europa* in 1931: the fellow who put on the steward's jacket and cap. I needed no warning. I only have to be told once. I knew the girls would be back. One of them was a good-looking girl. As their car drove away from the villa, she kept looking back. They circled the driveway once and came right back, but were severely waved off by the Secret Service this time.

The villa was on high ground. The guard which was maintained by the Secret Service and by ourselves covered every approach. It was therefore even more surprising, since they had been driven away, to see these women some distance away on the beach, coming in our direction. One of the girls stopped, poked a beach umbrella into the sand and sat down. The other one took off her shoes and stockings and began wading up toward us, carefully not looking our way. We made ourselves invisible, only one of us remaining within sight.

The barefoot girl was the good-looking one. She was the first person to pass along the beach since our arrival seventy-two hours earlier.

When she reached our part of the beach, she got into conversation with one of the young Secret Service men. From one of the windows, which was my station during the informal watches that we set up, I could see and hear her. As a newspaper person she was very determined and as a woman very direct. She told the Secret Service man that she knew someone of great importance was in that villa. He said, "So what?" She said, "If you can tell me who it is, I will go away and just print that and no more. If, however, you can arrange to get me an interview with him, you may spend your nights with me—in case I happen to appeal to you in that way." "How many nights," he asked. "A week?" she suggested.

I had not yet reached an age where my contemplation of

this young man's dilemma was one of philosophical detachment. In fact I was plain fascinated. But I am happy to report that after a searing inventory of himself, followed by some of the most interesting dialogue I ever heard in America, the Secret Service came through in a fine, though battered, show of self-denial. And I'm sure it wasn't easy. She looked very nice with her shoes off, a condition recommended by one of my own countrymen, Bea Lillie.

But the strong man did the strong, noble, uninteresting thing. He did more. He gave her a folding camp stool so she could get her stockings back on and it was during this rather delightful operation I had to remind myself that I also lived by a harsh code.

So the privacy of the Prime Minister was never penetrated. The press everywhere else had been splendid. They were very much for him. On January 6, the President, in a speech to Congress, referred to Churchill's visit in this way: "All in our nation have been cheered by Mr. Churchill's visit. We have been stirred by his great message to us. We wish him a safe return to his home." This remark tended to give the impression, at home and abroad, that the Prime Minister was on his way home.

But secretly we returned on January 10 to Washington.

The last morning at the villa, though it was raining, Winston decided to take a final swim in the ocean. While walking down to the water we all heard a loud shout. A shark had been sighted. Indeed it could be very easily seen, not twenty feet from the shore line. It was at least fifteen feet long. It coasted lazily past, a gentle-moving terror if ever there was one. He was told it was probably a sand shark and that it would do no harm. In Florida, I discovered that every shark is a sand shark and no sand shark is ever hungry. I told Churchill to stay out of the water; that my usefulness ended at the edge. The shark was big enough to eat a horse. Even Winston was impressed. "Sand shark? I am not so sure about that. I want to see his Identification Card before I trust myself to him." But he went in anyhow, though not far. "Keep sending me bulletins, Thompson," he shouted. "Keep him classified as inoffensive!" The shark turned in a slow half circle, looked at the Prime Minister, and swam away.

"My bulk has frightened him into deeper water," said Winston, and pawed about happily.

Back in Washington the Prime Minister worked under cover with the President and the Chiefs of Staff for five days. On the night of the 15th we were taken by a secret route and put on an unmarked sleeping train. We did an hour's trip on this train, all the blinds drawn. It was full of Secret Service men. I was mighty glad to see so many of them about. A killing would have materially and tragically altered history.

We went to Bermuda by the flying boat *Berwick*. Captain Kelly Rogers was in command. I marveled at the accommodations. It was not only large but luxurious. The dining room would seat twelve. Churchill can't resist airplanes, and though he's poor at the controls, he doesn't know this. Once aboard, he appropriated the copilot's seat, cigar and all. For purposes of easy movement he was wearing his well-known siren suit, which he calls his "rompers." Winston was as delighted to be at the controls ("I have just reappointed myself Minister for Air, Thompson") as I was nervous to have him there.

He was to speak in Bermuda, then we were to return to England on the *Duke of York*. But it was apparent he'd fallen in love with the *Berwick*.

"I need to save the time, Thompson," he rationalized, sensing my objections before I made them. It was altogether unnecessary for Winston Churchill to fly back to England but fly he did—without me.

We met up again in six days. He reported his visit to the United States to the House of Commons. German broadcasts were trying to show that the government in Great Britain was about to collapse. To answer this, Churchill decided he would make the debate on the war's progress an issue, for the purpose of obtaining a vote of confidence. He got it—464 to 1.

Nineteen forty-two was rough. Hitler, in his New Year's message to the German people, said: "The year 1942 will bring the final decision and will mean the salvation of our people."

Indeed, we still had to take our worst blows, some in the belly, some in the heart. Some of them doubled us clear over. While Russia was hitting back at Sevastopol and Rostov, the danger to Singapore was becoming daily more critical. Almost all the Pacific news was bad.

In Africa, Derna and Benghazi were lost to us. Rommel

seemed irresistible. During these months, he was too. After Churchill dispatched the *Repulse* and the *Prince of Wales* to Far East waters, the *Scharnhorst*, *Gneisnau*, and *Prinz Eugen* escaped through the English Channel to the safety of German waters. It was a brilliant and daring piece of seamanship and made us all look like chumps. It needed a lot of explaining.

But the fall of Singapore staggered the English spirit. And the Japanese treatment of civilians there, including the wives of English subjects and civil servants, was sickening in the extreme. Many were raped. Many committed suicide. Some were mercifully shot by their own husbands before the Japs could get at them. The fall of Singapore was a truly damaging military defeat of far-reaching and in some ways irreparable effect. It shook Churchill worse than did the evacuation of Dunkirk. At Dunkirk, we saved the majority of the army. But at Singapore, we could not make replacements. We lost a whole army.

In England I fear we were under a false impression that Singapore was impregnable. From remarks which the Prime Minister had made at various times—as recently as six weeks before at a press conference in Ottawa—it would appear today that he also shared that opinion. He was dumbfounded. During my period of guarding him—beginning in 1921—I have never seen him so disheartened. He could take the worst sort of knock, but this seemed one that was beyond his control. It was almost as if, through an unexampled carelessness, he had caused the death of one of his own children. These were bitter days. He could not sleep or eat.

When about to crack, he was urged to take some few days off. This he did, with Mr. and Mrs. Ronald Tree as his hosts. We arrived on a Friday evening. Phones were cut off so he could sleep. About thirty minutes after he retired, I was notified that he wanted to see me. I went right up. He told me that the telephone had awakened him. He was not angry. He was just pathetic. In a miserable voice, and with a face as pale as paper, he rose unsteadily and went over to a desk. "Sleep for me is finished. I will do some work." I later found that although I had asked the house operator to stop all calls to the Prime Minister, a switch that transferred calls from the secretaries' room to that of Mr. Churchill had not been taken off.

I then had a talk with Mr. Rowan, one of the Prime Minister's secretaries, and told him my secret fear: that Winston was so despondent, I actually felt if some relief to his mind were not soon discovered, he would descend into despair. It was agreed we should speak to his doctors and urge a longer holiday, and do so right away.

While dressing the second morning, he listened to my suggestion about a trip. "Yes, you are quite right, Thompson." He was, as I could tell by his physical actions in the mere matter of putting on his clothing, completely spent. "I should go soon," he said.

He then and there promised me he would do so. And he did.

The war thickened. Hitler was now engaging Stalingrad and finding that a smashed city can be the hardest thing in the world to take. But he was telling the world he *would* take it and stay in it. Rommel was still going where he pleased in Libya. Malta was defiant, though nearly pulverized from the air. Spitfires, for the first time, began to engage the Luftwaffe over Malta. This helped. The Germans said we couldn't get them there. They came from the decks of the U.S.S. *Wasp*. And the spirit of the Maltese was lifted immeasurably when His Majesty the King bestowed the George Cross upon the island.

We kept on taking losses in the Pacific. The *Exeter*, *Dorsetshire* and *Cornwall* were all sunk. Our small Far Eastern fleet had been annihilated. The British aircraft carrier *Hermes* had been sunk, as far away as Ceylon.

As the Americans would say, we were taking a shellacking. Certainly our prestige was. A year had passed since we had lost all our equipment at Dunkirk, and much of our heavy equipment dispatched to the Far East had never got east of Suez.

Churchill stiffened in the presence of all these horrors. His jaw came out again. "We must hold on."

Churchill made an accounting of the war to his countrymen after his first two years as Prime Minister. He said our reverses had been greater than our gains. But he looked forward to better days, and with good reason. American troops were pouring in, not only to the Far East, but also into Northern Ireland and to England too.

Earlier despondency had begun to clear. Fight was coming back. During these months our own heavy bomber strength had been growing. On May 30 soon after midnight, the Bomber Command had attacked the city of Cologne with more than one thousand bombers. The Germans were beginning to get it back. It was just a start. But it was the biggest air raid in history up to that time. Winston personally sent his congratulations to the whole Bomber Command on their wonderful feat of organization. Two nights later they did it again, plastering Essen and the Ruhr, with more than one thousand planes in the air.

But if we got ahead in one spot, we fell back somewhere else. Rommel had launched his Afrika Korps attack. We lost Tobruk. We had to pull back to El Alamein.

It was mid-June. Another talk between President Roosevelt and Winston Churchill was called for. Winston took a very small party this time. Its principal members were Sir Alan Brooke and General Sir Hastings Ismay. We flew from the north of England to the Potomac River in the *Bristol*, reaching Washington in twenty-six hours.

Winston caused much amusement on the trip over. He was relaxed. He loved flight. He did not much care what he looked like. This time he looked unbelievably ludicrous. He lay back in the rear of the plane, seeming to occupy most of the space there, absolutely flamboyant in baby blue siren suit and the gaudiest dressing gown ever seen on an Englishman. He changed hats a couple of times as the draughts seemed to change in the plane, and chewed a six-inch cigar most of the way across the Atlantic. It was better for me not to look at him.

The President was at the airport to meet the Prime Minister. We went at once to the White House, and Winston sat down immediately with his party and General George C. Marshall and Lieutenant General Arnold.

The meetings were barely started when the heavy news came to us that the British ships, containing armored vehicles to reinforce our armies in Libya, had been sunk. As you will remember, the Mediterranean was almost impassable, and supplies had to be sent thousands of miles around the Cape of Good Hope, then through the Suez Canal.

President Roosevelt looked up at this news and, as if declaring advantages he could see in a hand of whist, he said: "I have a number of Sherman tanks just being issued to our army. You shall have them at once. We'll send them for you right away." Without an instant's delay, without even waiting for Winston to thank him or any of the admirals and generals to react, he picked up a telephone at his side and issued the order then and there.

These tanks—minus a single shipload which a U-boat got —enabled us to drive the Germans back from El Alamein.

This alone would have made the trip more than worth while.

Things got very rough for Churchill, the politician, in London. While we were still in the United States, it was moved in the House of Commons by Sir John Wardlaw Milne, a member of Churchill's own party: "That this House while paying tribute to the heroism and endurance of the armed forces of the Crown in circumstances of exceptional difficulty, has no confidence in the central direction of the war."

We were all stunned by this. I was especially pricked to discover that the seconder of the motion had been Admiral Sir Roger Keyes, a great personal friend of the Prime Minister's, certainly a man who could comprehend the size of the problem Churchill dealt with.

Everyone in the White House corps kept asking me what it meant.

"Does it mean they want to get rid of Winston?" In the American opinion, and that of the world, too, Mr. Churchill was the principal director of the war. It was difficult for me to reply. I could only say what I thought was the truth of it, that many in the House of Commons were disaffected by our reverses in Libya.

The American newspapers had headlines hard to look at: COMMONS DEMANDS CHURCHILL RETURN TO FACE ACCUSERS. That was one. Here's another: CHURCHILL RETURNS TO SUPREME POLITICAL CRISIS. A third: WILL CHURCHILL RESIGN?

This news was staggering to the Prime Minister and cut him deeply. He thought the motion poorly timed in the extreme, while he was representing his own country abroad. It made it most awkward for him. Perhaps that was intended.

As is well known, Churchill replied at considerable length. The "no confidence" motion, offered by Sir John Wardlaw Milne, was defeated, 475 to 25.

June 11 was a day of momentous decision for Great Britain and Russia. On that day Molotov and Churchill signed a treaty providing for full collaboration between the two countries for twenty years. One of the items of significance about this signing was the fact that Churchill had been known for many years to be most antagonistic toward Russia. It was clear in everything he said, inside and outside the House. He hated their leaders and loathed their principles.

With the signing, however, it seemed an opportune time for the Prime Minister to see Marshal Stalin. Stalin wouldn't leave Russia. You went to him.

We flew out of England on August 1st in a Liberator Commando. It was piloted by an American, Captain Van de Kloot. Its copilot was Captain J. Ruggles.

Flying at this stage of the war, via Gibraltar and Cairo, was far from safe.

It was still light when we took off from Gibraltar. We arrived safely in Cairo, where Field Marshal Smuts was waiting. It was their first meeting since the war began. It was also the first time I had ever met this most remarkable and lovable man. Churchill loved him beyond all other humans and felt toward him as he might for his own father, were he still living then.

Smuts was in perfect health, very bouncy.

The High Command in Libya needed drastic change. Churchill intended that the army should have a new start under new leaders. In arriving at a decision so difficult, he relied on what he called—and what has since become the characterizing sentence that sums up Churchill's full attitude regarding Smuts as a political and military figure—the "massive judgment" of the Field Marshal.

After a visit to El Alamein, General Alexander succeeded General Auchinleck, with General Montgomery given command under Alexander of the famous 8th Army.

We went on then across the wastes of southern Persia, having picked up our full complement for the Stalin talks. Accompanying Churchill were Mr. Averell Harriman, General Maxwell, commanding U.S. forces in Egypt, General Sir Archibald Wavell and Air Marshal Tedder. We rested and refueled in the oriental capital of Teheran.

We reached Moscow in the early evening. The Moscow airfield was crowded with dutiful Russians. There was a great deal of mechanical smiling.

Molotov had a secret destination for us some miles from Moscow. We got in cars and were driven off, myself close to the Old Man.

I was struck by the width of the streets; some were four hundred feet wide. What amazed me more was the speed of motor vehicles in the city of Moscow itself. They went sixty or even seventy miles an hour, screaming around curves. The streets were nearly empty. Windows looked blank. Expressions on faces were gawking and incapable of communication. As the motor cavalcade passed by, the small groups that we would be near merely stared at nothing, not the slightest bit interested in anything or anybody around them. They were not even talking among themselves. They seemed impervious to human approach of any kind.

Though we were surrounded with the most important men in all Russia except for Joe himself we were everywhere challenged by soldiers. Outhouse and grounds were surrounded with armed sentries. They stood on walls and on the roof and in windows. I thought of going to church with the President in Washington.

Later I found how difficult it was to move about. You had to make application by telephone and a period of thirty minutes always elapsed before any move could be made. The Russians seem cosmically indifferent to bathrooms. We moved everywhere under guard and escort and under the thrust of perpetual challenge, even though Molotov was with us all the time.

At six that evening we left for the Kremlin. We passed seven guards to get in. On entering, we then met members of the OGPU. They followed us to the Marshal's room. Here we were separated from Winston Churchill and taken to another room.

A few moments after we were seated, we were ushered out again. Churchill had had his first row with Joe and was banging down the corridors of the Kremlin looking neither to right nor left. He struck a match on the Kremlin wall and still walking, lighted a cigar, puffing angrily. Stalin had tried to crowd a decision out of Churchill a little sooner than the Prime Minister wanted to give it.

We went to the villa assigned to Churchill. The following day the rest of our party arrived.

On Friday night the whole British Mission was invited to a banquet at the Kremlin. I have attended hundreds of dinners and banquets while serving Winston, but I never saw so much food laid out anywhere in the world—not even in Saudi Arabia, where they once slaughtered five thousand sheep for Winston. There was so much to eat you couldn't start: caviar soft or pressed, whitefish, salmon, sturgeon (pails of it), garnished herrings, dried herrings, cold ham, whole hot hams, game suffocating in gondolas of mayonnaise, salad payar, white mushrooms in sour cream, forcemeat of game, eggplant meunière, crème de Poularde, bathtubs of borsch, turkey, chicken, partridge, suckling lamb, suckling pig, thirty desserts and ices, and a rack of liqueurs bigger than the layout in New York's Astor Hotel bar.

The Russians ate everything and ate all the time. I'd heard of this. Now I dived into it. But a short-rationed Englishman can only have a good time for a few seconds at such a feast. My stomach was small, and even in peacetime I was never a heavy eater. I was soon through, very disappointed I could not do better. My seat was directly in front of the two principals. Stalin wore a kind of smock pulled together in the middle with a beautiful handworked leather belt. He wore breeches and jackboots. This was in sharp contrast to the military uniforms all around him. He was having a fine time. The first spoon had hardly been sent on his first mission into the bowls of vichysoisse when Joe was up toasting people. He was very democratic in this little ritual. He toasted everybody on earth, one at a time. Then he would toast them all over again, starting on the other side of the world and working back. It took many hours. Then he toasted everybody at his own table, then everybody at all the other tables. He moved around from one table to another like a fiddle player in a gypsy restaurant in Soho.

Dinner and toasting went on for several hours. About midnight the party repaired to the champagne room where there were more toasts. Winston had been a good sport for the first three or four hours of this. But there was work to do. Many of the Russians were drunk and singing, mistaking me for the "Minister from Scotland," or for nearly anything. They didn't want to do any work. Churchill became more and more ill at ease and kept his eye on Stalin. Photographs were taken.

I saw Churchill whispering to Sir Alexander Cadogan, who in turn spoke to an interpreter, a Mr. Pavlov, to convey to Mr. Stalin the request that the Prime Minister wanted to see Stalin alone, and now.

Joe Stalin would not hear of it. He dismissed the request and the person of Pavlov with a shove and went on drinking.

Churchill was disgusted. He got up and strode out. Sir Alexander Cadogan went with him. Naturally I did too.

When Stalin saw the British leaving the party, he did have the courtesy to come to the door of the great chamber to say good evening. Churchill was furious. There is a time when diplomats must keep their temper—most of the time. And there is a time when it is mandatory for them to lose it. And now was the time. Churchill's voice rose. He shook a finger at Pavlov, then shook the other one almost in Joe Stalin's face and he told Pavlov to tell Joe that if there was to be any "discussing," it better happen before the early part of Sunday morning as he (Churchill) and his party were leaving for Cairo then whether anything was accomplished or not.

The next day Mr. Churchill was respectfully informed that Marshal Stalin was most anxious to have a private visit with the Prime Minister and would he be so kind as to come to the Kremlin for dinner at 6:00 P.M. Churchill said he would.

We went through much of the same rigmarole as before. Winston and I were alone this time, however. I was not allowed to go in with him, when the Prime Minister was ushered into the Marshal's private study. I said I would wait at the door; the OGPU said I would not. Here we argued. I opened my coat and showed my guns. Pavlov came up with a big man I recognized as Molotov's special bodyguard whenever Molotov traveled abroad. Pavlov was asked to find out what the trouble was. I said I would no more budge from this location than he (pointing to Molotov's bodyguard) would budge from the side of his charge in London. It turned into a hell of a show. But I was as big as they were, a free man, well armed, and very cross. I talked with great force and unbelievable speed directly to the Russians, knowing that Pavlov could not pick up everything I was saying, then emphasizing it the more by crowding in while the amazed Pavlov was trying to make me understood. Then I took out my guns, transferred them to my side pockets and stood with back to door, facing them all. I stuck out my elbows. I looked tough. I can look very tough. I looked as tough as them. I stood there till 2:00 A.M.

I did not like the Russians at all. But then I did not like all the Englishmen who worked with and around Winston. Neither did he, I am sure. But they were all unusual, energetic, morally brave. Many of them were mental marvels. Lord Cherwell especially. Cadogan was the coldest I encountered—a real oyster. In the Kremlin, with my nerves frayed, wondering why Winston was being so long sequestered, dreading the worst and then running into the austere Cadogan, I had thought the momentary fellowship of a kindred soul on the same mission and in the same misery would have extracted a little cheer. But Cadogan, though as worried as I, was as silent as the Russians around us; mute as Pavlov, cold as the Kremlin's masonry. I cannot this day recall one single word that came out of this man.

That night in the Kremlin I'd have given a month's pay for a smile from an Englishman but Cadogan was all that penetrated my vigil and he has a look that can wither croupiers.

Suddenly the door opened and Churchill came out, smiling broadly. We returned to the villa. Churchill had come up with something he had gone down for. I never knew what it was. But his artifice in being furious, and *in showing his fury*, had won him a big point.

As we left, Winston pointed to something. It was the upper part of one of the buildings in the grounds that had been destroyed by the Germans. Scaffolding had been erected and a number of women could be seen working with the men on the roof. Women were in all the work groups I saw in Russia and worked clear round the clock, with the men, on any rush job such as this repair.

We flew back to Teheran, where Churchill lunched with the Shah of Persia. Then on to Cairo and twenty-four hours later, a second visit to the troops at El Alamein. He spent the night in the headquarters of General Alexander. He produced his prodigious ten-gallon hat and also an umbrella. He went about with both, as protection against the terrible sun, much to the amusement of the troops.

Someone shouted, "There's Winston!—hat, umbrella, cigar and all!" One soldier, somewhat bolder than the others, directly asked Mr. Churchill for a cigar. "Of course you shall have one," Winston said at once, handing over a fresh one.

He addressed the troops at El Alamein. He told them that the tanks they should have received had been sent to the bottom. Then he said that through the immediate reaction of President Roosevelt, new tanks—Shermans—far more powerful than those which were first sent—were already arriving. This was cheered with great excitement.

Rommel at this time had his first big setback. He attacked the southern flank of the Qattara depression. We were ready for it.

Back in London Churchill said this of Joe: "Stalin is an outstanding personality of inexhaustible courage and will-power, direct and even blunt in speech, with a sense of humor, cool wisdom, and absence of illusions." He said that the Russians in general did not think we had done enough for them, to take the weight off them. They should have seen London. Or Singapore. Or the fleet. Or the North African coast we had just been to. I thought what Churchill permitted himself to be quoted as saying about Joe Stalin was more than generous. There were other comments from the British as well as the Americans coming back from the Kremlin that the Marshal would not have cared to hear. But I can't set them down here. There would be a good many among us who could also claim "absence of illusions."

A very large U.S. Mission came to London. In it were Admiral King, Harry Hopkins, Ambassador Winant, Mr. William Bullitt, and Admiral Stark. After about six weeks of heavy consultations, satisfactory agreements were reached as to the further prosecution of the war and Mr. Churchill had a big dinner for everybody at Greenwich where they were met by the First Lord, Mr. A. V. Alexander. It was a great and noisy affair. Everyone relaxed. The First Lord entertained his visitors by playing the piano: well-known melodies that English-speaking people on both sides of the Atlantic have been singing for a couple of centuries. Winston tried to join in this. But while Churchill can undoubtedly make speeches he definitely cannot sing.

In late October Mrs. Roosevelt arrived in England. Unfortunately she was not accompanied by the President. The First Lady was met by Their Majesties at Paddington, and on leaving the station she received a hearty welcome from a great crowd in and around the station. She stayed for awhile with Their Majesties and, after the official visit, toured around London visiting bombed areas and various women's services and organizations.

Mrs. Churchill went with her on several occasions. Mrs. Roosevelt is a woman of inexhaustible energy and on many of these journeys, her pace was too much for the Prime Minister's wife. Weather made no difference to Mrs. Roosevelt. She had been told that the weather would mostly be bad and the thing to do was to ignore it. Since Mrs. Roosevelt had come to see things for herself, she fully intended to do so, weather or no weather.

In changing generals in North Africa, Mr. Churchill's foresight became manifest. Rommel was now beginning to retreat, a retreat that took him, eventually, out of Libya, Cyrenaica, Tripolitania and Tunis—with the loss of his army and his equipment.

Hitler was not yet desperate but things were not going the way he had predicted the year before. Or even the month before.

Because of our intensified bombing, Germany announced a form of reprisal to be called the "Baedeker raids." This merely meant that the German Luftwaffe would pick out towns and small cities and wage war on noncombatant populations without mercy.

Agonies like this were forgotten when greater news like the invasion of North Africa and Morocco could be announced. The incredible armada from America had traversed the Atlantic—837 ships—without the loss of a ship! The impact of this would not be immediately felt but the political and psychological impact was instantaneous. Hitler ordered the occupation of the southern half of France. Meanwhile Admiral Darlan arrived in Africa and put himself at the disposal of the Free French authorities.

On November 27, Darlan called upon the French fleet to come to North Africa, or to put in at British ports. A large number responded. It now became apparent that Darlan wanted to assume power, for he soon elected himself Chief of State and later on Leader of the French Empire.

Questions were at once put to the House of Commons as to what the British position vis-à-vis Darlan was. They were never answered. Darlan was assassinated in Algiers. It was Christmas Eve.

As the 8th Army neared Tripoli, Allied troops began to occupy most of the territory of North Africa. It was time for another meeting, one that would, it was hoped, effectuate what Roosevelt had been insisting upon: unconditional surrender.

For this meeting the Prime Minister, accompanied by Sir Charles Portal and Mr. Harriman, left England by plane in utmost secrecy. We arrived at Casablanca the following morning, January 12, 1943. The Allied authorities had commandeered a large hotel, the Angfa, for our use, together with its attached villas. The whole layout was on top of a hill.

Barbed wire surrounded the place and American sentries patrolled everywhere. The Prime Minister was housed in a villa just previously vacated by members of the German Armistice Commission and evidence of their quick getaway was everywhere. The oven was still on in the kitchen and there was a burnt roast in it. Unopened boxes of cigars were about.

The Chiefs of Staff of both England and the United States went to work right away. By now we had become pretty good at this sort of thing. But after a few days it became clear to all that something was wrong. An important cog somewhere needed some oil. It was the French—more specifically the friction between General Giraud who had become High Commissioner, and General de Gaulle whose position, while indeterminate for Allied purpose, was not sufficiently eminent to suit him. Efforts were made to bring these two patriots together. They failed. Churchill got very fidgety. He could never stand the unsmiling chill of de Gaulle anyhow. It was not new.

The friction which began some time after de Gaulle came to England, I feel, was the outcome of his continued demand to be placed in charge of some form of attack against the enemy. De Gaulle appeared during these terrible days to resent any action which did not coincide with his wishes. He was probably suffering inside in a most awful way: disappointed, only half recognized. Sour people never understand why others don't like them, and if they also have a fine record, their resentments can border on the neurotic. De Gaulle had no personality whatsoever. And he was most brutally brusque. The Germans could also be most brutally brusque —Rommel and Kesserling to mention two—but there was something almost picturesque, something at least superbly military about those two. But de Gaulle somehow never looked like a man of war. He was colorless and humorless. He was not even a second-rate leader in terms of those indefinables that draw and hold other men.

It was evident following the invasion of North Africa and the escape of General Giraud, that the time was coming when de Gaulle could come more into the picture. However, there existed considerable bad feeling between the two generals most of it on de Gaulle's side. De Gaulle had very few true feelings of any kind. He was a grouch and a sorehead, a bitterly disappointed idealist with a far more personal concern about what was to happen to his conception of France than what was to happen to France itself.

He was now afraid that Giraud would take his place with the armies as well as with the Allies. De Gaulle, to me, always seemed more concerned over de Gaulle than he did over France. This may be unjust but it did not seem so in military conferences where he resembled a disaffected woman whose dog had taken a poor decision in the field trials.

The two generals were brought together at Casablanca. Giraud was the guest of President Roosevelt, de Gaulle the guest of Sir Winston. I was called upon by Churchill, the day de Gaulle arrived at our villa, to keep watch around the place so that no person could interfere with what the Prime Minister told me would be "long and difficult conversations."

After what indeed seemed a long and difficult conversation, Winston told me that he and de Gaulle would be walking across the lawns to the President's villa. I do not yet quite know what the dodge was; perhaps some sort of "change partners" reshuffle. In any case, as we left our villa and made toward the President's, Mr. Murphy, Roosevelt's aide, left the presidential villa with General Giraud, both parties meeting midway as if by prearrangement. The prearrangement had not taken in de Gaulle, who seemed to crest up when he saw his own brother general approaching. He looked with quizzical hostility at both Winston and me, then rammed his long legs into the earth like a stork and stopped walking. He just stood there in a bony sulk, like a balking horse determined to bedevil its driver. But Churchill is a much better sulker than de Gaulle is. Churchill can be a champion sulker. He jabbed de Gaulle sharply with his thumb right in the General's backside and reinforced this indelicate gesture with a shove that set the angry Frenchman in motion again. "*Allez! Allez!*" Churchill snarled in his horrid French, and he stuck his own bulldog face right into General de Gaulle's. Maybe it was a rapprochement, but there was no French kissing about this one, I can testify.

That night, retiring late, Churchill stopped at my door. "Sorry to have kept you up so late, Thompson, but we have to marry these two fellows somehow!"

It happened. And right there.

Churchill broke a lot of the local rules at Casablanca, going down each evening to the ocean, often for a bath. Once trudging back up the hill to his villa, we encountered a large group of American sailors. One of them had a guitar. They recognized Winston at once and stopped and began to talk with him. He liked this. "Aren't you going to give me a tune?" he asked, pointing to the guitar. "You bet, sir," they said at once. And they sang several choruses around us, Churchill trying to get into it somewhere.

We picked up our jeep and the driver made a wrong turn. He drove us around to the far side of the compound where we were compelled to stop, owing to the barbed wire in our path. Winston could see his own villa from here. Looking at the barbed wire, he turned to me. "We can climb over that, Thompson." He began pushing down the wire and started to swing his leg over. There was a click of a rifle, and a shout of "Halt!" Guns from four different places were leveled at us. I shouted it was Churchill. The sentries came down to see. They were disgusted. They cursed and swore. They should not have done this. But then, neither should the Prime Minister have ignored the meaning of the barbed wire. We were extremely lucky not to have been fired on.

Later, Churchill had to visit the French battleship *Jean Bart*. It was being refitted in Casablanca harbor. The French sailors really gave Churchill a cold shoulder. I could not blame them. How could it be otherwise? He was the man who had shelled their fleet, when we were supposedly Allies.

The Casablanca Conference was coming to a close with "unconditional surrender" being written in as one of the terms of the end of fighting. Tripoli was captured by the 8th Army while the meetings were still in progress. Churchill and Roosevelt took leave of each other again. We packed and got in a plane for Cairo.

We toured back across North Africa. At Tripoli Winston spoke to the troops of the 8th Army and, in his simple imperishable English, he said: "After this war is over, it will be quite sufficient to say, when he is asked, 'What did you do?' to reply, 'I marched with the 8th Army.'" What a roar! What a man!

Churchill was suddenly taken ill with pneumonia in the third week of February. Five other members of his staff also came down the same day, with influenza, myself among them. We must have brought the germ back from Africa. Winston was ill for nearly a month but his recuperation was hastened, I am sure, by the good news that kept coming out of Africa. The American armies and our own gradually were closing in on the Germans from all sides, causing the enemy to retreat toward Tunis. The Germans had to give up the Mareth Line. On May 12 the campaign in North Africa came to an end, with the surrender of over one hundred and fifty thousand prisoners, including their commander, General von Arnim.

We went aboard the *Queen Mary* for our next trip to Washington. President Roosevelt seemed glad to see us all again and to greet new faces. He was very cordial to me as usual. I renewed my pleasant association with Mike Reilly and Gus Gennerich of the White House Secret Service staff, while the Chiefs of Staff sat down to decide how to deal with Japan. This took twelve days of conferring. Then we were in motion again, this time traveling by flying boat to Newfoundland, Gibraltar, and across to Algiers.

Our stay here was short and intensive, for Churchill had one meeting after another. Mr. Eden joined Mr. Churchill. Others present, including our own generals, were the two American generals Marshall and Eisenhower, and four French Generals: de Gaulle, Giraud, George and Catroux. "The cross I have to bear," said Churchill, coming out of a meeting with the French one afternoon, "is the cross of Lorraine," meaning, of course, de Gaulle.

We were delayed a day in our official plans to get back to England and there has been speculation all over the world that this delay saved Winston Churchill's life.

A civil aircraft, flying to England from Lisbon—a plane similar to ours—was shot down over our route and at about the same time the day before. One of the passengers was the famous actor, Leslie Howard, whom Winston had seen perform many times and some of whose films he owned and frequently showed in his private projection theatre at Chartwell. It occurred to us all at the same time: Was that plane mistaken for ours? We were actually supposed to be at that spot at that time and even at that altitude.

Before the House of Commons Churchill dealt with his visits to Washington and North Africa and described Stalingrad and Tunis as the greatest military disasters which had ever befallen Germany in all the wars she had ever made.

Preparations for our move across the Mediterranean were fast approaching completion. Sicily was being bombed daily and several small islands off the Cap Bon Peninsula were captured as loading and transfer points. His Majesty the King visited North Africa, covering much the same ground we ourselves had just been over.

Sicily was invaded on July 10. There was a most unfortunate high run of American casualties due to a mistake in signals and premature firing, with many of the paratroopers killed by their own gunfire. But the island was taken nonetheless, and a few days later, both the President and the Prime Minister appealed to the Italian people to throw over Mussolini, who, the message said, was the cause of their betrayal. On July 28 Mussolini resigned. The King of Italy took over supreme command, with Marshal Badoglio as Prime Minister.

I reminded Winston of that day, far back now, when we had stood together on the terrace of the Semiramis Hotel in Cairo, when the information had been brought to him there that an Italian General called Badoglio was moving into Libya ostensibly with an army of "agrarians." "We will have to come back here sometime," he had said. Now, he shook his head slowly, in bitter recall, thinking back to that moment. He had been only forty-seven years old on that trip.

The first big crack in the Axis partnership had come.

On September 3, the British 8th Army invaded Calabria, almost unopposed. Calabria is the toe of the boot.

On that day too, though it was not published to the world, an energetic warrior signed a secret agreement for the Allies, securing the signature of Badoglio for Italy, culminating in unconditional surrender of the Italian forces. This was General Dwight Eisenhower.

Italy's days of trial and turmoil were far from over. The Germans had no intention of allowing Italy to be so easily taken. German troops occupied Rome. The German press described Italy's surrender as "open treason."

The Italians now appeared desirous of helping the Allies. Admiral Sir Andrew Cunningham, Commander-in-Chief, Mediterranean, called upon the Italians to sail their ships to Allied ports. The Italians did so. Italian ships created a line over five miles in length when they surrendered.

You remember the painful but steady trek up the spine of Italy by General Mark Clark to Salerno, Cassino, Rome. The

U.S. and the British, with a few unforgettable Gurkhas, went up together till Kesselring, beaten down everywhere, gave up. The Allies eventually triumphed here—the first unconditional surrender of German troops, numbering just a million.

An Anglo-American Conference at Quebec was called. This time the Prime Minister took his wife and his daughter Mary. Sir John Anderson and Anthony Eden joined the Premier at a later date.

There was the customary load of meetings but these were a pleasure, not only because the war was beginning to quiet down, but because the War Cabinets were meeting at the famous Château Frontenac Hotel. I have never seen a place more beautiful. I was sorry when it broke up but the schedules of both Prime Ministers were very crowded. They said goodbye to each other here, and very soon Mr. Churchill was at Hyde Park again, week-ending with the President.

We stayed several days. I hated Hyde Park. There is no peace there. It was penetrable from a security point of view. There were other aggravations. Roosevelts always became superactive in the country. The President wanted to fish. Or he wanted to visit his own museum. Or Mrs. Roosevelt wanted everyone on a picnic. When the Roosevelts want something, they get it. They are worse than Winston himself. Day and night I was on the alert, chasing over the damn acreage with a creel on my hip or an abominable hot dog in midair or a whole hamper of sandwiches on my head, and mustard on my trousers; festooned with cameras, aswarm with Roosevelt grandchildren, myself not infrequently challenged by unfamiliar American police (this was the worst!), and a bad bed at night right under a revolving floodlight.

By God, I will take Chequers in the blitz to a Roosevelt week-end-with-the-children.

Anyone could walk right into Hyde Park. Millions were doing so then. It was becoming a sightseer's shrine. Searchlights were rigged in tree boughs, poles, ridges, roofs. The place looked like a *stalag* after a break at midnight. Daytimes it was a sort of bucolic Brighton with all of America's underprivileged children determined that every grownup was Santa Claus.

We then went to Niagara Falls where the press, who knew of our visit, awaited us in force. Cameramen surrounded us so thickly it was not possible to walk. Winston, with his wife Clementine and daughter Mary, stood in a hundred poses but there were never enough. One of the newsmen asked in a loud voice, upon learning that Churchill had seen the Falls in 1900: "Do the Falls look the same to you as when you first saw them so many years ago, sir?" Many tittered but all waited.

Winston looked out at the mighty chasm as if giving his questioner the compliment of a considered answer, then said: "I'm not absolutely certain as to the Falls, but the principle remains unchanged!" Everyone loved it and laughed.

We were to have a few days of rest and fishing in Canada, arranged for us by Prime Minister Mackenzie King and through the direct invitation of Colonel F. W. Clarke. We went to Snow Lake, renowned for its fishing.

Churchill entered into this sport as into anything else and his excitement was intensified because of his proximity to water again. We got up at five and were fed and fishing by six. It was cold and marvelously exhilarating, just the thing the Old Man needed. During our stay he had varied luck, catching a number of fair-sized trout, but no records of any kind. Sir Charles Portal and Field Marshal Sir Alan Brooke also fished and had the most success. But I landed the biggest one, a beautiful 3½-pound rainbow. As a reward, Colonel Clarke allowed a Royal Marine and myself to go out in a canoe.

I had never been in one and did not know they were tricky. Neither did the Marine. We paddled off shakily but happily and began to fish, but one of the hooks got caught in some pickerel weed and we made the mistake of trying to get the hook loose, both of us leaning over the same side of the canoe. We of course disappeared at once and came up again, plastered with bottom, weeds and humiliation. Churchill roared and sat down on a stump, the better to enjoy the spectacle we made. Our holiday was over too soon but it restored the Prime Minister.

We flew to Halifax and boarded H.M.S. *Renown*. As we neared the English coast the Prime Minister, with some of his secretaries and myself, computed the total mileage for journeys taken since the war started. What do you think it was? One hundred and eleven thousand miles—and fifty-four thousand of them by air.

The prelude to the Teheran Conference was just concluding at Moscow, where Mr. Anthony Eden, Mr. Cordell Hull and Mr. Molotov were meeting. The main meeting was scheduled for late November. We left Plymouth on the *Renown* and went to Malta. Here there was a delay. The American Secret Service agents, who had come on ahead of President Roosevelt, were far from satisfied with the security arrangements in Teheran. It was suggested the conference take place right here at Malta. Churchill was agreeable. Obviously President Roosevelt would have been most relieved. Stalin said no. We went ahead, this time by plane, to Cairo. Here Churchill became very agitated when the President was some hours overdue, and was noticeably relieved when his plane's safe arrival was announced. Meantime Generalissimo and Madame Chiang Kai-shek had arrived and had had a couple of preliminary talks with Winston. It was Chiang Kai-shek's first conference, and with Japan figuring as one of the principal subjects under discussion, Admiral Lord Louis Mountbatten was present.

The President arrived and work began in earnest. Roosevelt does not stay up late to work. He works all day. Churchill was anxious to get through this part and get on to Teheran. Roosevelt didn't seem in any hurry to get to Iran, nor to enjoy it once he got there.

Madame Chiang Kai-shek impressed us all. She was certainly a prime factor in the discussions attended by her husband in which his judgment was sought. She also acted as his interpreter. It was plain to see that not only was she a smart, well-dressed and attractive woman but also a worthy representative with her husband, able to put forth the claims of China. The delegates were attentive to her, affected not only by her wide knowledge and her tact, but by the manner in which she so forthrightly stated complicated situations in simple language.

It is interesting to note that while these virtues of Madame Chiang Kai-shek were manifest to all, they did not appeal to President Roosevelt. He simply could not stand this lady, disliking her even from their first meeting. No reason was ever attributed; just one of those deeply felt yet inexplicable personality antipathies. As to what she might have felt toward the American President, she was throughout inscrutable. Except for this antipathy, the Chinese representatives might have had wider influence than the Cairo meeting afforded. They would almost certainly have participated in the Teheran Conference.

We got a disturbing report that an attack on the Prime Minister and possibly on the President too was being planned and might be expected to erupt before the party had met with Stalin.

We went ahead with the plans for the conference anyhow, not telling the principals of the flash that had come to us. We left Cairo by plane on November 27 and arrived at Teheran without incident. We were met there by the British Minister, Sir Reader Bullard, and Major General A. Shelby, the officiating Commander-in-Chief.

Then we started for the Legation by the most unusual route. For security reasons, we traveled right across fields, scoured beforehand for land mines. We were escorted by armored cars. As we approached the center of Teheran many people were on the street corners. Some got too close and got knocked away. All entrances to the British Legation were guarded by troops. Many more troops were quartered in the grounds. But the measures taken still seemed to be inadequate.

Winston had heard his life was threatened here. He was very excited, even pleased. He looked into everyone's face with the happiest sort of suspicion. Our information was now a bit more exact. German secret agents, about sixty of them, had been parachuted into the desert country just south of Teheran, in two drops, during the previous two nights and were concealed, disguised, armed and supplied with plans of our intended movements. Many of them were caught by our own agents under command of Colonel Joseph Spencer as they floated to earth. Spencer nabbed the leader, let him set up shop at the point of rendezvous. In came the others, one by one, not knowing there was a British gun trained on their leader. It was a good roundup but we didn't get them all. And so the tension remained.

Most of us felt displeasure at many of the measures adopted for security, particularly as they dealt with the problem of moving a number of conference members from one location to another.

The American Embassy where the President was to stay was approximately one and a half miles from the British Legation. The Soviet Embassy practically adjoined the Legation. In view of the threat, Stalin invited President Roosevelt to be his guest and, following his acceptance and his removal there, the security problem eased somewhat.

On Sunday, November 28, the first session commenced. It was most noticeable and very striking to see Russian officers in full uniform, looking very smart, on duty at the entrance to the Soviet Embassy. As the various delegates arrived, military salutes in the British style were given to them by the Russian officers. This was a great difference from the salute given while in Moscow at a previous conference. The atmosphere at the conference was most cordial. There seemed an air of real hope.

The following day was the "Stalingrad Sword Day." Churchill was most dignified and impressive when he presented a steel sword to the Marshal. So were the words: "Marshal Stalin, I have a command from His Majesty King George VI to present you, for transmission to the city of Stalingrad, this sword of honor, the design of which His Majesty himself approved. This blade bears the inscription, 'To the steel-hearted citizens of Stalingrad,' a gift from George VI in token of homage of the British peoples."

Stalin seemed very moved by this and took it with grace. I had not seen this in him before. He smiled with quiet pleasure, lifted the sword to his lips, and in absolute silence kissed the scabbard, then handed the sword to Marshal Voroshilov, the hero of Stalingrad.

The conclusion of the Cairo and Teheran Conferences came on a happy note. Field Marshal Smuts, on his way home to South Africa, called upon the Prime Minister in Cairo. The Premier was overjoyed at seeing his old friend, and in the evening they both dined with President Roosevelt.

Then it was all over. The President flew away to America the day after. Winston now hoped to spend a night or two as guest of General Dwight Eisenhower and then visit troops in Italy.

Something happened. Too much work for too long, then a sudden letdown. He seemed to be bone tired and became listless. He seemed anxious to get to General Eisenhower's headquarters, to get down on the ground again. We weren't allowed to land at Tunis airport immediately. Finally we came down on a small field many miles away. General Eisenhower and several of his staff officers were there waiting.

On seeing the Prime Minister alight from the plane, I was struck by his appearance and mentioned it to Lord Moran, the Premier's physician. I thought he looked ill. Lord Moran thought he looked tired.

However, on arrival at the White House in Tunis where he was to stay, he went to bed at once. He was found to have a temperature.

This went higher as time passed. Undoubtedly he was developing some illness. I was asked to take a turn during the night in watching him. I suggested covering the whole night for him, something I was more accustomed to do. At eleven o'clock I took up this long vigil.

Lord Moran had instructed me to listen to the tempo of the Prime Minister's breathing. He told me if any change came in this tempo, to call him at once. I sat outside the bedroom door where I could hear very distinctly the Prime Minister's fast breathing. About 3:00 A.M., the sound ceased. I crept into the room. All was silent.

My heart came up into my mouth, for now I was at his bedside. Not a sound could I hear. I feared the worst. I thought he had slipped off quietly while in a high fever. I leaned down and listened very intently. At last I was rewarded by an almost inaudible yet regular intake of breath. Slower exhales now, too.

I cannot remember during my whole lifetime a moment like this. I slipped out and informed Lord Moran of the change. After visiting the bedside he said, "He is breathing better now. You were quite right to call me."

I went back and sat in the room, still as possible. Somewhat later Churchill rose up, then stood fully upright. I spoke softly. He said he was looking about for his sleeping tablets. They had been discreetly removed. He seldom used them. He looked at me with heavy eyes, weary with sickness, and asked me rather pitifully for the tablets. I felt so sorry for him, I evaded his question. I was relieved to see him walk back to his bed. After he had returned to it he said to me:

"Thompson, I am tired out, body, soul, and spirit."

I answered him: "No sir. Not spirit, sir. You have had a most strenuous time. I hope you will be able to rest a little more now the conferences are ended."

He lay back a moment or two with his eyes closed. Then he opened them and looked at me. "Yes, I am worn out, but all is planned and ready." I did not know what he meant by this and grew fearful. A strange light had come into his eyes and he looked through the window into the mystic night.

Glistening on the horizon line, miles away, was the marble finger of a minaret pointing to the sky. It looked ancient, immortal, almost supernatural. Winston was looking at it too, I think.

"What is this place?"

"It is Tunis, sir. We are with General Eisenhower."

"Tunis? Tunis—that is Carthage. The ruins of Carthage are close by. The sound of the Romans and Hasdrubal." He got part way up on his pillows by using his elbows. "What better place could I die than here? Here in the ruins of Carthage?"

"Don't say that, sir!" I pleaded with him. "Everyone in the world needs you. Even your enemies. And England needs you."

He sighed deeply, fell down on the bed again and went off to sleep.

At eight, Lord Moran and his staff took over. I learned that the Prime Minister's physician had not been idle. Nurses and specialists began to arrive like magic. They flew in from all over. General Eisenhower had a whole laboratory put at our disposal.

Churchill was terribly ill, close to death, but the critical peak had been reached and passed as I sat there in his room; as he passed, for those few moments, from lucid thought to a happy and strange transport of hallucination that saw him dead in Carthaginian ruins. Gloom hung over the villa. All members of his party stood about, waiting for the posting of bulletins or for verbal reassurances from the doctors and nurses.

Then a wonderful thing happened. Mrs. Churchill arrived. Her sudden appearance at his bedside gave him great comfort. From then on, he started to come back

My colleague on this trip, Sergeant Cyril Davies of Scotland Yard, and I continued our security duties, patrolling around the villa many times a day; many times an hour. Great was my surprise, when after his convalescence was well advanced but before he was about on his feet, Churchill looked up at me and said cheerfully: "I saw you and your colleague carrying on just the same while I was ill, Thompson. It was pleasing and comforting to see you pass and repass the windows."

These little mentions have great meaning.

It was decided he could go to Marrakesh to complete his

rest. Great care was taken on this journey as to height and weather and an RAF doctor, with special oxygen apparatus, accompanied the party.

We flew at about seven thousand feet. As the journey progressed, and we were making a large detour to avoid the Atlas Mountains, Mr. Churchill seemed to sense this detour. He complained of the extra time it would take, said he felt fine, and insisted on the more direct route, over the Atlas Mountains.

When he insists on these things, they get done. Those in attendance upon him all opposed this idea, but he had his way. We increased the altitude slowly, one thousand feet at a time, at half hour intervals, till we were going over the peaks or through the high passes. The doctors kept checking his pulse and breathing. On being told by them that he was all right, he roared with gusto, "Of course I'm all right! I don't need to be told this! I'm announcing it!"

But on arrival he was exhausted and went to bed straight off. So he remained for a few days, later on sitting out in the sunshine in a most beautiful grove of orange and lemon trees. He went on with his paperwork as usual and began having a large number of people come visit him.

A very high tower formed a part of the building in which the Prime Minister slept. It was reported to him that a most remarkable view could be had from the top of this tower. Churchill insisted upon being carried up it. So we improvised a sort of chair with jutting handles. It was very difficult to maneuver this chair around the steep corners of the ascent, the architects of this Moorish place not having made much room for it. And it was terribly tiring, though both my colleague and myself were unusually strong and in perfect condition. But we did it willingly enough and were happy to do anything that would hurry his recovery or make him happy.

As he got stronger, he wanted more and more to get about into the mountains and foothills. Picnics were being held daily in various places nearby, all picturesque spots. On one of these picnics Lord Beaverbrook, who had flown out from England especially to be with Winston during his convalescence, accompanied us. Winston was very fond of His Lordship.

A very large party attended this one. It was a glorious day. We came to a small plateau near a bridge. Below us, one hundred feet perhaps, a wild stream splashed through rocks in a rough gorge in the mountain's side. You know about Churchill and moving water. After lunch, Churchill, who had been peering down at this cataract and listening to the challenge of its plangent sound as it came up to us, expressed his intention of descending.

Lord Moran, who had done so much to bring Churchill back to health so quickly, demurred. But the Prime Minister said he felt strong enough. And down he went, carefully keeping to the path. It was a dangerous path, being cut out of the cliffside some centuries before, from the looks of it. He went right to the spot where the water foamed and pounded through the side of the cliff. -

It was finally time to start up again. I went ahead of Mr. Churchill, instructing him to hold on to me. Our progress was very slow. Up above, our situation was being studied by the others. I got behind Winston and pushed, but this did not seem very appropriate and didn't solve the problem. He was just too tired out and too heavy. And though I could have physically picked him up and carried him on level ground or even up a smooth incline, it was not possible on this precipitous cliffside.

Suddenly a woman called down to us. It was Lady Diana Duff Cooper. She with her husband came hurrying down to meet us, Lady Diana carrying the large tablecloth which had been used for the picnic. She suggested we put it round the Prime Minister and use it as a rope, Sergeant Davies on one end and me on the other.

So, amid general amusement, that is the way we got Winston Churchill back to the top without causing him much unnecessary exertion. And so back to the villa.

The day came when Lord Moran thought the Prime Minister had sufficiently recovered to be able to return home. He cautioned against flying and restricted the return to one flight only, from Marrakesh to Gibraltar. Here we went on board the *King George V*. In this fine ship our journey home was uneventful. Mr. Churchill took it easy. He lived in the Admiral's cabin on the bridge. On this journey he did not once visit the cinema—the only time in my long years with him when he put aside this temptation—and instead walked daily and for hours about the bridge and the decks. This was good for him.

On several occasions, when touring the mighty ship, considerable amusement was caused by the problem of getting the Prime Minister up the various gangways. It was like the picnic tablecloth and the gorge, only this time there was a sergeant of the Royal Marines with his shoulder heaving powerfully at Churchill's rear. The Prime Minister saw the funny side of this and joined the roars and cheers and the happy grins of the men as the ladders and inclines, one by one, were ascended.

Back in London, rested, Churchill was all action again. By the end of February, he warned the House of Commons and England that German air retaliation would be terrible. He warned of new forms of air attack, alluding to pilotless aircraft and rockets. Some scoffed at the warnings. Churchill's life is crowded with records of men who scoffed at his warnings only to turn into the face of the very horrors he had predicted.

In the same war review Mr. Churchill referred to Poland. He reported he had raised the Polish question with Marshal Stalin at Teheran, and that Stalin had replied he wanted to see created "a strong, unified, independent Poland." The Premier reminded the House that we English had never guaranteed a particular frontier line to Poland. "The British view in 1919," he stated, "stands expressed in the so-called Curzon Line which attempted to deal with this problem."

In view of the decisions taken at the Yalta Conference, this statement has importance and refutes claims that Mr. Churchill had let the Poles down.

But we were at the meeting of waters—the opaque waters of gloom and the shimmering waters of our next struggle.

We were gathering our strength for D-Day. Five years before, in 1939, there could be no question but that Goering's Luftwaffe was the strongest air force in the world. Through the midyear of 1943, the Germans had had their own way for two years and a half in the air. But now the challenge was being more equally met in direct engagement. German bombing squadrons were measurably depleted. Their peak force of first-line fighters was not above three thousand. In 1944 one thousand German planes were destroyed in January and February alone. Essen and Schweinfurt were gratifyingly reduced from the air. From an air point of view, in the quoted opinion of the Prime Minister, the week of February 20-26 was "the most decisive of the war."

At this time we could not of course see how enormously

our advantage would grow, but by the end of the war, for every ton of aerial bombs British cities had taken from the Germans, the Germans had received *315 tons*. Three hundred and fifteen to one. The American contribution here, plus the Canadian, as well as token assistance from the Free Poles and occasional help from the Free French, is naturally a huge part of this story. Of interest to Americans is this: As of January 1, 1945, German plane losses were 51,858; U.S. plane losses, all fronts, 17,790.

When Churchill recovered enough to work full days again back in London, he, as Prime Minister, together with his Chiefs of Staff, had to stand up against an increasing barrage of demands for "the Second Front." In reality, both a second and a third front were already in being. Slogans were chalked up all over the city on boards and pavements demanding the Second Front and the suspense grew each day, seeming to follow the fantastic advances being made by our (then) Allies, the Russians.

Churchill of course saw these scribbled instructions all the time. On one occasion he turned to me, more musingly than in irritation, and said: "Yes, we will start the Second Front the minute we are ready. But we will not throw thousands of lives away on any project until the time is ripe. Then our losses, by the careful preparations made now—and the restraint shown—shall not be too heavy, God willing." He seemed to be speaking to all of England, all the world. And his eyes filled.

We went on a mad sequence of visits to docks. Do you know about the enormous concrete caissons? I am sure you do, except for one thing: you have no idea how enormous they were! Unbelievable. These were being built now in many places, and were new to warfare. These dramatic improvisations of artificial harbors were to make the D-Day landings possible, for the troops were going to breach a bare coast, as you now know.

Churchill was all about, with me hanging onto his coat-tails. All his friskiness was back, a disease with him now, but not of attrition—more of overstimulation.

Hundreds of blockships and concrete caissons, constructed in as many places on the British coast, east, south, and west, were towed through the Channel in dead of night, floated to location, and there sunk. They created breakwaters, floating pierheads, pontoon causeways. Troop carriers of all kinds could bring in combat units and beach them, it was hoped, in calm or nearly calm water.

By the end of March we'd been to Newbury, Tidworth and the Winchester areas with the tireless, sternly cheerful Eisenhower with whom Winston was increasingly impressed. After inspecting a huge parade of U.S.A. paratroopers, Mr. Churchill and General Eisenhower attended a large military exercise where the General showed the new bazooka and American carbine to the Prime Minister. It was suggested that they fire at a target. You cannot ever suggest such a thing to Mr. Churchill without his at once getting to it. He loves a contest. The troops gathered round by hundreds. General Eisenhower, General Bradley and Mr. Churchill stood in a row and all took aim with carbines on targets ahead. Mr. Churchill stood up very well against the younger men. He also fired several rounds with the bazooka, a gun which interested him enormously. He addressed a great concentration of American troops at Winchester and reminded them they were occupying barracks that had been the home of famous British regiments for more than fifty years. The troops loved the Prime Minister but, from the looks on their faces, they had never heard of the regiments referred to.

After this we came right back to town. Churchill in a broadcast to all the people, spoke of the approaching struggle, and of the gigantic preparations being made; of the visible strength in the mighty U.S. army that was forming and toughening. "There will be false rumors," he said, "feints and many dress rehearsals. We may also ourselves be the object of new forms of attack from the enemy. But Britain can take it."

And he spoke of the rebuilding of English homes.

SHAEF was getting into its stride. Churchill visited it constantly, consulting with those in charge of the armies that were going to punch into France. SHAEF was situated on the outskirts of London, in ideal surroundings except for the necessary brick wall all round. Secret telephones were installed and links could be made with Washington and Moscow. Direct contact was in service with the army within a very short period after the landing in Normandy. They had their own secret radio wave lengths which enabled them to contact military chiefs and even bombers in flight in various parts of Europe.

General Sir Frederick Morgan was the man appointed to be in charge of the British and American Joint Planning Staff whose one great job was the invasion of Europe. At this time he actually *was* SHAEF.

Ceaseless meetings were held with Prime Ministers of the Commonwealth: Mr. Mackenzie King, Mr. Curtin, Mr. Fraser, Field Marshal Smuts, Sir Godfrey Huggins. It was agreed and announced that after the war a world organization to maintain peace and security should be set up.

The days were whirling past. "D" Day was near. Three days were spent in the south of England, visits being made to the docks at Southampton and Portsmouth. We went aboard fast motorboats here. On every side were landing craft of every kind. We were later shown piers which were to form part of the landing stages in Normandy. Southampton docks held hundreds of the mighty concrete caissons finished and half finished—some ready to be taken in tow and already in the grip of hawsers. Hundreds more were moored at Itchin, Southampton. What an opportunity for the Luftwaffe! But she never struck at the caissons, not once. We never knew why.

I did not know the actual date of D-Day. But the Prime Minister was terribly keyed up. Those around him knew that something big was on us. It was most noticeable when we left London by special train on June 3. We took with us certain maps that were fixed up in a locked saloon in charge of Captain Pim. He had been the genuis who had built the "Map Room" that Churchill took all over the world and set up in the White House.

We went to a secret destination on the south coast. The day was fine. There was a tank review, then bulldozers, then an unimaginable mass of stores being loaded into the landing craft there.

As Churchill passed along the ranks of troops, we encountered a detachment of 8th Army men of Libyan fame. Every man in the 8th Army knew Winston even from a distance. Many, unable to speak, touched his coat as he passed.

We put out into Southampton water and on to Portsmouth. Here was an endless spread-out of ships of all types: liners, warships, monitors. Everyone we passed cheered loudly. It is not possible to visualize an armada of this depth without actually seeing it. We went aboard a cipher ship which we were told was the heart and center of communication and would play a great part in the control of the various invasion plans. We got a bad weather report while on this ship, one which visibly concerned General Eisenhower with whom Churchill went into a long series of discussions.

We went back to town. Sunday came. So did de Gaulle. After a long conference with him the French General returned for conferences with Eisenhower. No matter what the subject or the occasion, any conversation with de Gaulle is always tense. But it was ascertained the invasion fleet could not leave that night because of bad weather. Churchill came down to Southampton again. The same three had another conference. Winston and I went back to the train, followed shortly after by de Gaulle in his car. The Prime Minister had to return immediately to London and asked the General to come along with him, and to dine with him en route.

The invitation was refused. I felt at the time that de Gaulle was put out about something, as he would have reached London far sooner by taking advantage of the Prime Minister's offer. And as he would be traveling in comfort as well, he could have the valuable opportunity to converse for a few hours with an Englishman who had been almost as good a friend to France as de Gaulle himself. But de Gaulle was seriously displeased about something. One expected him to stamp his foot.

De Gaulle is brilliant and brave. He is also petty.

The Prime Minister lunched with the King at Buckingham Palace, then visited General Eisenhower at SHAEF.

That night—June 5 and the following dawn, June 6—was D-Day.

Four years of hardship, death, misery and terror by night. All the enslaved peoples of Europe must have wept with feeling when they knew. Now the mighty German was to meet a liberation force that Hitler had scoffed at. "Those military idiots!" So often he'd screamed this. "Had I before me a serious opponent, I'd know where the Second Front would come! But with military idiots one never knows!"

How right he was!

Eisenhower had had a terrible decision to make: whether to go in with bad weather and with a promise of worse to come. He had decided. It was an awful chance, a crushing risk. But it was taken without flinching.

You all remember what happened. In six days, the U.S.

and British forces had taken sixty miles of the Normandy coast! The artificial harbors functioned well. They did what they were built for. Then many of them got smashed into uselessness by gales. I saw this damage with Churchill. Most desolating sight, but the British went to work reconstructing, with somewhat the same kind of skill and resourcefulness that made the American Seabees world famous in the Pacific.

Twenty-one days after D-Day, Cherbourg fell. We had our first continental port, if you could call it that—the demolition job of the Germans was their very best. But in the first one hundred days, 2,200,000 troops had landed. Four hundred and fifty thousand vehicles had landed. And four million tons of stores.

U.S. and British joint planning made this possible. Nothing else. Lessons learned in amphibious attacks in Africa and Italy, and one vital and seldom mentioned item: the instant replacement of all smashed or damaged equipment.

The long conferences that Churchill and his staff had so often held in so many places all over North Africa with Generals Bradley, Eisenhower and Marshall, paid off. And how!

It was the greatest amphibious operation in history. Air cover was maintained by ten thousand planes: the RAF and the U.S. 8th and 9th. Four thousand ships crossed the Channel. Eighty battleships and cruisers put eight hundred heavy guns on the German fortifications.

It was a busy summer and fall for Mr. Churchill, and also for me.

A week passed. The good news continued. Then the Prime Minister decided the moment had come for him to see the show for himself. It was a sudden decision. We were in the country. We left by special train and overnight went to Portsmouth. By early morning of June 12, we were embarked in H.M.S. *Kelvin*. Field Marshal Smuts and General Sir Alan Brooke accompanied the Premier. Churchill, as usual when off on something dangerous, was twitchy to be in motion.

As we left the dockside, all about could be seen ships loading. The sky also was amarch with aircraft. We saw unnumbered concrete caissons again, being towed, then later twin pieces of the landing piers. One of these had been broken adrift from its tug, and we sank her with gunfire.

As we approached the Normandy coast a screen of small ships could be seen in semicircular formation. These stopped U-boats penetrating and sinking the landing craft. Beyond and ahead could be seen the monitor *Roberts*. We could hear her guns as she threw shells into German positions inland.

Two ducks came alongside. Our party, with Admiral Vian, descended by the gangway to the ducks and thence to the beaches of Normandy.

I landed with the Prime Minister. Here again was a moment when it was hard to belong to Scotland Yard; hard not to complain. My disappointment over not inspecting the Maginot Line came back to me quite bitterly. But this was worse. There was no transport for me. I was left on the beaches, a solitary civilian among a million troops.

Some press correspondents I knew came to my rescue. They told me where I might later on meet the P.M., gave me some food, and together we walked along the beachhead for many hours. Melodramatic results of the bombardment could be seen everywhere, but most of the smashup was ashore, few damaged ships being in evidence at this part of the coast. We came upon the grave of a Canadian soldier, hastily dug. At the end was his rifle and his steel helmet. A small wooden cross, neatly whittled, read simply: "Here lies a Canadian soldier."

We continued walking, finally arriving at Courcelles, a little village where I rejoined the Prime Minister. Here the troops really mobbed him. As they pressed about, patting him, slapping his back and punching his ribs, three German fighter-bombers dashed over the coast, dropped some bombs, then suddenly found themselves engaged by our Spitfires. One of the Germans came blazing and hissing to earth, crashing in a huge roar nearby. A great cheer went up, a sort of continuation to the welcome Winnie was getting there.

We returned to the *Kelvin* but instead of steaming for home, we ran at right angles to the shore, cutting our speed as we stood off the German defenses. An order rang out. Our guns fired several salvos into the German position. We provoked no reply from them and set course for Portsmouth.

In the railroad journey back to London, I sat directly behind Mr. Churchill, who was having an animated talk with Field Marshal Smuts.

General Smuts said: "I think the *Kelvin*'s captain is rather cross with you." Churchill turned to the older man at once and asked why. "For your ordering the firing on the German positions," Smuts told him.

"Well, I admit I'm only the Prime Minister and had no right to take over his vessel, but—"

"That isn't the way of it at all, Winston."

"Well, what is the way of it then?"

"When you ordered the *Kelvin* to fire, she was in full range of German guns."

Then Churchill began to grin. "That's what I did it for! I wanted response!"

Suddenly both the men laughed uproariously, others in the car turning to peer at them. For a moment it did not seem like the awfulest war in the world.

Yet only twelve days after the invasion of Normandy, the Germans commenced to send their flying bombs to London and into southern England. This was an unholy monster. No one can deny the hideous impartilaity of such a weapon, but it was soon known all over England as the "doodlebug."

These were grim days. They have been recorded a thousand times by as many writers. For us, the flying bomb set up a series of Alerts that nearly cripped our energies. One got used to the continuous gunfire, but the humming of the flying bomb and the austere silence which followed the cutting out of its engine and the heavy molar crash of its landing—these were noises that set up patterns in my patience most disquieting. The humming could be heard right through heavy gunfire, even as the shrill bleat of an E-Flat clarinet can pierce the full symphony.

London was on fire.

We were standing at the site of the wrecked Guards Chapel. Churchill for the most part had been taking the main events through which we were passing with noble restraint, but this spectacle—and the dead still unclaimed—was hard to look at. A flying bomb had slipped through the defenses and crashed into the Guards Chapel at a time when a service was in progress. As at times he would cheer out loud watching a fight in progress overhead, so he would sometimes look and shudder and weep. So it was here. His pity was always greater than his fury.

We left the scene of rescue and he and Mrs. Churchill paid a visit to AA gun sites in the south of England. Here at one of these their youngest daughter, Mary, was in charge of a plotting battery. She was glad to see them but too busy to give them her time. By now the guns in London itself were no longer being brought into action during an Alert. The system of defense and attack worked outside the London area. Flying bombs which escaped it pursued their course unchecked; unchecked, that is, until they were intercepted by our fighters.

The Germans chose two time periods to make these attacks: evening hours, and very early morning. Although an Alert usually lasted throughout the night, the All Clear would generally sound between five and six. From then until nine would be an almost continuous series of Alerts. These heralded the approach of an increased number of buzz bombs, and at those hours when a majority of people were getting up, having breakfast, or making their way to work.

Intensity of these raids mounted during the summer. There were a few moments of relief. One was the afternoon of July 26. Mussolini resigned. He was rescued, as you recall, by the Germans who didn't much want him. Churchill called him a name then that will stick all through history—"that tattered lackey." Tojo resigned, a great gratification to the Americans in the Pacific. The Germans capitulated in Paris and armed civilians liberated their own city. It was turned over to de Gaulle. I am sure this pleased Churchill.

One Friday evening in late summer, out of the blue, there was a colossal explosion, the worst I heard in the whole war. It took place at Chiswick. It made a deeper crater than the flying bomb. The noise was heard in London many miles away. A complete security blackout was laid down. The cause was put down officially to a burst gas main! It was the first of a series of "burst mains." Somehow it never affected the gas supply. It wasn't long, therefore, before Londoners knew that the Germans had a new one. It was the V-2, infinitely more terrifying than the blitz or the flying bombs.

I say terrifying for many times I felt the terror of it. It was terrifying even to contemplate. The reason is simple. It traveled at a velocity so great as to make advance warning altogether impossible. No Alerts therefore, since none could be sounded. People went about their normal business knowing that at any moment a rocket would descend and the authorities were absolutely helpless in the matter. It was this sense of impotence that froze one.

The V-2 actually traveled so much faster than sound that the first indication of its presence was the crash of it hitting. After this came another slightly smaller or lesser explosion —its warhead blowing up—then a pause, and finally a long rumbling roar like thunder. This last noise, after the pause, was the sound of the rocket on its way, arriving somewhat after the rocket.

We took it all through the winter of 1944-45. We were also having our coldest winter in fifty years.

How did the British take all this? And how did Churchill take it? In our concentrated population there was little fussing. And never once did I see panic, or even the hint of panic. But the earlier contemptuous and even jocular attitude displayed in previous raids was lacking. We had had it. The people still held on, but the hours, the blackout, the queueing, the rationing, loss of rest and holidays, loss of homes and children, the great dead areas without fun or change—all this finally began to grind down our nerves. We became grim and ugly. Any Germans who might have invaded us would have met no pity. Englishmen who lived through this will not easily forget this last ordeal to which we had been submitted. Among most Englishmen there will never be a "Let bygones be bygones" attitude toward the Germans. I had lost one of my sons, but Churchill's attitude seemed typical and he had not lost any of his immediate family.

His hatred was expressed to President Roosevelt at the Quebec Conference and on our next trip to Moscow only a few days after we'd come back from America. Roosevelt had not come to Moscow. After a gala performance at the Bolshoi Theatre a party was given later by Stalin marked by tiresome toasts of "future collaboration and eternal friendship"; Churchill suddenly seized a goblet of wine and returned a compliment that Stalin had paid the British with these words: "I have always believed and I still believe that it is the Red Army that has torn the guts out of the filthy Nazis." When Pavlov translated this sentence, the Russians seemed to go crazy, and Joe Stalin clapped Winston over the back and shoulders so hard the two spilled liquor all over each other.

On October 14, at another gala performance, Mr. Churchill entered the theatre with the Polish Prime Minister. The whole audience rose. The Marshal, who was standing to the rear, was called forward by Mr. Churchill, who insisted that all should be seen together. At this point Mr. Eden and Mr. Molotov moved in, and there was a new outburst of cheering as the five were photographed together.

We got back to England just in time to take off again, this time for Paris. The liberated city was going to celebrate its first anniversary of Armistice Day of World War I, the first it was able to observe in four years. Paris was aquiver. Her citizens did not know that Mr. Churchill had arrived.

The crowds were oriental in their congestion. Just before eleven o'clock the Prime Minister, in a Royal Air Force uniform and accompanied by General de Gaulle and Mr. Eden, left the Quai d'Orsay in an open car. I stood on the runningboard. We proceeded to the Arc de Triomphe and were in turn preceded by several cars filled with French police. Flags of the Allies were fluttering from most of the buildings. Window frames were jammed. It was the greatest day of rejoicing I have seen.

On the stroke of eleven, a single gun was fired for silence. The crowd congealed. There was not a murmur. Another gun announced the end of the two minutes. Mr. Churchill and General de Gaulle, each carrying a huge wreath, walked side by side to the Tomb of the Unknown Soldier.

After this ceremony, Churchill, de Gaulle, and Mr. Eden walked abreast—refusing the cars that had brought them—from the Arc de Triomphe down the Champs Élysées through crowds which the French police found almost impossible to control.

The party finally reached the saluting base where Mrs. Churchill, Mrs. Eden, Mme. de Gaulle and Mary Churchill were waiting. For an hour and a half a great military parade passed us, led by General Koenig, Commander-in-Chief of the Free French Infantry.

After the parade there was an elaborate luncheon at which our party was entertained by de Gaulle at the War Ministry, and where General Giraud and many prominent Frenchmen spoke. All stressed the need for a French-British entente. It seemed a long way from *"Allez! Allez!"* and I knew Winston thought of it here.

On the way back to London, we got the good news that Hitler's best battleship, the *Tirpitz*, had been sunk by twelve thousand-pound bombs from our Lancesters. Churchill told me he could not ask for a better birthday present. He was seventy.

Greetings poured in from all over the world but there was always some mess that had to be taken care of. We went to Italy, then Greece, where we spent Christmas, our headquarters being the H.M.S. *Ajax* of *Graf Spee* fame. Here for the first time I saw the energetic and brilliant Harold Macmillan—now England's Minister of Defense—in action.

After the unbelievable complex of Greece was brought to working resolution, we had a few weeks in England that were presently interrupted by our flight to the Crimea and thence to Cairo. The Cairo interval was reminiscent of our first visit there and many old memories came up. Our stay was too busy and Churchill was constantly in the presence of one king or other, the Emperor of Ethiopia, the King of Egypt, the King of Saudi Arabia, the President of Syria. President Roosevelt was on hand for most of these talks but he would break off conversations, looking suddenly weary, and ask to be taken back to his suite. For the first time, Mr. Churchill and I shared a deep concern over how very badly President Roosevelt was looking. It was hard to believe he was the same man we had seen so recently in Quebec.

Our spirits stayed up, however. All sensed it was "the beginning of the end." Big battles were occurring in the West. Troops under Montgomery were clearing the enemy from the west bank of the Rhine. Churchill felt the urge to plant his feet on conquered German soil. He visited General Eisenhower, Field Marshal Montgomery, and units of the American 9th Army. Before a group of Highlanders and massed pipers, I got a thrill when he said: "Anyone can see that one good strong heave, all together, will end the war in Europe." Then, at defenses near Aachen in the Siegfried Line at one of our artillery posts, he picked up a piece of mechanic's chalk and printed out in great capitals: FOR HITLER PERSONALLY. Then as a cheer went up he fired the 2400-mm. gun and sent the shell toward Berlin. While we were still there we got the electric news that the Americans had captured the Remagen Bridge intact. We went over the Rhine.

On the way back to London, and I can say this now that I am toward the end of this story, I believe Winston Churchill knew that his own work was about over; that the end of war might also detach him from public office. I believe he was prepared to take what came, even though it might be as bitter as Dundee had been so many years before. But I also believe he welcomed dismissal for on our return to Chartwell in early April the Prime Minister sat down in the doorway of one of the cottages and said with a glint of humor: "Well, Thompson, there's a Cabinet meeting tomorrow. If they throw me out, I'll come right back here and be happy as a sandboy." And actually when it did happen, it wasn't so very different from this.

I went to London with him. Everyone was looking older. And was older. I never look at myself in a mirror. Even when shaving I try not to look too directly at anything but the operation itself, but I knew my face was changing. Unfortunately I was not growing into a resemblance of Churchill through this long and intimate association, but I was feeling the years; feeling life closing in on me from many sides.

The Greek civil war had hit Winston very hard. Six weeks had cost us about two hundred million dollars that we didn't have. And the lives of two thousand British troops. The Yalta Conference had been successful but extremely wearing. (Historians are questioning how successful it had been. The questioning of everything Churchill ever did will begin any minute.) But diagrams for the complete destruction of Germany as a fighting nation were drafted in detail. Stettinius, who had replaced Cordell Hull, was appointed to carry the constructive plans into fruition at a United Nations Conference to take place in San Francisco in late April.

"Things are coming our way, Thompson," he said one morning to me and there was a sad peace in his voice. "I hope nothing disturbs this sequence and that we shall happily pass Friday the 13th."

He often joked about Friday the 13th, but the joking was never quite a joke with him. I do believe it was his one obstinate superstition. I do not know that he had any other. He played hunches at gambling and I suppose that is a superstition.

But the Germans were getting shoved back so hard and

so fast on all fronts where they were still fighting that I looked forward to any Friday the 13th with joy.

However, there was a Friday the 13th, and it was in April, 1945. It was 3:00 A.M. and my night bell rang. I was instantly up. Winston seldom calls this late unless I have left him within the last few minutes. This night he had turned off his light a little before two. I was reading the newspapers. I was not restless but I was wakeful.

"Can you come quickly, Thompson," Churchill said weakly. I grabbed my guns and rushed in. I had horrible dreams of Tunis and his hallucinations during fever, his visions of being dead in the ruins of Carthage, and the nearness of it that is still dreadful to me, even today.

He was up and pacing about his bedroom. His head was sunk down. He kept looking at the rug. He would go from one wall to another. He never stopped.

"Have you heard the terrible news, Thompson?"

"Oh, no, sir," I said, protesting. But he seemed all right and that was the main thing. "Nothing in your family, sir?"

"It is the President of the United States. Your friend and mine, Thompson."

"Stricken?" I asked quickly, thinking of Yalta, and later, the dead look the President had when they took leave in North Africa and flew away.

"It is far worse, Thompson. He has passed away." For a long time Winston Churchill just walked about his room, talking of Roosevelt—weeping, reminiscing, smiling, going over the days, the years; recalling conversations, wishing he had done this, wondering what had been meant when Roosevelt said this or that; agreeing, disagreeing, reliving. Then I realized Winston could not stop talking—here in the middle of the night—because he could not bear the agony. Now that the great American was no more it was all a terrible, unbearable loneliness for him. He suddenly felt there was no one. And in a strange sense this was true: there was no one left but Churchill.

I remember some of his sentences. "No one realized what that man meant to this country. No Englishman can ever quite know it altogether. They can only half sense it. Perhaps, in time. In later years." He went over to a dressing table and opened a drawer. I did not look up at him, for I

knew what he would do there. He kept his fresh handker-
chiefs there.

"He was a great friend to us all. He gave us immeasurable
help. We would have surely gone under. We would have
lost the war. Without him and the Americans behind him,
surely we would have been smothered. There was just too
much." Then he wept, and finally recovered. "I do not know
just now, but I will try to fly across the ocean tomorrow.
The funeral is to take place at the weekend. I do not know
for certain. I must ask the King and the Members of the
Cabinet. There is so much. You will come of course, if I
go?" And he looked shyly at me.

"Of course, sir. Whatever is needed."

He walked over to a carafe and poured a glass of water.

"He was loved by millions. Inside and outside the United
States. Hated too, as who isn't who gets things done! I'll be
hated. But I'm composed about it. It requires no resignation
on my part. I'm sure it took none for Franklin." Then he
drank the water and set down the glass. "I have lost a great
friend. One of the greatest ever. And now—" and here the
pacing slowed and he went into deep thought "—we have to
start all over again. And it is Friday the 13th."

I must say I was so stunned a shiver jumped down my
back and a tremble went right through me.

"He has the peace and the satisfaction to know his work
is done. To see it done just before the end. His task was completed at Yalta. He died on the eve of victory but he saw
the wings of it. And he heard them."

Never will I forget that night. He seemed to want to go
on talking. I stayed with him for some time.

I did not see how it could be arranged that the Prime Minister get to America for the President's funeral. If the fact
of peace were at hand, yes. But there was fighting yet, and
much of it. We were approaching the final climax in the
West. Militarily, Churchill could not leave.

He knew this himself the next day. I believe he truly
knew it that night and that he was drawn to the picture in
America by his great love for Roosevelt while knowing
that the exigency of his own schedule would forbid the trip.

The war in Europe was now approaching its final phase.
In attempting to escape, Mussolini was captured by anti-Fas-
cists and executed, but not before he begged for his life.
"Only spare my life, and I will give you an Empire!" This

was his last sentence. Then he was shot. So was Signorina Petacci, his most recent mistress. Both were stripped and hanged upside down and spat upon.

Winston received this news just as he entered the Great Hall of Chequers for the weekend. A few guests had already arrived, friends he knew well and to whom his expressions were not a shock. With considerable pleasure and much emphasis he rolled it out: "Ah, the bloody beast is dead!" Only three days later, we received the news of Hitler's death as well. Churchill went to the window and looked out at the lawns for a long time, his back to the rest of us, and said no word. He never did have a word to say about Hitler's self-destruction. Later, when he was asked if he thought Hitler had committed suicide, Winston said quietly: "That is the way I should have expected him to have died."

The Italian campaign came to an end with the first unconditional surrender by the Germans—this to that genius of military efficiency, Field Marshal Sir Harold Alexander. Soon after the mass surrender in northern Germany took place, Field Marshal Sir Bernard Montgomery taking the surrender.

On Sunday, May 6, retiring at 4:00 A.M., he gave no sign that things were truly over but he said: "The end is near. But we still have a tough struggle in the East."

The "Cease Fire" was signed the next day, Admiral Doenitz surrendering unconditionally.

The Prime Minister waited throughout the day, hoping for such official confirmation as would permit him to release the news at 6:00 P.M. when all of England listens to the BBC news broadcast. Winston was in touch with President Truman and Marshal Stalin and a decision was finally reached that the statement be made the next day at 3:00 P.M. The public was then notified that Tuesday, May 8, would be V-E Day, and that told them all they wanted to know.

At dawn on the 8th, large crowds were already gathered in Whitehall, outside the House of Commons, and around Buckingham Palace. They knew Churchill would visit Commons. They waited in thousands to see him. At 10:45 he drove to the House of Commons. At least we drove part of the way. No engine power was necessary. The car was literally lifted and pushed along by the crowd.

We traveled as far as Parliament Square with little difficulty, the crowds cheering wildly as we passed. They were all determined to see him and touch him. To congratulate him personally. Millions seemed to get their wish! I hadn't been so scared for him and his safety as that day years before in Cairo when the Egyptians mobbed us.

Mounted police came upon the scene. How welcome! The excitement was stupendous. Winston had wisely come into the front seat now, with myself and my other colleagues around him. What a wonderful day for him!

Eventually we somehow got to the House, but it was the worst struggle I'd ever been through with him. He enjoyed every inch of it, every smiling face, every shout. So did I.

Later we walked in procession with other Ministers and Members of the House of Commons, to St. Margaret's Church for a Thanksgiving service. Then we returned once more to the House. On leaving the House, we were due to go straight to Buckingham Palace, where the War Cabinet and the Chiefs of Staff were received by His Majesty the King.

En route, the Prime Minister asked for a cigar.

But, awful to report, I had come without his case! For the first time in my life! What a day! But he was not put out. He was quite charming. "Let us go round to the Annex," he said. "I will get one there." I thought he must have wanted to smoke very badly indeed, but should have known better, and did, thanks to his next sentence: "I must put on a cigar. They expect it!" How he laughed. How I did!

And once he got it, he stood up conspicuously and conspicuously lighted it. They all cheered. And cheered him on into Buckingham Palace, where he had lunch with the King.

At three he broadcast to the nation, then returned to Number Ten Downing Annex where Mr. Churchill went to the Ministry of Health. He went through the glass doors and out upon the balcony. The crowd was beside itself. I have never heard such cheering, except at the Coronation and the Queen's return. He made a speech, the people meanwhile cheering for all they were worth. They kept calling him out. And he kept coming out. Once he brought his little grandson with him—young Julian Sandys. This broke them all up. They began to sing "Land of Hope and Glory."

And they laughed at everything he said: "Why don't you

take the day off tomorrow as well!" They roared. At another point he said, "The lights went out"—and for just an instant, right then the floodlights did dim. And the crowd screamed with delight, although I think he was started upon a serious sentence. It never was finished. Winston looked over at me and his eyes asked me what they were laughing at. It was just the way the crowd felt. It was what they wanted to do. And mostly, it was because they so loved and honored Winston Churchill. He shrugged and smiled and waved and came back in.

The next day—V-E Day plus 1—was another hard one for us all. I was asked early in the morning to chart the drive through the west end of London. It was to include in its route the American and Soviet Embassies, and a visit to the French Ambassador. We left for these visits in an open car about 4:00 P.M. We had an escort of four mounted police. The journey was triumphant. I felt safe with the mounted police about the car. I felt safe at the sight of the fine horses. We came back about 6:00 P.M. He immediately went to a meeting at Number Ten. He walked there, although a large crowd waited for him outside the Annex. Thinking he did not require an open car again, I sent it away.

At 8:30, he left Number Ten. He saw the closed car waiting. A large crowd was at the bottom of Downing Street. He asked for the open car. When he was told it was not available, he said, "I will walk through them."

"It will be impossible, sir," I said quickly. "The crowd is too dense."

But he started. On reaching Whitehall he realized he could not get through. "I will walk between the two cars," he said. He then began walking at the rear of the first car with the other following. But immediately the crowds closed in. I begged him to wait for the mounted police. But he was so sure of himself, he would not wait. He was quite peeved over the open car having been sent away.

Meanwhile we had a terrific struggle to keep the crowd from engulfing him. He saw he was in danger, that he might be overrun, knocked down, and trampled. He climbed up on the rear bumper of the car. Our control was improved by this. But the crowd kept pressing in on behind, trying to pat his back or shake hands with him.

Suddenly he decided to climb up on top of the car. With

our assistance, he was able to get a good position there. Then, once there, he saw better possibilities. He crawled along the top of the car on all fours until he could sit in the front with his legs dangling over the front windscreen.

Here he looked very funny. And very happy. He gave the impression of a schoolboy on an outing. The crowd liked the posture. So through the ecstatic mob to Number Ten Annex. We went to the balcony in Parliament Street where there was another huge crowd. He spoke for some moments. He led them all in singing a verse of "Rule Britannia." They did not need to be invited to join in. It rang over the whole city of London.

We got to bed about 5:00 A.M.

In this book of my experiences with this noble man, I know I have told very little that can have interest to the historian, but I have tried to set down my impressions of the man as I saw him day by day.

In the evening of his life and work (his eightieth birthday was November 30, 1954), I hope that the peoples of the world will long remember him as the one who, when all seemed about to crack, hung on; that his eloquence and his determination and his honest endeavor to keep this world together, and keep it right, did vitally help bring us through to victory in Europe—where my story ends.

You know he lost the election in another month. My duties as his bodyguard came to an end the same day. I returned to Scotland Yard for another assignment. On the way, I realized that I too was weary, that I didn't at all want another assignment; that I'd had my best one. And I felt, too, that I had done my best. Churchill was alive. That is all they had asked of me.

Now I just wanted to retire. And I did.

I think it is fitting to mention here the crowning honor of Winston's life, the bestowal upon him of the title Knight of the Most Noble Order of the Garter. As you probably know, the origin of the Order dates back to the fourteenth century. Legend has it that Edward III, on retrieving a garter dropped by the Countess of Salisbury, coldly reprimanded his tittering courtiers with the remark: *Honi soit qui mal y pense*"—the present day motto of the Order.

The ceremony took place in the Throne Room of Windsor Castle, where Her Majesty invested Sir Winston with the insignia of the Order. The Garter King of Arms, Sir George Bellow, handed the jeweled garter to the Queen, who, assisted by the Marquis of Salisbury and Earl Alexander, buckled the garter just below the Prime Minister's left knee.

As the ceremony continued, the Riband and the Star, the mantle collar and the chain were bestowed upon Sir Winston. The ancient oath was administered that "Wittingly or willingly you shall not break any statute of the said Order," and in reply Sir Winston said, "So help me God." The traditional lunch was then held in the castle, followed by the colorful pageantry of the procession of the knights to the chapel, walking in reversed seniority, two by two, Sir Winston being first and alone, smiling and appearing extremely happy. Her Majesty, escorted by the Duke of Edinburgh, ended the procession, beautiful in her dress of white and gold. The Household Cavalry Band played until Her Majesty passed under the lintel. Then silence, followed by a fanfare of trumpets and the ringing of the bells in the Curfew Tower. The assembled company then went to their respective stalls, surrounded by the hundreds of armoural plates of knights long since passed away. After the National Anthem had been sung the Queen commanded: "It is our pleasure that the Knight Companion be installed." Earl Halifax then called out: "The Right Honorable Sir Winston Leonard Spencer Churchill," and the Garter King of Arms conducted the Prime Minister to his stall.

A moment of absolute silence followed. It was as though the ghosts of the knights of the past were looking down on this most memorable occasion. For the Queen, it was the first Garter ceremony of her reign; it seems right that the Prime Minister should be the first so honored.

A short service followed, closing with the Te Deum. This concluded the investiture and installation of one of the most colorful men of our century; one who richly deserved the honor conferred upon him, and who will bring to the Order dignity and chivalry.

It has been a privilege to live during the lifetime of such a man, and to have been his protector over so many years, and to have received such friendship from him.

When shall we find another Anglo-American to take his place?

Other Important Reference Books Published by POPULAR LIBRARY

★★★★★★★★★★ WITH A ★★★★★★★★★★

Franklin D. Roosevelt
NOTHING TO FEAR

The living words of a
great and gallant man
who led his countrymen
through depression,
world crisis and global
war . . . "a truly
important book"
—*Boston Post*

Edited by
BEN D. ZEVIN

Preface by
HARRY L. HOPKINS

With a special
introduction by
ALLAN NEVINS

Here is a history of our times, in the living words of its greatest
spokesman, F. D. R. When he died, one message to the American
people was left undelivered. It is published here in full — and
significantly, the last word in that message is "faith."

A POPULAR LIBRARY SPECIAL — 75¢
Available wherever pocket-sized books are sold.